G. T. Clark

*Scholar Ironmaster
in the Victorian Age*

George Thomas Clark, 1809–1898
Oil on canvas by Henry Wyndham Phillips, 1865/6
National Library of Wales.

G. T. Clark

*Scholar Ironmaster
in the Victorian Age*

edited by

Brian Ll. James

UNIVERSITY OF WALES PRESS
CARDIFF
1998

© The Contributors, 1998

British Library Cataloguing-in-Publication Data.
A catalogue record for this book is available from the British Library.

ISBN 0–7083–1500–3

Typeset at University of Wales Press
Printed in Great Britain by Henry Ling Limited, Dorchester

Contents

List of Illustrations

Colour Plates
between pages 102 and 103

Maps, Pedigrees etc.

Foreword

Even in an age like the nineteenth century, when human migrations were so frequent and widespread, few incomers can have contributed so lavishly and diversely to the county of their adoption as George Thomas Clark (1809–1898). And although Victorians were proverbially no less versatile than energetic, there cannot have been many among them to rival this prodigious individual in the breadth and variety of their interests, or the intensity with which they pursued them. Descendant of a long line of articulate, high-minded and morally upright parsons, brought up in an evangelical atmosphere where duty and obligation were assigned the highest priority, and blessed with profound and wide-ranging inborn intellectual instincts, Clark fully lived up to the criteria instilled in him by inheritance and nurture. By the 1850s he had acquired an extensive familiarity with men and affairs, industry and commerce, transport and communications, sanitation and housing. He had already successfully revealed his capacity in three professions: as surgeon, railway engineer (in England and India), and public health inspector and reformer in a number of towns in England and Wales. Nor had this achievement as a practical man in any respect cramped his delight in learned and artistic enterprises, or his desire to satisfy his scholarly curiosity and indulge his literary bent. During these years he had simultaneously given evidence of a consuming passion for archaeology, history, genealogy, literature and the visual arts. In 1850 he married into the historic Lewis family of Glamorgan, by taking Ann Price Lewis as his bride. If, literally, he married one of the daughters of the shire, he might figuratively be said to have married the county itself, bringing to it an unparalleled endowment of mind, energy, vision and discernment.

It was as manager of the Dowlais Iron Works from 1855, when he was forty-six years old, that Clark really entered on his years of greatness. He now became one of the foremost industrialists of south Wales; an influential force in its politics, especially its local government; and a prominent figure in contemporary military, religious and charitable activity. As if that were not enough, his prowess in the sphere of scholarship was equally impressive: his monumental publication, *Mediaeval Military Architecture*, was the foundation for the serious study of castles in Britain; his encyclopaedic *Limbus Patrum* laid the basis of Glamorgan genealogy; and his six-volume *Cartae* have no equal as a compendium of the county's manuscript sources. As an employer, he was humane, considerate and mindful of his workmen's rights and needs in characteristic Victorian patriarchal fashion. As a savant, he was industrious, thorough and many-sided, with a talent for expressing himself in a style in which precision and accuracy vied with elegance and lucidity. As architect and dilettante, he has left abiding testimony to his insight, taste and discrimination in the house and gardens, and the church of St Ann, at Tal-y-garn.

The year 1998 marks the centenary of the death of this Triton among the minnows, after a long and prolific life of eighty-eight years. It is worthily commemorated in the volume compiled by Mr Brian Ll. James and his collaborators, to whom we are all immensely indebted. They have succeeded in presenting an admirably rounded and authentic portrait of a multi-faceted genius. It was fitting that Clark should have been enamoured of Italy and its Renaissance, for he was himself a true scion of that great awakening. Here, indeed, was a veritable nineteenth-century *cortegiano*: a man of action and sensibility; politician and critic; connoisseur of architecture, furniture, painting, and the arts in general. His parson-ancestors must surely have been familiar with the character in the New Testament parable who was favoured with five talents; they can hardly have foreseen that the greatest of their progeny would be a man blessed with ten!

Glanmor Williams

Preface

Historians in Glamorgan are aware of their great debt to G. T. Clark of Talygarn for his contributions to the study of the past of his adopted county, and of antiquities beyond its boundaries. The idea of commemorating the centenary of his death, however, came from someone who had been Administrator at Talygarn, long after the departure of the Clark family, when the house had become a Miners' Rehabilitation Centre. That person was Derrick Kingham. In company with Peter Leech, who was researching Clark's contacts with Venice and use of Venetian craftsmen, he succeeded in securing the involvement of several others who had a profound regard for Clark's achievements. The result was the formation of a G. T. Clark Centenary Commemoration Committee, consisting of the two prime movers, Brian Ll. James, Professor Henry Loyn, Donald Moore and the undersigned. The Committee set itself a task not hitherto attempted, namely the production of a book about Clark which would give an extended account of this many-sided genius.

The Committee began its work in April 1996, holding monthly meetings, usually at Talygarn itself, with the ready assent of the East Glamorgan NHS Trust, which had become responsible for the Rehabilitation Centre. A list of names of possible authors for a series of articles was drawn up and these persons were approached. At the same time a circular was distributed to test the market for the proposed book, and individuals were invited to commit themselves in advance to purchasing the work. The names of those who responded are printed in the volume. Their support was very encouraging, and the Committee was emboldened to pursue its negotiations with the University of Wales Press, which had expressed a willingness to undertake publication.

It was realized from the outset that the readership for a relatively specialized volume of this kind would not be large and unlikely to produce the funds necessary to publish a book of the quality the subject deserved. Appeals were therefore sent to individuals and institutions for financial contributions towards the venture. Here again, the response was generous and encouraging. Particular gratitude is expressed to Mr Guy Clark, GKN plc, the Manorial Society of Great Britain, the Ethel and Gwynne Morgan Trust, the Glamorgan County History Trust, the Pontyclun Community Council, the Honourable Society of Cymmrodorion, Mr George Williams, Mr Mark Birley and Sir Glanmor Williams.

During more than two years of planning and intensive research, the authors and Committee have received advice, information and assistance in various ways from many people. The following deserve special mention: Mrs Juliet Coyne, Madame Alys Cattoir-Clark, Mr L. H. W. Williams, Mrs Tydfil Thomas, Dr R. Brinley Jones, Dr Michael Siddons (Wales Herald Extraordinary), Mr Stephen K. Jones, the staffs of the National Library of Wales, the Glamorgan Record Office, the Library of the University of Wales Cardiff, Westminster Archives and Cadw: Welsh Historic Monuments, and Mr George McHardy of the Society of Antiquaries of London, Lieutenant-Colonel R. J. Redford and Mr Gordon Philbrook of the Duke of York's Headquarters, Chelsea, and the late Mr John A. Owen of Dowlais.

Finally, the Editor and Committee wish to express their warm thanks to the University of Wales Press for its work, and especially to Ms Susan Jenkins, its Senior Editor.

Patricia Moore
Chairman,
The G. T. Clark Centenary Commemoration Committee.
November 1998.

Contributors

Andy Croll, Lecturer in History, University of Glamorgan, Pontypridd.

J. Barry Davies, retired civil servant, Cardiff.

Richard Hewlings, an Inspector of Ancient Monuments and Historic Buildings at English Heritage, and editor of the *Georgian Group Journal*.

Brian Ll. James, formerly Sub-Librarian, University College, Cardiff.

Ieuan Gwynedd Jones, formerly Sir John Williams Professor of Welsh History, University College of Wales, Aberystwyth.

John R. Kenyon, Librarian, National Museums & Galleries of Wales.

Derrick C. Kingham, formerly Administrator of the Miners' Rehabilitation Centre, Talygarn.

Peter Leech, sometime Head of English, Penarth Grammar School/Stanwell Comprehensive School, Penarth.

Donald Moore, formerly Keeper of Pictures and Maps, National Library of Wales, Aberystwyth.

Sir Glanmor Williams, Emeritus Professor of History, University College of Swansea.

L. J. Williams, Emeritus Professor of Economics, University College of Wales, Aberystwyth.

Abbreviations

Arch. Camb.	*Archaeologia Cambrensis*
Arch. Cant.	*Archaeologia Cantiana*
Arch. J.	*Archaeological Journal*
B	*Builder*
BL	British Library
BLG	Burke's *Landed Gentry*
BM	British Museum
BQR	*British Quarterly Review*
Bristol & Glos. Trans.	*Transactions of the Bristol and Gloucestershire Archaeological Society*
CCM	Cyfarthfa Castle Museum
Coll. Top. & Gen.	*Collectanea Topographica et Genealogica*
CP	*Complete Peerage*
Cumb. Antiq. Soc. Trans.	*Transactions of the Cumberland and Westmorland Antiquarian and Archaeological Society*
DIC	Dowlais Iron Company
DNB	*Dictionary of National Biography*
DWB	*Dictionary of Welsh Biography*
GEC	General Electric Company
Gent. Mag.	*Gentleman's Magazine*
GKN	Guest, Keen and Nettlefolds
GRO	Glamorgan Record Office
GWR	Great Western Railway
ICOMOS	International Council of Monuments and Sites
MMA	*Mediaeval Military Architecture in England*, by G. T. Clark
Mont. Coll.	*Collections Historical and Archaeological relating to Montgomeryshire*
MR	*Monthly Review*
NLW	National Library of Wales
NLWJ	*National Library of Wales Journal*
NMW	National Museum of Wales (now National Museums & Galleries of Wales)

NPG	National Portrait Gallery
NS	new series
OED	*Oxford English Dictionary*
PP	*Parliamentary Papers*
PRO	Public Record Office
QR	*Quarterly Review*
RAI	Royal Archaeological Institute
RCAHMW	Royal Commission on Ancient and Historical Monuments in Wales
RHS	Royal Horticultural Society
Somerset Arch. Proc.	*Somersetshire Archaeological and Natural History Society's Proceedings*
Sussex Arch. Coll.	*Sussex Archaeological Collections*
THSC	*Transactions of the Hon. Society of Cymmrodorion*
TVR	Taff Vale Railway
V. & A.	Victoria and Albert Museum
VCH	*Victoria County History*
WFM	Welsh Folk Museum (now Museum of Welsh Life)
WGRO	West Glamorgan Record Office
Yorks. Arch. J.	*Yorkshire Archaeological and Topographical Journal*

A Note on the G. T. Clark Papers and Printed Books at the National Library of Wales, Aberystwyth

This very large collection of family and personal papers was presented by Wyndham Damer Clark between 1922 and 1959. Only part of the collection is fully listed, as NLW MSS 5171–5234 and 14,991–15,061, but useful descriptions appear in the Library's *Annual Reports*; see *Guide to the Department of Manuscripts and Records, the National Library of Wales* (Aberystwyth, 1994), 68. A major portion of the collection consists of G. T. Clark's incoming, with some outgoing, letters, which are arranged and calendared by date. These letters are cited in the chapters by L. J. Williams and Ieuan Gwynedd Jones by year and running number, e.g. Clark MSS, 75/323.

W. D. Clark also gave some printed books and sets of periodicals from his grandfather's library. The most valuable printed material consists of G. T. Clark's own copies of his pamphlets and offprints which he had bound into volumes. These items are entered individually in the Library's catalogues.

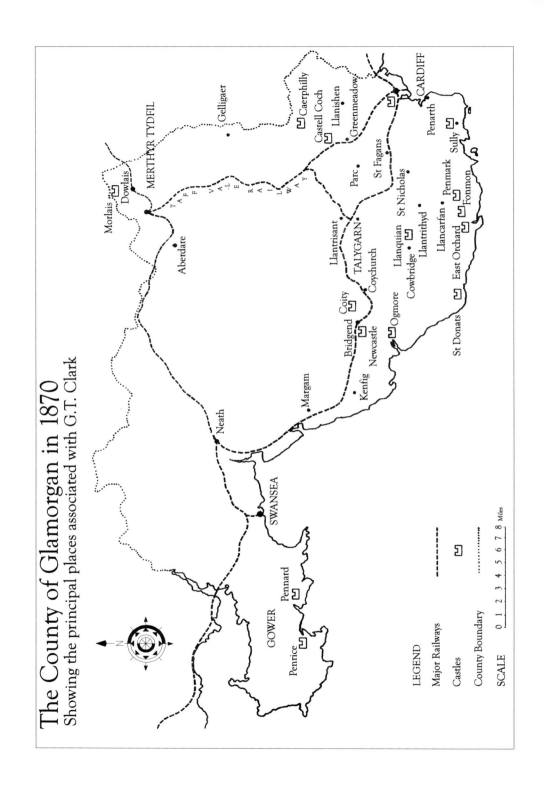

The County of Glamorgan in 1870
Showing the principal places associated with G.T. Clark

LEGEND

Major Railways

Castles

County Boundary

SCALE 0 1 2 3 4 5 6 7 8 Miles

MERTHYR TYDFIL

Morlais

Dowlais

Aberdare

T
A
F
F

V
A
L
E

R
A
I
L
W
A
Y

Gelligaer

Caerphilly

Castell Coch

Llanishen

Greenmeadow

CARDIFF

Penarth

Sully

Parc

St Fagans

St Nicholas

Penmark

Fonmon

Llantrisant

TALYGARN

Coychurch

Llanquian

Cowbridge

Llantrithyd

Llancarfan

East Orchard

Ogmore

Bridgend Coity

Newcastle

Kenfig

Margam

Neath

St Donats

SWANSEA

GOWER

Pennard

Pennice

N

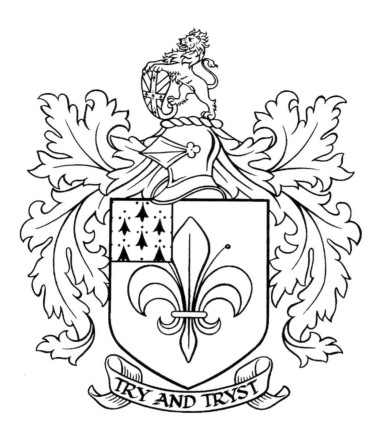

Coat of arms of the Clark family

Drawn by Marie Lynskey.

Arms: *Gules, a fleur-de-lis or, a canton ermine.*

Crest: *A lion rampant or, supporting a shield gules charged with a cross ermine placed upon a saltire or.*

G. T. Clark used these arms and they are depicted in carvings and coloured glass at Talygarn. They were borne by earlier generations of the family, as the seventeenth-century engravings of the Reverend Samuel Clark confirm. The College of Arms, however, can find no evidence of their official recognition. Perhaps because of this, Clark's grandson, Wyndham Damer Clark, obtained a formal grant in 1924, retaining the arms of his forebears but with the canton engrailed.

Ancestors of G. T. Clark

Based on Burke's Landed Gentry and G. T. Clark's writings

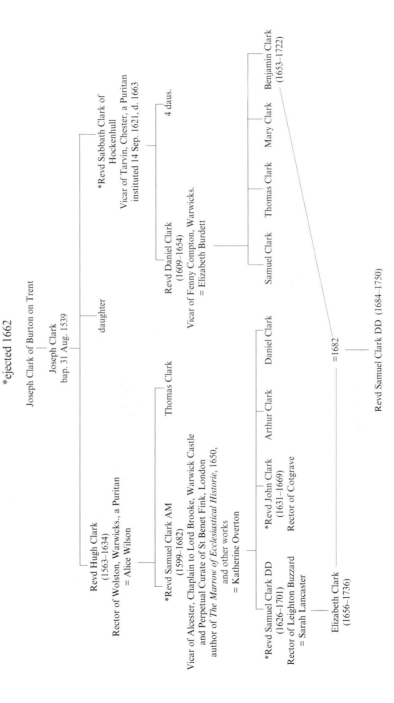

*ejected 1662

Joseph Clark of Burton on Trent

Joseph Clark
bap. 31 Aug. 1539

daughter

*Revd Sabbath Clark of
Hockenhull
Vicar of Tarvin, Chester, a Puritan
instituted 14 Sep. 1621, d. 1663

Revd Hugh Clark
(1563–1634)
Rector of Wolston, Warwicks., a Puritan
= Alice Wilson

Thomas Clark

Revd Daniel Clark
(1609–1654)
Vicar of Fenny Compton, Warwicks.
= Elizabeth Burdett

4 daus.

*Revd Samuel Clark AM
(1599–1682)
Vicar of Alcester, Chaplain to Lord Brooke, Warwick Castle
and Perpetual Curate of St Benet Fink, London
author of *The Marrow of Ecclesiastical Historie*, 1650,
and other works
= Katherine Overton

*Revd John Clark
(1631–1669)
Rector of Cotgrave

Arthur Clark

Daniel Clark

Samuel Clark

Thomas Clark

Mary Clark

Benjamin Clark
(1653–1722)

*Revd Samuel Clark DD
(1626–1701)
Rector of Leighton Buzzard
= Sarah Lancaster

Elizabeth Clark
(1656–1736)

=1682

Revd Samuel Clark DD (1684–1750)

Revd Samuel Clark DD (1684–1750)
Dissenting Minister of Independent Chapel, St Albans
author of *Scripture Promises* and other works
= Sarah Jones

Revd Samuel Clark of Daventry
(1727–1769)

Joseph Clark of Northampton (1738–1807)
Distributor of Stamps
= Sarah Rudsdell

Charlotte Clark
b. 1778, d. unm.

Revd George Clark AM (1777–1848)
Chaplain of the Royal Military Asylum, Chelsea
= 1806 Clara Dicey

George Thomas Clark
(1809–1898)
= 1850
Ann Price Lewis of Greenmeadow

Charles Rudsdell Clark
(1810–1836)
d.s.p.

Henry MacGregor Clark
(1813–1850)
= 1843 Ann Robertson

Frederick Guy Lestrange Clark
(1818–1883)
= 1841 Emma Terry
d.s.p.

Clara Ann Wilhelmina Clark
(1827–1903)
d. unm.

Charles Dicey Clark
(1844–1849)

George Rudsdell Clark
b.1846

Charles Henry Clark
d. inf.

Frances Elizabeth Clark
d. 1849

see separate pedigree

G. T. Clark's Descendants

Based on Burke's Landed Gentry and information from the family

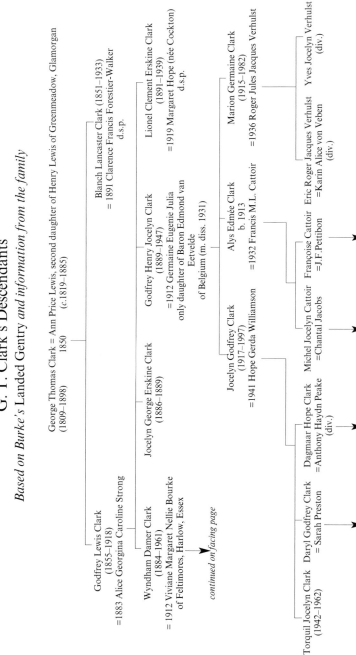

George Thomas Clark = Ann Price Lewis, second daughter of Henry Lewis of Greenmeadow, Glamorgan
(1809–1898)   1850   (c.1819–1885)

Godfrey Lewis Clark
(1855–1918)
=1883 Alice Georgina Caroline Strong

Blanch Lancaster Clark (1851–1933)
=1891 Clarence Francis Forestier-Walker
d.s.p.

Lionel Clement Erskine Clark
(1891–1939)
=1919 Margaret Hope (née Cockton)
d.s.p.

Wyndham Damer Clark
(1884–1961)
= 1912 Viviane Margaret Nellie Bourke
of Feltimores, Harlow, Essex

Jocelyn George Erskine Clark
(1886–1889)

Godfrey Henry Jocelyn Clark
(1889–1947)
=1912 Germaine Eugenie Julia
only daughter of Baron Edmond van
Eetvelde
of Belgium (m. diss. 1931)

Marion Germaine Clark
(1915–1982)
=1936 Roger Jules Jacques Verhulst

continued on facing page

Jocelyn Godfrey Clark
(1917–1997)
=1941 Hope Gerda Williamson

Alys Edmée Clark
b. 1913
=1932 Francis M.L. Cattoir

Yves Jocelyn Verhulst
(div.)

Torquil Jocelyn Clark Daryl Godfrey Clark
(1942–1962)   =Sarah Preston

Dagmaar Hope Clark
=Anthony Haydn Peake
(div.)

Michel Jocelyn Cattoir
=Chantal Jacobs

Françoise Cattoir
=J.F. Pettibon

Eric Roger Jacques Verhulst
=Karin Alice von Veben
(div.)

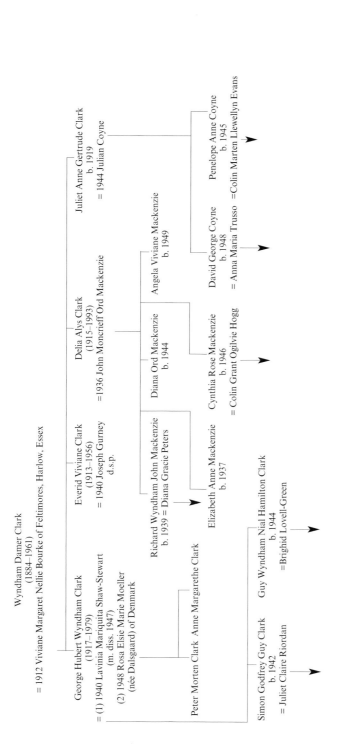

Wyndham Damer Clark
(1884–1961)
= 1912 Viviane Margaret Nellie Bourke of Feltimores, Harlow, Essex

George Hubert Wyndham Clark
(1917–1979)
= (1) 1940 Lavinia Mariquita Shaw-Stewart
(m. diss. 1947)
(2) 1948 Rosa Elsie Marie Moeller
(née Dalsgaard) of Denmark

Everid Viviane Clark
(1913–1956)
= 1940 Joseph Gurney
d.s.p.

Delia Alys Clark
(1915–1993)
=1936 John Moncrieff Ord Mackenzie

Juliet Anne Gertrude Clark
b. 1919
= 1944 Julian Coyne

Richard Wyndham John Mackenzie
b. 1939 = Diana Gracie Peters

Diana Ord Mackenzie
b. 1944

Angela Viviane Mackenzie
b. 1949

Penelope Anne Coyne
b. 1945
=Colin Marten Llewellyn Evans

Peter Morten Clark   Anne Margarethe Clark

Elizabeth Anne Mackenzie
b. 1937

Cynthia Rose Mackenzie
b. 1946
= Colin Grant Ogilvie Hogg

David George Coyne
b. 1948
= Anna Maria Trusso

Guy Wyndham Nial Hamilton Clark
b. 1944
=Brighid Lovell-Green

Simon Godfrey Guy Clark
b. 1942
= Juliet Claire Riordan

CHAPTER 1

The Making of a Scholar Ironmaster

An Introduction to the Life of G. T. Clark

BRIAN LL. JAMES

George Thomas Clark's life spanned the nineteenth century. He was born in 1809, the same year as Gladstone, Darwin and Tennyson, when George III was king, the Napoleonic Wars were at their height and Napoleon was the virtual master of Europe, and he died in 1898 when the reign of Queen Victoria was only three years from its end. It was a long and a remarkably varied life, for Clark pursued several different professions, he controlled a great ironworks, he travelled extensively, he distinguished himself through his antiquarian studies and his writing. He was described by one of his closest friends, the first Lord Aberdare, misquoting Dryden, as 'a man so various he seems to be not one but all mankind's epitome'.[1]

The biographer who sets out to chart the life, to assess the achievement and to portray the character of such a man will be presented with a whole array of difficult problems. Hitherto there have been only obituary notices or brief entries in biographical dictionaries and the like, and these secondary sources have proved to be both inaccurate and deficient. Even the memoir by Godfrey Lewis Clark appears to betray ignorance of many aspects of his father's early life. One of the reasons for this, if not the whole explanation, is Clark's own reticence. 'Able conversationalist as he was, Mr Clark was little given to talking about himself, even with his most intimate friends', was the comment of the second Lord Aberdare,[2] who had known him well, but was not of the same generation as Clark. There is almost nothing by way of autobiography, unless the notes which describe the building and beautifying of Talygarn, Clark's country estate near Llantrisant in Glamorgan, can count as such.[3] But if he gave no thought to writing his memoirs, he did preserve a vast private archive – documents, diaries, notebooks, many thousands of letters – as if he had a care for posterity and for his posthumous reputation.[4] The materials for a comprehensive biography exist.

The present work, a collaborative enterprise, is not the definitive biography that is merited by the importance and diversity of Clark's achievements. It does not deal with every aspect possible. Its main emphasis is upon the professional life and the historical and artistic interests of the mature man, from the time that he began to work for the General Board of Health in 1848 down to his last years in the 1890s. It may be that readers will find that the treatment is commemorative rather than critical and that some kind of 'devil's advocacy' is needed to show the other side to a character that not everyone will deem benevolent and well meaning. So be it.

We begin with a brief account of Clark's early career, up to the time of his marriage and his taking control of the Dowlais ironworks in the 1850s. An opportunity is taken in this 'introductory' chapter to sum up the character of the man, or to *attempt* something of the kind since the task is as easy as grasping quicksilver. A group of chapters follows in which the several authors deal with aspects of Clark's career as engineer and industrialist – the inspector for the General Board of Health, the ironmaster at Dowlais, his role in the politics of Merthyr Tydfil which required him to maintain the 'interest' of the ironworks and the Guest family. The next three chapters take up the antiquarian theme: Clark's seminal contribution to the study of castles, his great service to the history of Glamorgan in publishing its medieval charters and the pedigrees of its older families. The last group of chapters is concerned with the artistic and literary achievement, the family portraits, the exquisite house in Berkeley Square, the building of Talygarn and the patronage of the remarkable, mainly Italian, craftsmen, who decorated and furnished the house. The book concludes with a bibliography of G. T. Clark's output of published writings which demonstrates an astonishing quantity and range of subject-matter sustained over sixty-two years.

Heritage

The pedigree of the Clarks is traced back to Joseph Clark of Burton upon Trent in the sixteenth century.[5] Through several generations they were Anglican clergy – among the Puritan tendency – serving in parishes mainly in the Midlands and the Home Counties. In 1662 at least four (possibly six)[6] members of the family who had held pastorates during the Commonwealth were ejected from their livings because they could not accept episcopacy and the Book of Common Prayer as re-established by the Act of Uniformity passed in that year. The two most important were G. T. Clark's direct ancestors, Samuel Clark I (1599–1682), who had been vicar of Alcester,

Ætatis Suæ 50 Octob. 1659

All that thou - fees't and readest is Divine:
Learning thus vs'd is water turn'd to wine :
Well may woe then despaire to draw his minde,
View heere the case ; ith Booke the Jewell finde .
T Cross Sculpsit   P. V. A. M. fecit

2 The Revd Samuel Clark (1599–1682). Engraved
by Thomas Cross, 1654. *National Library of Wales.*

Warwickshire, and curate (minister, or pastor) of St Benet Fink in London, and his son Samuel Clark II (1626–1701), rector of Leighton Buzzard, Bedfordshire, and of Grendon Underwood, Buckinghamshire. They became Dissenters or Nonconformists, though unwillingly since they had been moderate Puritans and among those that had promoted the Restoration, with the forlorn hope of 'comprehension' within the Church of England thereafter. Samuel Clark III (1684–1750), the grandson of Samuel II, was a Dissenting minister and schoolmaster at St Albans. The three Samuels were all noted authors of devotional, biographical and scriptural works – several of which were reprinted by their descendant – and they were proud to own the friendship of leading Dissenters, Baxter, Watts and Doddridge.[7] Samuel Clark IV (1729–69), was a protégé of Philip Doddridge and a tutor at Daventry Academy where Joseph Priestley was one of his pupils; he died relatively young, and the line of descent continued through the younger

3

3 The Revd George Clark (1777–1848), father of
G. T. Clark. Engraved by William Holl the Elder after
Joseph Slater, 1816.
National Library of Wales.

brother, namely Joseph Clark of Northampton (1738–1807), distributor of stamps for the counties of Northampton and Rutland and the town of Birmingham. Whether he returned to the Church of his more distant forebears is not at present known but, as a minor government official, it is likely that he did.

His son, George Clark (1777–1848), did return, entered the University of Cambridge in 1796 and was ordained by the Bishop of Peterborough in 1800. After briefly serving as curate of Kingsthorpe, near his native town, the Revd George Clark was appointed chaplain to the Royal Military Asylum through the recommendation of Sir Harry Calvert, the Adjutant-General of the Forces. Newly founded in Chelsea by the Duke of York, the Asylum was an orphanage for the children of soldiers killed in the Napoleonic Wars. Clark was in fact responsible for the education as well as for the spiritual and moral welfare of the children, and the Asylum also became a place for the training of army schoolmasters.[8] As might be expected of a man with a Nonconformist ancestry, the Revd George Clark was an evangelical clergyman; he was on friendly terms with members of the Clapham Sect – Wilberforce, Hannah More, the Macaulays, Gisbornes, Babingtons, Stephens – and was a supporter of the abolition of the slave trade.[9]

4

THE ROYAL MILITARY ASYLUM AT CHELSEA.
For Soldiers Children of the Regular Army ...Intended for 500 Girls & 500 Boys.

4 The Royal Military Asylum, Chelsea. The Clark family's apartments were probably in the block on the left. Engraved 1805; published by Laurie and Whittle. *National Army Museum, London.*

In 1806 he married Clara, youngest daughter of Thomas Dicey of Claybrooke Hall, near Lutterworth. Although the proprietor of a modest country house on the borders of Leicestershire and Warwickshire, Thomas Dicey's business was actually in Northampton where his grandfather had founded the local newspaper in 1720.[10] Four generations of Diceys owned and edited the *Northampton Mercury*, though Clara Clark's brother, Thomas Edward Dicey (1789–1858), who married the daughter of James Stephen MP, extended his interests into railways. Edward James Stephen Dicey (1832–1911), one of their sons, carried on the family's tradition as editor of the (London) *Observer* from 1870 to 1889.[11]

George Thomas Clark was born in Chelsea on 26 May 1809, the eldest son of George and Clara Clark. He was brought up in the Royal Military Asylum in a family that was benevolent, loving and religious without being 'puritanical', and in surroundings governed by military discipline. The inheritance from Puritan and evangelical forebears showed itself in the sense of duty and obligation, the tenacity of purpose, the compulsion to write; all these qualities can be traced to his upbringing and family tradition. The Diceys had a similar evangelical – though not in their case Dissenting – background; Hannah More had been *their* friend too; and the example of

5 Charterhouse Schoolroom. Aquatint by J. Bluck after A. Pugin, 1816; published
by Rudolph Ackermann. *Charterhouse School.*

this remarkable dynasty of provincial journalists must have encouraged in
the young George Clark the urge to write. Writing and publishing were,
indeed, in his blood. The military context of his early life was certainly a
continuing influence which is seen in his later involvement with the
Volunteers. Clark also gained some advantage from the powerful circles to
which his father had access – the upper echelons of the military, the royal
family, and perhaps most important of all, the Clapham Sect and what Lord
Annan called the 'intellectual aristocracy'.[12] Although not as affluent as all
these, the Clarks were in no doubt that, by birth and education, they were
gentlemen and that they might consort with the highest in the land; this was
fundamental to G. T. Clark's outlook on life.

Education

His schooling began perhaps at home with his father. In 1819, when he was
ten, Lord Erskine, a former lord chancellor, nominated him a 'gownboy' at
Charterhouse, which was equivalent to a scholarship providing him with free
tuition, board and lodging. Charterhouse, then located in London – close to

Smithfield Market – was one of the most prestigious and successful schools of the day, under the somewhat harsh regime of Dr John Russell. The public schools were as yet unreformed – Dr Arnold went to Rugby in 1828 – and Thackeray, a younger contemporary of Clark's, referred to the school as 'Slaughter House', though his picture of it in *The Newcomes* was a good deal kinder.[13] Clark makes no reference to his schooldays at Charterhouse, but undoubtedly he was well grounded there in the ancient languages, and he thought well enough of it in later life to present a reredos to the chapel when the school moved to new premises at Godalming in 1872.[14] But it can hardly be otherwise that, as far as concerned his wide knowledge of science, history and modern languages, Clark was entirely self-taught.

From Charterhouse Clark did not go on to university but was articled in 1825 to Sir Patrick Macgregor, personal surgeon to the Duke of York. Sir Patrick died in 1828 and Clark was 'turned over' to another leading London surgeon, George Gisborne Babington of Golden Square, whose names proclaim his connection with the Clapham Sect. He pursued his medical and surgical studies and spent periods at St George's Hospital and the infirmary of the Marylebone workhouse; on 14 December 1832 he was admitted to the Royal College of Surgeons.[15]

Bristol and the GWR

Having qualified, Clark moved to Clifton, Bristol. He was beginning on a career in medicine but there are few facts about it and his name does not appear in the medical section of the annual *Bristol Directory*. He did, however, write in his diary a draft of a letter applying for the post of surgeon at the Bristol Infirmary in 1834, but noted 'not sent'.[16] It is nevertheless possible to view his three years spent in Bristol as significant, even if the details of his professional life at that time must remain indistinct. There was a group of distinguished men of science in the city who had founded the Bristol Institution and the Philosophical and Literary Society. A leading figure was already a family friend of the Clarks, the Revd William Daniel Conybeare,[17] a notable pioneer in geology, and others were Dr John Addington Symonds and the ethnologist, Dr James Cowles Prichard.[18] In March and April 1834 Prichard and Clark gave a course of lectures on Egyptian antiquities at the Institution where the theatre was 'crowded to excess with scientific and reflective persons'.[19] It was this group of provincial savants who invited George Clark to edit a quarterly periodical entitled the *West of England Journal of Science and Literature*. Five issues appeared in 1835–6, many of the articles – on castles, geology, physiology, chemistry and philology – being written by the editor himself, showing him to be, already at twenty-six, something of a polymath. The *Journal* was discontinued early in 1836, by which time Clark had returned to London; he attributed its failure, over-modestly, to his own shortcomings as a writer. In reality he had a remarkable facility with the pen[20] and by 1836 had published a number of articles and reviews in the *Gentleman's Magazine*. The Bristol years had seen the start of the astonishing flow of publications that continued unabated throughout a long life.

The Bristol period was also one in which old friendships were consolidated and new ones begun. The Frere family, living at Bitton halfway between Bristol and Bath, were particularly hospitable. The father, Edward Frere, had been a partner in the Clydach ironworks in Breconshire, and it was there that his numerous children were born. The second son, George Edward, had been an older contemporary of Clark's at Charterhouse; he was one of Brunel's chief assistants on the construction of the GWR. But it was a younger son, Henry Bartle, who was to become Clark's life-long friend.[21] This was Sir Bartle Frere, the future colonial governor and a major – if controversial – figure in the history of British imperialism.

While in Bristol Clark was a fairly frequent visitor across the Channel in Glamorgan – at the rectory in Sully and at Dowlais House, Merthyr Tydfil. The rector of Sully from 1822 to 1836 was the same W. D. Conybeare who was prominent in the intellectual life of Bristol, where he held another church appointment. For example, Clark stayed with the Conybeares for several days in August 1834 and was one of their party attending the Gwent and Dyfed Royal Eisteddfod and Musical Festival in Cardiff Castle.[22] Mrs Conybeare was the sister of the first Mrs J. J. Guest of Dowlais – the unfortunate Maria Ranken who had died in childbirth at twenty-three, less than a year after her marriage.[23] It seems that it was through the Conybeares that Clark was first invited to Dowlais; he and Conybeare went there in September 1833 and assisted in the excavation of Morlais Castle. The consequences of this introduction for George Clark's later career were immense, for the acquaintance quickly developed into a close friendship with Josiah John Guest and his second wife, Lady Charlotte. Lady Charlotte's journal indicates that both Guests enjoyed his company – he was one of the few visitors at Dowlais House who could talk to her about 'ancient literature'. In November 1835 Clark stayed at Dowlais for ten days and accompanied the family party to the eisteddfod at Abergavenny, where Sir John Guest presided.[24] Thus Clark got to know Glamorgan and some of its principal inhabitants twenty years before he came to live in the county, and it was on these visits in the 1830s that he had his first opportunity of studying the local castles.[25]

For the immediate future what was more significant was a chance meeting with Isambard Kingdom Brunel, in a half-finished tunnel on the Coalpit Heath Railway (officially the Bristol and Gloucestershire Railway), probably sometime in the winter of 1834–5. What Clark was doing in the Staple Hill tunnel is never explained; Brunel was there to make detailed observations as he prepared himself for the great challenge of building his first railway, the Great Western, and 'when a shaft in which we were suspended cracked and seemed about to give way, I well remember the coolness with which he insisted upon completing the observations he came to make. Shortly afterwards I became, at his request, his assistant.'[26] It was perhaps in the autumn of 1835 that Clark agreed to join Brunel's staff, and it must seem to us a surprising change of career for a recently qualified surgeon to transform himself into a civil engineer. Of course, he was already an amateur student of geology and military architecture, which would have given him some knowledge necessary to his new profession. The rest he learnt in Brunel's office in London, and from the actual practice of building a railway. There did not exist a body of civil engineers from whom Brunel might recruit; he had to find and train his own assistants. In this, as in most things, he was remarkably skilful.[27]

Brunel's management of his staff and of his numerous engineering projects was authoritarian and paternalistic. No one could doubt that he was in command, and yet most accepted his authority and came to regard this many-talented man with something like veneration. Clark admired him enormously for his ability in all branches of engineering and in negotiation with contractors and landowners, in his handling of his employees, for his 'sustained power of work', and also for his human qualities – 'his light and joyous disposition'.[28] The entire design of the GWR was Brunel's, and that included every structure, 'from the smallest culvert up to the Brent viaduct and the Maidenhead bridge'. Clark's comment shows that he was conscious of this as perhaps a weakness, that his old chief would allow no independence of action, for 'the consequence was that though he trained several excellent assistants, few of them ever rose to be engineers-in-chief, or executed any great or original work'.[29] If, as seems possible, Clark attempted to model himself upon Brunel then he explicitly rejected this aspect of his style of management – the unwillingness to entrust responsibility to others.[30]

It has been stated and often repeated that Clark was assigned two 'divisions' of the GWR which included the original terminus at Paddington (adjoining Bishop's Bridge Road) and the bridges over the Thames at Basildon and Moulsford, above Reading. Proof that he was responsible for the construction (though not, of course, for the design) of these is elusive, but there are indications that it may be so. The statement first appeared in

6 Approach to the original GWR terminus at Paddington.

7 Basildon Bridge, Berkshire/Oxfordshire. G. T. Clark supervised the construction of this bridge on the GWR in 1839.

Lithographs by J. C. Bourne, 1840/1; first published 1843. *Stephen K. Jones.*

print in 1877 in an article on G. T. Clark in a series entitled 'Industrial Celebrities',[31] and it is probable that this article would have had Clark's prior approval. There is support also from Clark's known presence at the right time: in London in 1838, and at Streatley in Berkshire in 1839. Streatley, on the Thames, is midway between the villages of Lower Basildon and Moulsford. Almost certainly Clark was never promoted to 'resident engineer' of the forty-four-mile section of the line opened from Reading to Swindon at various dates in 1840, but that he was the assistant engineer in charge of the two majestic brick and Bath stone bridges over the Thames seems close to being proved. They stand today.

What can be proved to a certainty is that Clark was the author of the anonymous *Guide Book to the Great Western Railway*, which came out in 1839 when only the first section of the track from Paddington to Taplow was operational.[32] This booklet appears to have been officially sanctioned by the Company and is dedicated to Brunel, although there is nothing in the author's preface to suggest that he had been commissioned to write it. A second, and much more ambitious, publication, *The History and Description of the Great Western Railway* (1843, 1846),[33] had text written to accompany the famous lithographs of J. C. Bourne. According to Clark, writing fifty years later, the text had been written, and the subjects of the drawings selected, by 'one of the engineers employed on the construction of the line', though his name – at his own request – did not appear on the title-page.[34] He stops short of naming himself as author, but it is virtually certain that it was he who was the 'engineer' in question.

Clark would probably have been working on this book in the early months of 1843 when the line had been fully open through from London to Bristol for less than two years. Although he was no longer employed by Brunel by then, it is difficult to pinpoint the date when they parted company. Two letters from Brunel to Clark, dated 27 October and 2 November 1840, indicate clearly enough that the latter had recently ceased to be employed on the GWR, but was apparently then working on the Taff Vale Railway, another of Brunel's many projects. The first section of the TVR (from Cardiff to Navigation, the present-day Abercynon) had been inaugurated by Sir John and Lady Charlotte Guest on 8 October; it was completed to Merthyr Tydfil the following April.[35] It may well be that with the completion of work on the TVR Clark severed his connection with Brunel (or was dismissed), but no evidence has so far emerged to allow one to explain in exactly what circumstances they parted company. The parting must surely have been amicable – it was otherwise with George Edward Frere in August 1841[36] – in view of the high regard for Brunel that Clark expressed throughout his life.

India and engineering

There followed another abrupt change of career, for on 22 January 1842 George Thomas Clark was admitted to the Middle Temple.[37] Nothing more is known about his legal training and he was never called to the Bar. Instead, in the summer of 1843, he set out on a long and leisurely journey overland to the Mediterranean, down through Italy, by sea to Sicily and Malta, then on to Egypt and thence by ship for Bombay, staying long enough *en route* to view numerous cathedrals in France and Italy, to visit friends in Malta, and to explore the antiquities of Egypt: 'but a month is a short time even to get a general notion of them'.[38]

Bartle Frere, secretary to the governor of Bombay, had suggested to his friend Clark that he might come out to Bombay, 'for there seemed to be a good opening for him there as a civil engineer'.[39] He took with him a letter of introduction to the chief engineer at Bombay from Sir George Stephen, whose father had been so prominent a member of the anti-slavery movement and of the Clapham Sect. Old friendships and family connections[40] proved crucial at this juncture. In India Clark settled easily into the small English ruling class, was appointed a magistrate and is credited with various engineering works but, without doubt, the most significant of these was the survey he began to find a route for a railway from Bombay, over the Western Ghats, on to the Deccan plateau. He became engineer to the grandly named Great Indian Peninsula Railway Company. Returning to London on the Company's business in 1847, he printed his *Report . . . on the Engineering Features of the Concan and Great Western Ghauts*, but for some reason he never returned to India. Godfrey Clark believed that his father's health had suffered from the climate and that this explained his decision to remain in England.[41] Some years passed before the plans laid by George Clark for a railway out of Bombay came to fruition, the first stretch as far as Thana being completed in 1852.

There is little detail about how G. T. Clark made his living in the years between his return from Bombay in 1847 and his taking command of the Dowlais Iron Company in 1855. In a general way it is probably correct to describe his profession during that time as 'consulting engineer'. He was based in London, and until 1850 often gave his club, the Athenaeum (to which he had been elected in 1844), as his address. He afterwards lived in Gloucester Terrace, Regent's Park, before moving into a country house, Frimhurst – which he may have built for himself – at Frimley Green in Surrey.[42] It is, of course, possible to be much more exact about Clark's employment as a superintending inspector under the Public Health Act from 1848 to 1850: this

8 George Thomas Clark.
Photograph by Arthur Pendarves Vivian, 1854.
National Library of Wales.

aspect of his career is discussed in the next chapter by Dr A. J. Croll. Clark still retained his own private practice and was being paid three guineas a day when engaged on work for the General Board of Health. It may be that, privately, he was employed by some of the local boards of health to implement his own official recommendations for drainage and water supply.[43] But for at least three, quite lengthy periods of time in the early 1850s, Clark was abroad, presumably engaged in civil engineering of some kind – in January 1852 he was in Heidelberg;[44] in February 1853 Lady Charlotte Guest regretted the loss of his sound advice and encouragement on account of his departure from England;[45] and the January 1854 issue of *Archaeologia Cambrensis* reported that G. T. Clark 'being on the Continent' had resigned his place on the committee of the Cambrian Archaeological Association.[46]

The Guests, the Lewises and the Dowlais Iron Company

To understand how a consulting engineer should suddenly find himself responsible for one of the largest industrial concerns in the world, with some 8,000 employees, we have to return to Clark's friendship with Sir John and

9 Ann Price Clark. Drawing by Helen Shaw,
undated. *Glamorgan Record Office.*

Lady Charlotte Guest which had been firmly established in the 1830s. Josiah John Guest's family had been connected with the Dowlais Iron Company for three generations; their control of the Company had been gradually strengthened, though it was not until 1850–1 that Sir John had bought out the last remaining partners: Wyndham William Lewis and Edward John Hutchins.[47] The success of the enterprise under his management had made Guest immensely rich, and correspondingly ambitious. He was elected to Parliament in 1826, and in 1833, then a widower of 48, he had married the twenty-one-year-old Lady Charlotte Bertie, daughter of the ninth Earl of Lindsey. His wealth was exchanged for her blue blood (*sangre azul*, as Lady Holland described it).[48] They had been introduced at a dinner party given by Mrs Wyndham Lewis,[49] the wife of Guest's partner. There can be little doubt that George Clark first met Ann Price Lewis, who was Wyndham Lewis's niece and Wyndham William Lewis's sister, in the Guest circle; their long-expected engagement was formally announced at Canford, the Guests' seat near Wimborne in Dorset, at Christmas 1849.[50] They married at St John's, Cardiff, on 3 April 1850.

14

George Clark was forty at the time of his marriage, and Ann was about ten years younger. They had thirty-five years of devoted marriage together. Their two children were Blanch, born in London in 1851, and Godfrey, born at Frimhurst in 1855. The marriage brought George Clark happiness and the son who would eventually carry on the Clark line. But we have to weigh up the social advantages that an alliance with the Lewises brought him, for although the Clarks were a distinguished family, with a long pedigree and a coat of arms, they had not previously married into the landed gentry. Ann Lewis's coat of arms had twelve quarterings and her pedigree, as later printed by her husband,[51] consisted of twenty-seven generations in the male line, beginning with a somewhat shadowy 'Gwaethfoed Fawr, Lord of Ystrad Towy, and Gwynvae, co. Caermarthen, son of Clodien, Prince of Powis', and continuing through the famous Welsh hero, Ifor ap Meurig, better known as 'Ifor Bach',[52] lord of Senghennydd in the twelfth century, down to the Edward ap Lewis who adopted 'Lewis' as a fixed surname in the first half of the sixteenth century.[53] This Edward Lewis built the 'fair place caullid Vanne', as Leland tells us, near to (and in part with stone pilfered from) Caerphilly Castle. Subsequently, the family established their principal residence at St Fagans Castle, near Cardiff. The main line of the Lewises ended with an heiress who married the third Earl of Plymouth (of the 1682 creation) in 1730, but there were junior branches, and of these there is one that has continued down to the present day, namely the Lewises of Llanishen and Greenmeadow. They were not great landed magnates, as the Lewises of the Fan and St Fagans had been, but were among those families of lesser gentry who, in each generation, provided high sheriffs for Glamorgan and serviced the magistrates' bench.[54]

Thomas Lewis of Llanishen (high sheriff in 1757) was one of several partners who in 1759 formed the Dowlais Iron Company. Two of his grandsons were Wyndham Lewis of Greenmeadow in the parish of Whitchurch, who has already been mentioned, and Henry Lewis of Parc, an old gentry house at Capel Llanilltern in the parish of St Fagans, leased from his kinsman, the Earl of Plymouth. It was at Parc that Ann Price Lewis[55] was born about the year 1819, and it was there that she and her brothers and sisters were raised until, on the death of Uncle Wyndham in 1838, their father Henry inherited Greenmeadow. It is probable that Ann herself lived there for only a few years; her parents did not survive long to enjoy Greenmeadow, and it seems likely that when her elder brother married in 1842 Ann went to live elsewhere, perhaps in Cardiff, where she was living at the time of her wedding. Nevertheless, she is usually, and not incorrectly, referred to as 'Ann Lewis of Greenmeadow'.

Such was the history of the family that George Clark had married into. As the nineteenth century wore on the Lewises became increasingly important as landowners; they were leaders in the social and hunting set of the Cardiff area, but their family pretensions were in fact underpinned more by income from the Dowlais ironworks than from their landed estate.[56] Ann herself was not particularly wealthy when she married, nor had she great expectations of an inheritance. As it happened her younger brother, Wyndham William, died without male issue in 1871, and this circumstance unexpectedly brought some valuable property in and around Llanishen to herself and her two sisters.[57] The absence of a substantial dowry did not mean that Clark failed to benefit materially from the marriage. It consolidated and secured his position in the Guest circle – and this led in only two years to his being named one of the trustees and executors in Sir John Guest's will – and it gave him a recognized status in Glamorgan society which, however able he might be and however rich he might eventually become, could never otherwise have been his.

For two or three years after Sir John's death in November 1852 it was Lady Charlotte herself who took on the management of the Dowlais works as trustee for her children. The third trustee, Edward Divett MP, resigned and his place was filled by Henry Austin Bruce (who had succeeded Sir John as MP for Merthyr Tydfil). Under the terms of the will, Lady Charlotte forfeited her rights as a trustee upon her second marriage in April 1855; her new husband was Charles Schreiber, fellow of Trinity College, Cambridge, and until lately her eldest son's private tutor. It was at this juncture that Clark assumed control of the ironworks and in March 1856 he and his family moved to Dowlais,[58] and into the plain but substantial house that Guest had built, about 1818, at the time of his first marriage.[59] Originally a little distance from the works, by Clark's time the environs of Dowlais House had been much encroached upon and only a few yards separated the garden from the furnaces.

G. T. Clark: an assessment

Perhaps for the first time in a career that had taken several different directions, Clark had great responsibilities thrust upon him. He was now in his middle forties. He devoted the rest of his professional life to the Dowlais ironworks, to the welfare of its dependent community and to the local government of Merthyr Tydfil. Would it be fair to say that his varied experience had prepared him for such a position of authority and influence? Few of the great industrialists of the mid-nineteenth century had his broad knowledge of the practical world, or his assured social position, or his high degree of culture and learning. Certainly no one in Merthyr could match

10 George Thomas Clark. Lithograph, artist
unknown, probably 1870s; published as frontispiece
in the 1910 edition of the *Cartae*.

him. And yet, for all his attainments, Clark had not previously had a part in
the management of a large industrial concern, nor was he a metallurgist. It
was the particular good fortune of the DIC that he proved to be an able
administrator and that this ability was coupled with the technical expertise
of the two successive general managers whom he appointed, namely William
Menelaus (1818–82) and Edward Prichard Martin (1844–1910), both of
them eminent men in their own right. The prosperity of the Dowlais
ironworks through much of the second half of the nineteenth century made
G. T. Clark a rich man. His accumulating wealth, combined with his policy
of delegating day-to-day responsibility to the general managers and the
hierarchy of departmental managers under them, enabled him to devote
time and money to his antiquarian interests. His wealth provided him with
the means to create at Talygarn a fine house, garden and landed estate, such
as befitted the family of landed gentry it was his ambition to found.

17

What manner of man was George Thomas Clark? How can we assess his character and personality, and understand his motives and ambitions? Different people undoubtedly saw him differently, or saw different sides to his character. The very lengthy obituary notice in the *Western Mail* was headlined 'The saviour of Dowlais. Creator of Dowlais-Cardiff. Our first archaeologist'. It went on to say that 'the people' – the inhabitants of Merthyr – frequently, though wrongly, considered him 'austere'. The writer considered that there was 'a geniality blended with the firmness and justice of his administration which commended itself to all'.[60] Lord Aberdare, approvingly quoting an 'old friend', described Clark as a 'man of the strictest probity, inflexible will, faithful and loyal to his friends'.[61] An obituarist in one of the learned journals to which Clark had contributed so often, referred to the 'genial author', and recalled his 'fine manly presence, his piercing dark eyes, and his singularly clear and eloquent discourses' at meetings of the Royal Archaeological Institute. The writer cherished the memory of a 'worthy scion of a worthy stock, of a man of rare gifts and ready tact and courtesy, such as the present generation of antiquaries is hardly likely to meet with again'.[62] Aberdare remembered a 'brilliant conversationalist, full of apt quotation, ready wit, and an inexhaustible fund of appropriate anecdote'.[63] David Jones of Wallington, a local historian and genealogist, experienced, however, 'a perfect explosion of temper' when he called on Clark at Talygarn without an appointment, but they soon struck a mutual understanding and parted on good terms.[64]

Clark was a man who was widely respected, by markedly different circles of friends and acquaintances. In the industrial world he was elected president of the newly formed British Iron Trade Association in 1876. In the world of antiquities he became a vice-president of the Royal Archaeological Institute and of the Cambrian Archaeological Association. In Merthyr Tydfil he topped the poll in elections to the School Board, and for many years chaired that board as well as the Local Board of Health and the Board of Guardians. In these associations and local authorities members and colleagues found Clark good company, wise, honourable, energetic, lacking in pomposity and self-importance unlike so many successful men in Victorian industry and commerce. He was nevertheless self-assured, seriously purposeful, ambitious and determined. No one without such qualities could have achieved so much in so many spheres.

The relations between G. T. Clark and the workforce at Dowlais were more complex and are difficult to characterize. His own attitude to his employees was both paternalistic and authoritarian. In a reply which he made when questioned before the Royal Commission on Trades Unions in 1867 he eloquently expressed his paternalism. Having already stated that there had been no trade unions or strikes at Dowlais in his time, he was asked if he was willing to talk to deputations of the men on the subject of wages:

> Certainly. My own men are like my own children, and I should as soon think of refusing to listen to my own child as of refusing to listen to any man who came from the works to talk to me on any matter, because I think it of equal importance that my men and I should be on good terms as that I should be on good terms with my own family.[65]

He certainly had a fine record of concern for the welfare of the men and for the town of Dowlais, maintaining and developing the schools, and the medical, social and recreational provision begun by Sir John and Lady Charlotte Guest.[66] The record of the DIC was far superior to that of the other major employers in the district. But paternalism had its limits, and it may well be that the harmony which had existed between the Company and its men since the strike of 1853[67] was already fractured by 1867, whatever Clark wished to believe.[68] Relations worsened in the 1870s, especially between the colliers and the DIC, and matters were complicated by Clark's chairmanship of the Board of Guardians. However sincere his sympathy for the plight of individual workers, when capital and labour came into conflict, Clark's first responsibility was to the Company and its interests, and when the Guardians were confronted with the crisis of 1875 when many thousands of strikers faced starvation, it was the rules laid down by the Poor Law and the interests of the hard-pressed ratepayers that were seen to be paramount.[69] Clark's philosophy of paternalism, presupposing as it did the deference of the workmen, was ineffectual in a situation of social disharmony.

And yet, there is not the least doubt that George and Ann Clark were charitable people, in the best traditions of Victorian philanthropy. They lent support to churches, chapels, schools, hospitals and individuals from their private means, as is well attested by Clark's correspondence and also by contemporary newspaper reports.[70] Obituary notices recorded that Mrs Clark's many acts of kindness had been done without ostentation. 'She saw with her own eyes what destitution existed, and administered the relief with her own hands.'[71] The vicar of Llantrisant wrote of George Clark that he had 'endeared himself to those around him by many acts of unostentatious kindness and generosity'.[72] It is easy to dismiss such remarks as merely conventional tributes, just as it is easy to disparage the philanthropy of the rich as no more than attempts at social control. Paternalism and the distribution of charity *were* such, of course, but until more generous and less condescending and discriminatory forms of relief and welfare began to be enacted by government policy early in the twentieth century, they helped to alleviate the privations of the poor.

It is not easy to know if the impulse to benevolence arose from Clark's religious convictions, but it is probably so. His religious upbringing within the walls of a charitable institution, and the evangelical fervour of his younger years,[73] would have certainly been a solid foundation for later humanitarianism. He remained a devout member of the Church of England throughout his life, though in later years the earlier fervency may perhaps have moderated. Religion for the mature Clark became a private matter, to be expressed in unobtrusive acts of charity, and to be given public expression in his support for the building of Anglican churches and Nonconformist chapels (most notably the new Welsh church at Dowlais, the enlargement of St John's, Dowlais, and the new church at Talygarn).

The portrayal of G. T. Clark that is found in this book – though readers are invited, indeed urged, to make up their own minds – is essentially favourable in the context of his times. We portray a man who was successful in several worlds that were usually separate: it was rare for a wealthy industrialist to make a significant contribution to historical studies, essentially the interest of his leisure time. As a person, we see him as a socially confident man, yet one who was also modest and reticent about himself, a man of genial temper, generous to his subordinates but, in the tradition of the nineteenth century which Clark would not have wished to overturn, one who commanded and expected obedience. His personal ambition seems to have found expression in the notion of 'family'. The house at Talygarn, while it would have excited the disapproval of the puritan ancestors on account of its size and grandeur, was designed to be a worthy setting for the family of landed gentry to be known as 'Clark of Tal-y-garn'.[74] But its interior decoration, with coats of arms and ciphers (the entwined Cs) almost everywhere, also commemorated the past glories of the Clarks and, to a lesser extent, the Lewises; it proclaimed the Clarks to be an old family (unlike the Guests and Crawshays). It might have been new money that had enabled G. T. Clark to create such a house, but he made in it an emphatic claim to *pedigree*. Talygarn was built for the Clark *family* past, present and future, and not for the personal vanity of its creator.

Notes

[1] Henry Austin Bruce (1815–95), quoted by his son in *Arch. Camb.*, 6th ser. 1 (1901), 49. The 2nd Lord Aberdare may well have been unaware of the source of this quotation in *Absalom and Achitophel*.

[2] Henry Campbell Bruce (1851–1929), *Arch. Camb.*, 6th ser. 1 (1901), 49.

[3] See Chapter 9.

[4] In NLW, but only partially scheduled. Another major archive, the records of the Dowlais Iron Company, is deposited in GRO. A number of other collections in NLW, GRO, BL, the Bodleian Library, and elsewhere, also contain relevant material.

[5] *BLG.*

[6] Six according to G. T. Clark, but only four are identified by A. G. Matthews in *Calamy Revised* (Oxford, Clarendon Press, 1934), 117–20. George Clark, *Sermons Preached in the Chapel of the Royal Military Asylum* (London, privately printed, 1872), p. vii.

[7] *DNB*, under 'Clarke'.

[8] T. A. Bowyer-Bower, 'A pioneer of Army education: the Royal Military Asylum, Chelsea, 1801–1821', *British Journal of Educational Studies*, 2 (1953–4), 122–32. The Asylum buildings are now the Duke of York's Headquarters, and the school has become the Duke of York's Royal Military School at Dover.

[9] G. T. Clark wrote a brief life of his father as a preface to *Sermons Preached in the Chapel of the Royal Military Asylum*, pp. v–xxv.

[10] G. A. Cranfield, *A Hand-list of English Provincial Newspapers and Periodicals, 1700–1760* (Cambridge, Bowes and Bowes, 1952), 15; and id., *The Development of the Provincial Newspaper, 1700–1760* (Oxford, Clarendon Press, 1962), 56 *et passim*. I am grateful to Mr Philip Riden, editor of the *VCH* for Northamptonshire, for information about the Diceys and Joseph Clark.

[11] Further information on the Dicey family is included in Chapter 8.

[12] N. G. Annan, 'The intellectual aristocracy', in J. H. Plumb (ed.), *Studies in Social History: a Tribute to G. M. Trevelyan* (London, Longmans, 1955), 243–87.

[13] Gordon N. Ray, *Thackeray: The Uses of Adversity (1811–1846)* (London, Oxford University Press, 1955), 79–100. This biography gives a detailed and horrifying account of Charterhouse in the 1820s.

[14] Information kindly supplied to Mr Peter Leech by the archivist of Charterhouse School.

[15] A bundle of documents relating to his medical training survives in NLW, G. T. Clark MSS, unscheduled.

[16] NLW MS 15,003B. Covering the years 1830–40 this is not a regular diary; there are long periods without entries and much of the content is extracts from reading and notes of sermons.

[17] Dean of Llandaff, 1845–57. *DNB, DWB.*

[18] Both were physicians in Bristol and the authors of several influential books. *DNB.*

[19] *Memoir of the Bristol Institution* (Bristol, 1836), 9.

[20] See Chapter 11.

[21] See G. T. Clark's contribution to John Martineau, *The Life and Correspondence of Sir Bartle Frere* (London, John Murray, 1895), i, 44–6.

[22] *Romilly's Visits to Wales 1827–1854*, ed. M. G. R. Morris (Llandysul, Gomer Press, 1998), 24–5. The Revd Joseph Romilly was one of the Conybeares' house party and mentioned in his diary 'a very agreeable lively young surgeon of Bristol, Mr Clarke'.

[23] Revel Guest and Angela V. John, *Lady Charlotte: A Biography of the Nineteenth Century* (London, Weidenfeld and Nicolson, 1989), 141–2.

[24] *Lady Charlotte Guest: Extracts from her Journal, 1833–1852* (London, John Murray, 1950), 186, 233 etc. There are many more references to him in the unpublished journal, e.g. 9–20 September 1833, 8 and 10 December 1834, 19–28 November 1835, NLW, Lady Charlotte Guest MSS IX. See also Mair Elvet Thomas, *Afiaith yng Ngwent* (Caerdydd, Gwasg Prifysgol Cymru, 1978), 7.

[25] See Chapter 5.

[26] Isambard Brunel, *The Life of Isambard Kingdom Brunel, Civil Engineer* (London, Longmans, 1870), 94.

[27] L. T. C. Rolt, *Isambard Kingdom Brunel* (London, Penguin Books, 1989), 143; R. A. Buchanan, 'I. K. Brunel: Engineer', in Sir Alfred Pugsley (ed.), *The Works of Isambard Kingdom Brunel: An Engineering Appreciation* (London, Institution of Civil Engineers, 1976), 8.

[28] Isambard Brunel, *The Life*, 97.

[29] [G. T. Clark], 'The birth and growth of the broad gauge', *Gent. Mag.*, 279 (1895), 496.

[30] See Chapter 3.

[31] *British Trade Journal*, 1 April 1877; *Merthyr Express*, 14 April 1877.

[32] The BL copy has 'Compiled by G. T. Clark' in the author's own hand on the title-page. See also Chapter 11.

[33] Most copies are dated 1846, but there had been a limited edition in 1843. George Ottley, *A Bibliography of British Railway History*, 2nd edn. (London, HMSO, 1983), 358, Item 5930; id., *Supplement* (London, HMSO, 1988), 45; Jack Simmons, *The Victorian Railway* (London, Thames and Hudson, 1991), 123.

[34] [Clark], 'The birth and growth of the broad gauge', 489–90.

[35] The letters are in the Brunel Collection (Private letterbooks) at the Bristol University Library and the PRO (RAIL 1149, item 6) respectively. Mr Stephen K. Jones of Wenvoe very kindly supplied the latter reference, and much other information about Brunel and Clark. See also D. S. Barrie, *The Taff Vale Railway* (Lingfield, Oakwood Press, 1962), 10.

[36] Adrian Vaughan, *Isambard Kingdom Brunel: Engineering Knight-Errant* (London, John Murray, 1991), 193.

[37] H. A. C. Sturgess (comp.), *Register of Admissions to the Honourable Society of the Middle Temple* (London, Butterworth, 1949), ii, 492. There is no doubt that this is the same G. T. Clark since his parentage is correctly given. His youngest brother, Frederick Guy Lestrange Clark, of Lincoln's Inn, had been called to the bar in 1840.

[38] I am grateful to Mr Roy Denning of Cowbridge for the transcript of a letter dated 15 November 1844 from G. T. Clark in Bombay to the Revd J. M. Traherne of Coedriglan, Glamorgan, in which he described the journey out.

[39] Martineau, *Sir Bartle Frere*, i, 44.

[40] Sir George Stephen's sister, Ann Mary, was married to Thomas Edward Dicey of Claybrooke, Clark's uncle. See Chapter 8.

[41] G. T. Clark, *Cartae et Alia Munimenta*, 2nd edn. (Cardiff, William Lewis, 1910), p. v. Another possible variant on this is that Clark may have found his father in failing health, and decided to stay for that reason. The Revd George Clark died in January 1848.

[42] It seems fairly certain that Frimhurst dates from *c.*1854; G. T. Clark's name appears as freeholder at that address on the electoral register for 1854–5. I am grateful to the Surrey Record Office, Kingston upon Thames, and the Surrey Local Studies Library, Guildford, for information on this point. The house is now the National Family Centre, ATD Fourth World Movement.

[43] As at Penzance, see p. 34. Chadwick himself approved of the Board's inspectors being employed in this way. R. A. Lewis, *Edwin Chadwick and the Public Health Movement, 1832–1854* (London, Longmans, 1952), 297.

[44] GRO D/D MTh 202/32/1. Letter from Mrs Clark to her brother, W. W. Lewis, 26 January 1852. I owe this reference to Mr Keith Edwards of Aberthin, near Cowbridge.

[45] *Lady Charlotte Guest: Extracts from her Journal, 1853–1891* (London, John Murray, 1952), 4.

[46] *Arch. Camb.*, NS 5 (1854), 71.

[47] Madeleine Elsas (ed.), *Iron in the Making* ([Cardiff], County Records Committee, etc., 1960), pp. vii–viii.

[48] Guest and John, *Lady Charlotte*, 28. G. T. Clark angered Guest's daughter, Lady Layard, by recalling that her father 'had not been either well educated or of good family'. Gordon Waterfield, *Layard of Nineveh* (London, John Murray, 1963), 310.

[49] Mary Anne Evans (1792–1872) married Wyndham Lewis of Greenmeadow, near Cardiff, in 1815. He died in 1838 leaving his widow a life interest in much of his property, but the Dowlais shares passed first to his brother, and then to his nephew. In 1839 Mrs Wyndham Lewis married Benjamin Disraeli; she was created Viscountess Beaconsfield in 1868.

[50] *Lady Charlotte Guest: Extracts from her Journal, 1833–1852*, 233.

[51] *Limbus Patrum Morganiae et Glamorganiae* (London, Wyman, 1886), 38–75.

[52] Immortalized by Giraldus Cambrensis; see *The Journey through Wales*, trans. by Lewis Thorpe (Harmondsworth, Penguin Books, 1978), 122–3. The Guests had named their eldest son 'Ivor' after this medieval chieftain.

[53] RCAHMW, *An Inventory of the Ancient Monuments in Glamorgan*, iv, 1 (Cardiff, HMSO, 1981), 192.

[54] *A List of the Names and Residences of the High Sheriffs of the County of Glamorgan* (privately printed, 1966), 60–1.

[55] 'Price' was a baptismal name commemorating her descent from the Price family who had previously lived at Parc. Ann's great-granduncle was Richard Price (1723–91), the philosopher.

[56] Henry Lewis of Greenmeadow was credited with 2,882 acres in 1873 and his late brother, Wyndham William Lewis of Newhouse, with 3,549 acres. John Bateman, *The Great Landowners of Great Britain and Ireland* (Leicester University Press, 1971), 269. For the family's prowess in the hunting field, see Fred, Vida and John Holley, *Wyndham William Lewis, Esquire, the Heath, Cardiff: Master of Hounds* (Merthyr Tydfil, V. A. Holley, 1987).

[57] I am deeply indebted to Mr Keith Edwards for his exposition of the complexities of the Lewis inheritance. The Clarks ultimately bought out the interest of Mrs Clark's sisters.

[58] NLW MS 15,004B, G. T. Clark's diary, 15 March 1856.

[59] John B. Hilling, *Cardiff and the Valleys* (London, Lund Humphries, 1973), 72; Thomas Lloyd, *The Lost Houses of Wales,* 2nd edn. (London, Save Britain's Heritage, 1989), 95. Dowlais House, having long since been converted into offices, was demolished in the 1970s.

[60] *Western Mail*, 2 February 1898.

[61] *Arch. Camb.*, 6th ser. 1 (1901), 49.

[62] A. H[artshorne?], 'Mr George Thomas Clark', *Arch. J.*, 55 (1898), 106–9.

[63] *Arch. Camb.*, 6th ser. 1 (1901), 47.

[64] See Chapter 9.

[65] *Fifth Report of the Commissioners Appointed to Inquire into the Organization and Rules of Trades Unions* (London, Eyre and Spottiswoode, 1868), 84; *PP* 1867–8 [3980–I] xxxix, 90.

[66] Guest and John, *Lady Charlotte*, 63–74.

[67] Elizabeth Havill, 'The respectful strike', *Morgannwg*, 24 (1980), 61–81.

[68] Ieuan Gwynedd Jones, 'The Merthyr of Henry Richard', in Glanmor Williams (ed.), *Merthyr Politics* (Cardiff, University of Wales Press, 1966), 45–6; Tydfil Thomas, *Poor Relief in Merthyr Tydfil Union in Victorian Times* (Cardiff, Glamorgan Archive Service, 1992), 135–6.

[69] Tydfil Thomas, *Poor Relief*, 120–32.

[70] For Mrs Clark's hospital at Dowlais, see Eira M. Smith, 'Mrs Clark of Dowlais', *Merthyr Historian*, 8 (1996), 213–18.

[71] *Merthyr Express*, 11 and 18 April 1885.

[72] *Llantrisant Church Monthly*, April 1898.

[73] The major characteristic of entries in his diary 1830–40, NLW 15,003B.

[74] Such an entry appeared in the 1871 edn. of *BLG*.

CHAPTER 2

Writing the Insanitary Town:

G. T. Clark, Slums and Sanitary Reform

ANDY CROLL

> Without going quite the length of some who seem to think that, if men were
> properly drained and ventilated, they would never be sick or die at all, we
> do hold cleanliness, manliness, and godliness to lie very nearly together,
> and believe health to be, after religion and civil government, if not between
> them, of concern to the weal of the nation. On this account, and because we
> are willing to support, according to our power, the new commission, we
> shall enter, in some detail, upon this important but somewhat unsavoury
> subject.
>
> (G. T. Clark, 'Sanitary Reform', *BQR*, 1849)

George Thomas Clark was the quintessential Victorian polymath. He
was, amongst other things, a trained surgeon, a civil engineer, a
respected archaeologist and antiquarian, as well as being an astute and
successful manager of one of the world's largest ironworks. Such a willingness to experiment, to test one's abilities in so many different fields of
human activity, can pose the modern historian some problems. For in these
days of specialisms and 'experts', it can be difficult to gauge the significance
of someone who took so much delight in transgressing the boundaries
between one discipline and another. Yet, if the obituary which appeared in
the *Merthyr Express* is any guide, late Victorians seem to have had little
difficulty in assessing G. T. Clark's worth. According to the newspaper, 'Mr
Clark will never be remembered locally as a politician – but as the
regenerator of the Dowlais works, and the foremost sanitary reformer of
Merthyr Tydfil'.[1]

The latter accolade was certainly well deserved. Not only did Clark play
an active role in promoting the idea of public health in Merthyr (one of
the most insanitary of all Victorian towns), he was also a key figure in the
drive to sanitize other urban settlements in nineteenth-century Britain. This

chapter examines his involvement in sanitary reform, paying particular attention to those few years in the late 1840s and early 1850s when Clark gave himself over almost entirely to matters of urban hygiene. These were the years when he was a superintending inspector, an important position that had been created in the wake of the Public Health Act of 1848. The inspectors were charged with the duty of reporting upon the sanitary condition of many of Britain's most insanitary towns and cities, and were required to venture into some of the most disease-ridden, dirty and dangerous of all urban spaces. The documents that Clark and his colleagues produced have provided historians with some of the most compelling images we have of the urban landscape of the mid-Victorian town. It is suggested here that they also allow us to glimpse into the thought-world of their authors.

G. T. Clark: from Bombay to the Board of Health

G. T. Clark's rise to a position of importance in the public health movement was a direct consequence of his talents as a civil engineer. These 'folk heroes' of the mid-Victorian period were renowned for their abilities to constitute, manipulate and describe physical space.[2] As such they were extremely well placed to assist in the development and installation of a whole new sanitary technology. Clark's first foray into the field of urban hygiene was as early as 1843 when he produced a report on the provision of sewerage facilities in Bombay. Although we know very little about his experiences in India (apart from the fact that he found the climate unbearable), it seems that he relished the challenges of sanitary reform, for on his return to Britain he followed closely the fortunes of the public health movement which was growing in influence during the 1840s. This movement, with dynamic figures such as Edwin Chadwick to the fore, did much to publicize the appalling squalor of urban life. Numerous reports, surveys and government inquiries, all focusing on the health of the nation, appeared in this decade and convinced many of the need for concerted action. The Public Health Act of 1848 was the direct result of this growing concern.

Although not the first Act of Parliament to address the issue of public health, the Act of 1848 has generally been seen as a highly significant moment in the history of the public health movement.[3] It established a General Board of Health composed of three commissioners, one of whom was none other than the energetic Chadwick. The Board's powers – in theory at least – were considerable. In the first instance, it could institute inquiries into the sanitary condition of any town in which the annual mortality rate exceeded 23 per 1,000 inhabitants, or in which at least 10 per cent of the ratepayers requested such an inquiry. If either (or both) of these criteria were met, a superintending inspector was sent to hold a public inquiry and collect evidence. This evidence was then presented to the Board as an official report. On the basis of the findings of the inspectors, the commissioners could proceed to apply the terms of the Act and set up Local Boards of Health. These bodies, elected by the ratepayers, were granted extensive powers, including the ability to make arrangements for the supply of water, to lay drains and sewers, remove insanitary nuisances, regulate public streets and highways, lay out public parks, supervise lodging houses, maintain existing burial grounds and fix the sites of new ones.

That G. T. Clark was well informed about the problems posed by insanitary towns, and the legislation that had been passed to deal with them, is revealed most clearly in a lengthy article he contributed to the *British Quarterly Review* in February 1849.[4] In it he reviewed a number of official reports on the state of Britain's urban settlements, and discussed the implications of the Act of 1848. The article is interesting not least for its role in bringing Clark to the attention of the General Board of Health. Clark annotated his own personal copy of the article, observing that 'I believe it was to this review that I owed my appointment by Lord Carlisle as a sub-commissioner under the Board of Health'.[5] Exactly how the essay secured him the position is unclear given that it was published three months *after* he had taken up his duties as a superintending inspector. Most of the other inspectors were required to write letters of application to the Board of Health. If Clark wrote such a letter it has been lost. Perhaps the most likely explanation is that a draft copy of the essay found its way on to Lord Carlisle's desk. Whatever the circumstances of his appointment, we can be sure that he was in post by 24 November 1848, when he attended a meeting of the Board to report on the preparations being made for his first set of inquiries due to begin two weeks later.[6]

As an inspector, Clark found himself right at the heart of the venture to cleanse, regulate and rationalize the urban spaces of mid-Victorian Britain. The sheer number of inquiries that he oversaw is impressive indeed. Between December 1848 and March 1850 he had visited, inspected, and reported upon over forty towns and cities, and travelled the length and breadth of England and Wales in the process. He toured extensively in the south-west of England, the north, the south-east, the Midlands and Wales. By the end of his engagements he had inspected a wide variety of urban settlements ranging from new industrial 'frontier' towns, older centres of population, fishing towns, rural market towns, and sprawling, congested manufacturing and commercial settlements such as Preston and Bristol. His investigations into such a diverse group of towns and cities ensured that by the time that Clark submitted his final report in April 1850, he was one of the most experienced of all the Board's superintending inspectors.[7]

'Amassing certain facts': G. T. Clark – the silent author

On the face of it the reports produced by G. T. Clark are unpromising sources for the historian interested in uncovering the personality of their author. In terms of structure and content, his reports have much in common with those written by the other superintending inspectors. There is little that is distinctive. This conformity can largely be explained by the fact that all of the inspectors were issued with a detailed set of instructions advising them on how to conduct their inquiries and present their findings.[8] The problem is compounded by the way in which Clark was eager to silence his own authorial voice.

There were two important strategies which Clark used to distance himself from his reports. First, he assiduously avoided writing in the first person. As such his work was qualitatively different from the journalists who were to descend upon the rookeries and the slums in the second half of the century. They were always ready to sensationalize the delightful horrors of life in the courts and alleys in the interests of boosting newspaper sales. Part of their ability to dramatize their accounts rested upon the fact that they were sharing *their* experiences with their readers. Thus Henry Mayhew – an early exponent of the art – constantly punctuated his kaleidoscopic representations of London's street life with reminders that he had first-hand knowledge of all that he was writing: 'I talked with . . .', 'I visited . . .', 'I met . . .'[9] In contrast, Clark and his colleagues were intent upon letting the facts speak for themselves. Take, for example, his description of a run-down quarter in the town of Beverley:

> At the back of the *fish shambles*, the street is in a dirty condition, and the courts and houses all up *Lady-gate* discharge into the street gutters. The houses here are built back to back, or nearly so, in solid blocks, and the night-soil is removed in boxes, and, in practice, appears to be thrown out into the private lanes. The subsoil here is very wet, and some of the cellars contain water. There are no drains. *Sylvester-lane* is very narrow indeed. In one place cows and pigs are kept, and the premises are very filthy. Some of the yard drains are merely covered with flag-stones, badly jointed, and loosely laid.[10]

PUBLIC HEALTH ACT.

(11 & 12 Vict., Cap. 63.)

REPORT

TO THE

GENERAL BOARD OF HEALTH,

ON A

PRELIMINARY INQUIRY

INTO THE SEWERAGE, DRAINAGE, AND SUPPLY OF WATER, AND THE SANITARY CONDITION OF THE INHABITANTS

OF THE TOWN OF

BRIDGEND.

By GEO. T. CLARK,

SUPERINTENDING INSPECTOR.

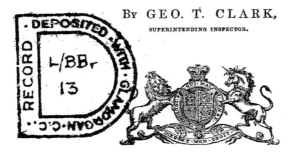

LONDON:

PRINTED BY W. CLOWES & SONS, STAMFORD STREET, FOR HER MAJESTY'S STATIONERY OFFICE.

1850.

11 Title-page of one of G. T. Clark's Reports to the General Board of Health. *Glamorgan Record Office.*

Such representations have a dramatic quality all of their own. However, their power to shock is dependent in no small measure upon Clark suppressing his own personal responses.

The second distancing strategy which the inspector used to great effect was the incorporation, wherever possible, of statistical material. The 1830s and early 1840s had witnessed something of an explosion in statistical surveys, as reformers, prompted by the outbreak of cholera and concerned by the rise of Chartism, began to focus attention on the 'Condition of England' question. Much work had been done on sanitary statistics in particular.[11] Edwin Chadwick's own *Report on the Sanitary Condition of the Labouring Population of Great Britain* was a prime example of a survey that used statistics, although there were others carried out by less well-known figures in towns and cities up and down the country.[12] Clark was quick to acknowledge both their achievements, and the need for such surveys. At a public sitting during his inquiry at Preston he explained why sanitary statistics were vital to his task: 'they showed, first of all, the extent to which improvement was necessary; and, secondly, they served as a point of departure'. Without precise information as to the condition of the towns, and the health of the population, 'it would be impossible to satisfy the public as to the good that was being done. Eight or ten years hence, people would hardly believe, without proper evidence, that they lived as they do now.' He was eager to cite such material where it existed, 'to quote it, and reason upon it as well as he could'.[13] By doing so, he was conveniently provided with another means of abstracting, anatomizing and representing the urban environment whilst minimizing the subjective content of his reports.

The objective nature of his reports is wholly consistent with Clark's views on the duties of an inspector. He stated publicly that, as he saw it, his role was simply to 'amass certain facts'.[14] During the course of the inquiries he developed this theme by proclaiming that it was not his task to apportion blame or to castigate particular individuals. When in Kendal, for example, he informed the gathered audience that though he was obliged to refer to specific cases, 'he wished to avoid, as far as possible, their identification with individuals, whom he looked upon as less in fault than the general system which had grown up'.[15] And at times it appeared as if he was willing to extend this philosophy to include institutions. At Bristol in February 1850, he announced that 'it was not his object to find fault with the local government, which had but very little power, but to point out the state of things that existed'.[16] Thus, the public persona that Clark tried to cultivate was one which consciously emphasized his role as an objective observer.

'The observation of a Lynceus': Clark as a chronicler of urban decay

This concern with objectivity has made his reports extremely valuable resources for urban historians who have been quick to exploit them in their quest to capture the sights and smells of the urban landscape.[17] Indeed, Ieuan Gwynedd Jones, the leading historian of public health and sanitary reform in mid-Victorian Wales, has singled out Clark the inspector for especial praise on the grounds of his 'power of observation and objectivity'.[18] There are good reasons for such enthusiasm. Each report represents an inventory of some of the most insanitary spaces to be found in the mid-Victorian town. Importantly, Clark made great efforts to inspect personally all the areas which appeared in the final documents. Thus, in his company we are taken on a tour through the choking miasmas, through the unpitched, dung-filled streets, right to the heart of the fever districts and the cholera dens.

It is clear that he was assiduous in ensuring that all areas of a town fell under his gaze. Upon arriving in Taunton, for example, he climbed up the tower of a local church 'for the purpose of commanding a bird's-eye-view of the district which he was about to examine'.[19] More commonly he contented himself with a series of lengthy walks, usually in the company of medical men, officials and members of the local police force. The route of these perambulations was in part determined by Clark's desire to see for himself the existing arrangements regarding sewerage and water facilities. He also made a point of seeking out any notorious 'trouble spots' that had been brought to his attention. Even in the smaller towns, these journeys through and around the built form could be time-consuming. For instance, during his three days in Penzance, Clark and assorted local notables walked around the boundaries of the borough, examined the site of a proposed reservoir, and looked at the borough gaol and the workhouse. According to the local newspaper, 'they perambulated the whole borough', taking in 'almost every court', the cemeteries, the slaughterhouses, the markets, 'and one or two venerable nuisances' along the way.[20]

More than one commentator was impressed by the professional manner in which Clark undertook his work. The editor of the *Kendal Mercury* paid tribute 'to the very business-like manner' in which he carried out his investigation of the town.[21] Another suggested that he 'manifest[ed] in his talent, assiduity, and discernment, a perfect competency to his onerous appointment'.[22] Meanwhile, his efforts in Bristol earned him high praise in one of the local papers:

[W]e cannot withhold our commendation of the masterly, searching, and thorough manner, in which Mr Clark . . . is performing his work. Physically and mentally, no man could be better qualified for the office. Rapid, keen, and penetrating, he has an ear for information from every quarter – a way of receiving and apprehending suggestions from all sides, and of separating that which is of use from that which is of no use. Sitting in open court, he has a faculty of comprehending the situation and circumstances of a locality he never saw, in a manner that surprises everyone . . .

Nevertheless, it was the sight of G. T. Clark at work during one of his tours of Bristol's slums that most caught the eye of the editor. In the report he was presented as an almost superhuman figure, constantly on the move, observing all the while:

[I]n his walks of personal inspection round the city, and in its most dense districts, he seems furnished with the fabled seven-league boots, while he possesses the observation of a Lynceus, who was said by mythologists to see through the ground, for all the subterranean ramifications of sewers and cesspools are as easily comprehended by him as though they were uncovered. To see him swinging along on his walks, and people panting to keep up with him, you would think he was performing an act of pedestrianism for a wager, yet he reads as he runs, and never loses a point however rapid his progress. It is only such a person that would do for the work: a man slow to sift his evidence, however sound, and unable to get speedily over the ground, however good his judgement, would take a twelvemonth to do that which Mr Clark will probably complete in a fortnight.[23]

If the comprehensive nature of Clark's inquiries makes his reports required reading for the urban historian, so does the sheer range of settlements covered by him and the other inspectors. A number of Victorian observers – most notably the 'social explorers' of the second half of the century – were bewitched by the magnificent squalor of London and of the large industrial centres, those 'shock cities' which mushroomed during the nineteenth century.[24] Their conclusions all pointed to the unhinging effects of unregulated urban growth. In turn, historians have been happy enough to follow the Mayhews, the Greenwoods, the Mastermans and the Booths into the slums of these great urban centres. Although such cities are perfectly legitimate objects of study, we should be aware that they represented just one of the many urban experiences of nineteenth-century Britain.[25] Because of the way in which the towns visited by Clark and his colleagues actually selected themselves (either as a consequence of the mortality rates or because the ratepayers requested an inspection) a number of these other experiences come into view.

When viewed from this altered – and wider – perspective, it becomes clear that rapid urban growth was not the only agent capable of creating the slums and rookeries. Clark's report on the cathedral city of Worcester makes the point neatly enough. The town was a long-established centre of the cloth industry, although by the early Victorian period the china and gloves trades had risen to dominance. At the century's mid-point, Worcester boasted a population of some 25,400, a figure which had been reached by a process of gentle incremental increases. As Clark remarked, 'Its defects are such as are found in most ancient towns': they were legion. Between 1838 and 1844 the average annual number of deaths was 675, or at a rate of 26.5 per 1,000, 'a proportion high in the mortalities of towns'.[26] And whilst the main streets were clean, neat and fronted by impressive public, commercial and residential buildings, they merely hid a congested jumble of slum dwellings. During his tours of inspection around these areas, Clark experienced nothing less than an assault on his senses. He saw – and smelt – overflowing cesspools, blocked drains, pumps dispensing polluted water, a court flooded with urine from an adjacent horse stand, and privies built in such a way that the 'night-soil' (the Victorian euphemism for human excrement) oozed through the walls and into the adjoining houses.[27]

Nor were such dilapidated areas the sole preserve of the larger towns and cities. Even much smaller older settlements could be touched by the ravaging effects of urban decay. In the Cornish assize town of Bodmin, there were a mere 3,850 inhabitants in 1841. However, as Clark discovered, a small population was clearly no guarantee of urban hygiene. Near the centre of the town was gathered a tangle of crowded court dwellings. These buildings were all damp, without adequate privy accommodation, and in a filthy state. The built form was peppered with numerous pigsties, open dung-pits and several slaughterhouses, while the streets were covered in offal, excrement and mud.[28] The only concession to anything approximating to a sewer was the town brook.[29]

A convert preaches the sanitary creed

Thus far the 'objective' qualities of G. T. Clark's reports have been noted. Clark was always willing to stress his objectivity, and historians have been eager enough to reinforce this self-assessment. A possible consequence of this objectivity has also been suggested; namely that the reports are more useful to the urban historian than they are to the historian interested in Clark himself. Yet there are good reasons for arguing that all of the above propositions are, to significant degrees, faulty. In the first place, the objectivity of Clark's reports is more apparent than real. Furthermore, we need constantly to be aware that we are in the company of a cultural outsider, someone who took a raft of assumptions, preconceptions and prejudices into the slums with him. As a result, it will be suggested that the reports shed as much light on the beliefs of Clark, and the class from which he was drawn, as they do about the urban landscape through which he moved. Even the idea that his reports can be used to recreate the horrors of the built environment needs to be interrogated. Clark's status as an outsider means that even his descriptions of urban space carry with them the very real possibility of his misunderstanding important aspects of what he saw.

The first point that needs to be emphasized is that Clark was both fully committed to the 'Sanitary Idea' and in total sympathy with Edwin Chadwick's often controversial theories. Indeed, if he had not been so-minded he would have failed to secure the appointment, no matter how great his talents as a civil engineer. Chadwick hand-picked the inspectors on the basis of their conformity to the principles which underpinned the Public Health Act.[30] Clark had, of course, presented his thoughts on this issue in his article on 'Sanitary reform'. It is an eloquent expression of the Chadwickian position. Like his mentor, Clark entertained an image of the sanitary city in which pure water circulated, rain water drained away, and excrement flowed harmlessly through sewers. Both men also believed that sanitary reform made economic sense. What upset Chadwick as much as the miasmas and the filth was the wasteful nature of the insanitary town. When he looked at the piles of excrement and ordure in the streets and the courts, he not only saw the sources of disease and death, he also saw potential sources of income. This led to his proposals to construct sewage farms that would convert detritus into manure. Clark fully supported this recycling scheme, and formulated a maxim which Chadwick himself would have been proud of: 'We believe that in all matters, as a general rule, it is both *better* and *cheaper* to do right than to do wrong . . .'[31]

As this pronouncement suggests, for Clark the promotion of urban hygiene was a moral good as much as it was an economic one. He saw it as incumbent upon members of his own class to take responsibility for the squalor in which many of the working class were living. Whilst he recognized that some of the problems facing the urban poor could only be rectified by God himself,

the gifts of free air, of the light of day, of the means of personal cleanliness, of unmolested exercise and innocent recreation, and of health untainted by physical abominations, these it is within the scope of the wealthier classes and of the government to bestow, almost at once, upon the people.[32]

If the 'wealthier classes' discharged their duties in this respect, then the '[very broad] line of separation between rich and poor' could be 'broken through', and 'internal peace, order and happiness' would be secured.[33] If they turned away from their responsibilities then social breakdown would result. He used recent history to support his case. In his report on Bristol, Clark referred his readers back to the famous riots of 1831, noting that the town 'felt severely, on one memorable occasion . . . consequences which may in great measure be attributed to the having allowed a large population to grow up in ignorance and to live in dirt and discomfort'.[34] Thus, as he saw it, he was engaged in a project that would ultimately 'knit together the hearts of the nation': the sanitary reformer was necessarily a social reformer.[35]

These statements should give us reason to pause. Clark was firmly convinced that the installation of a whole apparatus of sanitary technology – sewers, drains, pipes and taps – would result not just in an improvement in the physical condition of the working classes; it would also act as a stimulus to social peace and harmony. The alternative to sanitary reform was a descent into social disorder and possibly even revolution. Such beliefs allowed little room for compromise: sanitary reform was necessarily a desirable thing. Interestingly, there is evidence that, on his tours of inspection, he took the opportunity to propagate these ideas. Take, for example, his activities whilst in Penzance in 1849. Having already reported upon the state of the Cornish fishing town, he returned to oversee the implementation of his recommendations. In a letter sent to the Board, Clark was pleased to be able to inform the commissioners that great progress was being made, not only in the town itself but in the surrounding district: 'in consequence of this success [at Penzance,] Redruth has petitioned and I have good hope of St Ives and Helston'. His knowledge of the predisposition of these other towns to the Public Health Act was based on more than mere hearsay: Clark had actually used his time in West Cornwall to seek out potential sympathizers and win them over to the cause. He had arranged a meeting with the rector of Redruth and had done his best to spread the word: 'I explained the P[ublic] H[ealth] Act to him – gave him quotes of what would be wanted . . . He went away much supported, and I gave him a Kendal report to enable him to convert his flock to the orthodox sanitary creed.'[36]

Given Clark's enthusiasm for the 'Sanitary Idea', the suggestion that his reports are the work of an 'objective' observer seems somewhat suspect. More correctly, we should see them as political documents which, from the opening paragraph, set out to argue the case for sanitary reform.[37] Clark was certainly aware of the local political contexts in which his inquiries were held. Upon arriving in a town one of his first acts was to gauge the mood of locals and report back to the commissioners. For example, while inspecting

Rugby he wrote to Chadwick noting that the School and some of the 'resident gentry' were in favour of the Act, the principal solicitor and the canal engineer were 'neutral', while the doctors were all opposed, 'some avowedly, others practically so'. Moreover, he detected 'a great dread of expense existing in the minds of the general public'. Demonstrating a grasp of the political realities of the situation, he counselled Chadwick to move cautiously: as '[t]he people are somewhat at variance among themselves . . . great discretion will be necessary in any further proceedings'.[38] At Durham there was no such fine balance of forces. So hostile had members of the town council been during his inquiry, that Clark felt moved to complain to Henry Austin of the unscrupulous language they had used in condemning the Act.[39] Later, when asked by the council to advise them in writing of the cost of suitable drains, he refused, worried that they would wilfully misquote him. His patience with them was clearly running thin: 'The Durham people are particularly abusive at the meetings of their Council and thoroughly dishonest in their mode of quoting the report.'[40] His characterization of the different groups is in itself instructive. Thus while these opponents of the Act were 'thoroughly dishonest', members of the enlightened Penzance town council were deemed 'very intelligent and unprejudicial'. Meanwhile at Worcester the surgeon James Orwin, who attended Clark throughout his visit and was 'the prime mover in the whole business', was 'a clear headed and energetic man'.[41]

Morality tales: Clark writes the insanitary town

The degree to which Clark's reports mirrored the argument laid out in his review article is striking, as is the similarity of all of his reports, one to the other. We have, of course, already noted that the structure of the reports was laid down by the General Board of Health. Yet the similarities extend beyond a common structure. In every one, the same argument unfolded as Clark moved ineluctably towards his predetermined conclusions. Indeed, his rendering of the story of urban development (and subsequent degeneration) was akin to a morality tale that he told and retold more than forty times. The names of the characters may have changed, but the plot remained essentially the same, as did the principal heroes and villains.

Top of his hit list was bad government – local and central. In his article on sanitary reform he barely concealed his contempt for the generations of legislators in the House of Commons who had failed to grasp the nettle. Commenting on the numerous (and largely ineffective) local acts which had been passed to deal with street cleansing, drainage and the like, he took a swipe at 'our superseded friends at Westminster, Noodle and Doodle'.[42] The fact that they had been 'superseded', and that he was working for the newly constituted General Board of Health, suggests that by this time he was more sanguine about the state of central government.[43] However, as befitted someone employed by Edwin Chadwick, Clark cultivated a feisty dislike of the existing system of local government and took every opportunity to condemn it in his reports. In his view, power had to be consolidated and rationalized if the local authorities were to stand any chance of effecting improvements. The arrangements in Wrexham typified all that Clark detested. The government of the town was parochial, with the parish divided into fifteen different townships. Each township had two overseers of the poor, two surveyors of highways, and, in some cases, distinct gas inspectors. This system, Clark pronounced, was 'powerless for sanitary purposes; it is far too complex, and with responsibilities far too much divided'. To make matters worse, it was further hamstrung by the lack of skilled personnel.[44]

Other guardians of the 'public good' were also singled out for his opprobrious comments. Property owners in particular had much to answer for:

> [T]hey are the class who have perpetrated these abuses for gain, and who steadily oppose any amendment of them. As a class, they are perhaps more out of the reach of influence than any other. They are too high to suffer materially from the evils they create, and scarcely high enough, or sufficiently educated, to feel much shame from the exposure of their neglect of duty, and they are too near the condition of the poor to feel any great sympathy with them.[45]

As such, they were unwelcome brakes on sanitary progress. Importantly, though Clark criticized them, he did not see their indifference as an inevitable result of the pursuit of profit. Clark was no socialist, and he never advocated a suspension of the laws of the market-place. To the contrary, as he saw it, the problem was actually one of the property owners not being committed *enough* to the pursuit of profit. The landlords believed that their interests were different from those of the poor tenants. Clark thought they were mistaken in this, and told them so. He insisted that basic sanitary improvements, as well as improving the health of the tenants, would actually lead to the value of properties increasing.[46] Not to effect such reforms was both morally reprehensible *and* economically foolish.

When it came to dealing with the manufacturing classes, Clark was more ambivalent. This may surprise. As they were responsible for some of the worst pollution in urban Britain, one might have expected much of his time to have been spent considering how to deal with the problem.[47] He was certainly aware of the deleterious effects that accompanied prolonged exposure to noxious gases. Inhabitants of the St Philip's Marsh area of Bristol petitioned Clark, detailing their complaints against a nearby alkali works. Their houses were enveloped in a cloud of poisonous gases, 'so dense in damp weather as to check vision'. He inspected the area and sampled for himself the delights of the sulphuretted hydrogen clouds with their 'odour often mistaken for that from a herd of pigs just landed from the hold of a vessel'.[48] In Wrexham, written evidence was forwarded to the inspector complaining of the nuisances created by the gas works. Garden vegetables were rendered 'very unpalatable and unhealthy', while papers, linen and clothing were covered with 'blacks and flakes of soot'. In the same town, an inhabitant of Owen's Yard complained that one of his neighbours had turned his premises into a candle manufactory, erecting furnaces to burn animal fats. 'The result has been the most dreadful repetition of smells, which has occasioned the health of my family to be seriously affected.'[49] Despite noting the extent of the problem, and sympathizing with those affected by it, when it came to proposing remedies Clark remained silent. Doubtless aware of the manufacturers' importance as ratepayers (and their potential to be very powerful opponents of sanitary reform), the soon-to-be trustee of the Dowlais Iron Company was reluctant to suggest any measures that had the effect of curtailing their operations.

He was far more vocal when it came to expressing his views on the poor denizens of the courts and alleys.[50] Throughout his reports, Clark presented the working class as the unfortunate victims of the insanitary nuisances that had been allowed to proliferate unchecked. Whereas their social betters, to varying degrees, were held responsible for the condition of the rookeries and slums, he consistently argued that the majority of the urban poor were without blame. They were powerless to bring about the fundamental changes to their immediate environment necessary for good sanitation. 'It is impossible', he wrote, 'that [poor families] can successfully strive against the evils of a damp floor, an unpaved and undrained yard, an offensive public ditch adjoining the house, or a privy with an open cesspool in the yard.'[51] However, if the slum dwellers were victims they were not helpless ones. For no matter how appalling the scenes witnessed, Clark found reason to be hopeful. In his characterizations of the poor they generally appear as having the potential to live the good, clean life. They only needed encouragement from their social superiors. On his numerous tours of inspection, he peered into their dwellings and was always impressed with what he saw. In the filthy courts of Worcester he was struck by the cleanliness of the female glove makers.[52] In Bridgend the neat and tidy appearance of the interiors of the cottages was noted.[53] Even in 'the dirtiest quarters' of Brynmawr, he 'usually found the interior of the houses clean'.[54]

Notwithstanding Clark's sympathetic portrayal of the urban poor, one section of the working class was represented in his writings in very different terms: the Irish. His opinion of these poverty-stricken immigrants was most powerfully expressed in his review article on sanitary reform. Rather than being worthy of compassion, Clark suggested that they actually contributed to the process of urban decay. Thus, when discussing the evidence relating to the condition of some of Liverpool's courts and cellars, he observed that the situation was all the worse 'because the place is much infested with the Irish, who are very dirty in their persons and food, and very improvident'. Similarly, Bristol was 'a very dirty city, containing many Irishmen and Irish pigs'. When detailing the insanitary nuisances in Manchester, Clark developed the relationship between these slum dwellers and their animals. He noted that in 1843 there were 2,359 pigsties and 3,375 pigs in the city; 'and in 1841 perhaps an equal injury was done to its cleanliness by the presence of 4,683 Irish'. He continued, 'Your recent Hiberno-Celt, whether of the two-legged or four-legged quality, is an animal whose habits are not altogether Hygeian.'[55]

Such representations of the Irish poor, offensive as they are to modern sensibilities, appeared much less so to the majority of his mid-Victorian readers. The construction of racist images of the Irish immigrants had a long pedigree, and a number of different writers saw little wrong in deploying them in their texts. Even the young Friedrich Engels, passionate defender of the British working class, was content enough to conceptualize the Irish in the same animalistic terms.[56] That was in 1844. By the time Clark was writing, Britain's towns and cities were attracting ever increasing numbers of immigrants from the Emerald Isle, driven out of their home by the ravages of the Great Famine. This influx contributed, in part, to the strong current of anti-Irish sentiment that surfaced in these years.[57] Furthermore, Clark was by no means alone in suggesting that the Irish were a threat to public health.[58] However, if his views were typical in many ways, what is of interest to us is the fashion in which he had clearly taken his prejudices into the slums with him, and emerged with them still intact. His review article, after all, was published at an early stage of his inquiries, and was probably penned *before* he became an inspector. Yet Clark chose to represent what he saw in the crowded courts and close-packed streets in exactly the same language that he had used in his essay. His reports are littered with references to 'infestations' of the 'low Irish' who 'swarmed' in the slums. These unfortunates are contrasted with the 'English poor' who 'took pains to be clean in their persons and their houses'.[59] Nowhere do positive images of the Irish appear.

Clark's treatment of the Irish serves as another reminder of the highly subjective nature of what purported to be objective reports. Far from the experience of visiting the slums structuring his representations, it seems that those preconceived representations played a significant role in shaping his experiences. For whilst he doubtless did see many examples of wretched and debauched Irish, drinking to deaden their senses, one can be equally certain that he witnessed many English, Welsh, Scots (and others) engaged in similar pursuits. That he chose to ignore their ethnicity, and also ignore those Irish who did not conform to the racist stereotype, alerts us to the partial, and highly particularized, set of images of the mid-nineteenth-century town that emerge from the pages of his reports. At the same time, it is noteworthy that Clark's discursive strategy presented him with something of a problem. By referring to the potent stereotypes of the Irish immigrants he was employing 'Irishness' as literary device, a convenient shorthand for images of dirt, disease and demoralization. The very presence of 'the Irish' symbolized how bad things had become in the insanitary town. He had only to mention that a district was inhabited by this ethnic group and no further allusion to its condition was required. Yet, no matter how depraved Clark's 'Irish' were, if his overall argument about the virtues of sanitary reform was to retain its coherence he needed to keep open at least the possibility that they too could attain salvation. Thus he was forced to qualify his characterization somewhat:

> It had been said by some landlords that if they put the poor in palaces of gold or ivory they would not keep them clean. He differed with those who expressed that opinion. If they put the Irishman into a dirty place, dirty would he remain; but even the Irish, if placed in a clean place, and well looked after, would learn to improve; and as to the Saxon, place him in a cleanly comfortable dwelling, with the necessary conveniences, and he would, he was sure, keep it orderly and clean.[60]

Clark's representations of the poor denizens of the slums and rookeries thus supported perfectly his already formulated argument. The English poor would respond well to any reforms brought about by the socially responsible 'wealthier classes', becoming better, more peaceable, sanitary citizens in the process. Meanwhile, such was the civilizing power of properly laid drains, a pure and constant water supply, and an effective sewerage system, that *even* Clark's debased, inhuman 'Irish' could be rescued from the mire.

The partial gaze of the cultural outsider

For the most part, Clark's observations on the cultural habits of the labouring population were strictly limited. We should not be surprised by this: he was, after all, primarily concerned with the condition of the urban landscape. Nevertheless, there were occasions when he did remark, albeit obliquely, upon such matters. In so doing, his sensibilities as a cultural outsider once again came to the surface.

Throughout his reports we are presented with a bourgeois conception of urban space. All his descriptions of the courts and alleys, the congested streets, the insanitary slaughterhouses and so on were written according to the dictates of a middle-class common sense. This common sense categorized some forms of behaviour as acceptable, others as unacceptable. Partly because Clark's assumptions so closely mirror our own it is tempting to accept uncritically his various descriptions and assessments. Yet we have all the time to be aware that the superintending inspector may have related to the urban landscape in ways very different from the inhabitants of the slums and rookeries. The degree of difference should not be overstated, of course. Although direct evidence for the assumptions and thoughts of the working-class urbanites is scanty, there is enough to suggest that the overwhelming majority would have preferred to live in a much cleaner environment. When detailing a particular nuisance, Clark often noted that inhabitants 'complained greatly' of the problem. Furthermore, on rare occasions members of the labouring classes submitted written evidence to the authorities. One such letter, in careful handwriting, was sent to the General Board of Health from a court dweller in Bristol. Concerned with the supply of clean water, it indicates that the 'Sanitary Idea' was by no means one entertained only by the well-to-do:

> In some Courts there is 20 Houses which contains 40 families at the least. We are oblige to buy water by the Gallon or Buckett. We have no entermediate Sewers made[,] the Landowners says the Commissioners must make them[;] we are nearly sofficated and cannot get any relief.
>
> We the humble Classes of Life humbly prays by the *thousands* for your immediate interfearance if the Health Act has any provision on our behalf. We pay 3d. a family, 6d. per house, 10s. per week in a small court to be allow'd one Tap of water.
>
> But thousands have none at all. And the Labouring Man['s] hard earnings is going into the Owners Pocketts by such practices.[61]

Yet if such a plaintive cry from the slums of Bristol provides some evidence of working-class support for sanitary reform, we should remain aware that the urban poor could still think about the spaces through which they moved on a daily basis in ways which baffled the sanitary 'experts'.[62]

The task of recovering these working-class understandings of the slums is difficult, not least because the best evidence we have comes from middle-class individuals such as Clark. Their own bourgeois sensibilities, more often than not, rendered them insensitive to the thought-worlds inhabited by members of other social classes. Nevertheless, at times we are provided with telling glimpses of those alternative world views. For example, when visiting Brynmawr, Clark observed that 'It is customary to cast out into the road all the filth of every description, and to trust it to the wind in dry weather, and the rain in wet weather, to remove it'. He went on to remark that 'Some of the older inhabitants objected to privies, or regular dust-bins, or drains, and stated that the road was the best place for the soil and refuse!'[63] To Clark's mind, the idea that any mid-Victorians could seriously doubt the need for such pieces of sanitary technology was laughable and required no further comment. However, the fact that these 'older inhabitants' expressed such views should give us reason to pause. It is possible they were simply attempting to shock the inspector. If so, that in itself could be an important indication of working-class resentment at being placed under Clark's observing gaze. But perhaps his informants were expressing a genuinely held belief, one which saw the streets as perfectly acceptable sites in which to dump their refuse and excrement. That they were specifically described as being 'older' might mean that we are being presented with a tantalizing glimpse into the *mentalité* of a generation whose views were in the process of being superseded. Given Brynmawr's rapid growth, these inhabitants would not have been born in the town. It is likely that many may well have moved to the iron district from the countryside. As such, it could be that Clark was talking to people who had learned how to relate to space in a rural context, and who had transplanted those rules and codes into a new urban environment. Their willingness to dump what Clark and others of his class would have considered to be 'private' waste in 'public' spaces suggests they perceived their immediate environment in radically different ways from the inspector. Indeed, it could be that they were increasingly out of line with the perceptions of younger working-class urbanites who were learning newer codes of urban behaviour.[64]

Clark was most likely to notice other examples of distinctly working-class attitudes to urban space if they contravened the tenets of his own middle-class common sense. While visiting the courts and back alleys of Wrexham, he commented upon the way in which it was possible for some inhabitants of the slums to see the detritus which blocked the streets and yards as a positive asset. 'Many of the lower classes', Clark observed, 'collect dung and filth from the roads, and keep it up against their houses for sale, which is only removed once a year.'[65] He visited a lodging house, which although 'close and damp' did not dissuade the landlady, one Mrs Brewer, 'from accumulating a large dung heap, of three months' standing', which 'she values highly'. He also found an open cesspool which inhabitants supplied with straw. The 'large pool of soil' was worth between one and two pounds per annum.[66] What to Clark was an unmitigated evil, was a valuable source of income to the poor. When in Penzance, he encountered another instance of the inhabitants behaving in ways which upset sanitary logic. It had been common practice for the fish markets to be held in the public streets, a nuisance which Clark thought should no longer be tolerated. As such, he was glad to see that 'a new and commodious covered room' had recently been opened to house poultry and fish markets. Notwithstanding this improvement, the women traders had refused to use the new building, and continued to sell their fish in the street, picking a site in front of the town hall. In Clark's opinion, this was 'a less objectionable spot than that formerly occupied by them, but very inferior to the new market, out of which they should not be allowed to sell'.[67] The interesting point about this incident is the manner in which the women were displaying a preference for the public streets generally, and not one particular 'customary' or 'traditional' location. Thus, they were content to move from their previous venue to another street. Perhaps the streets appeared to be sites of freedom compared with a market which the authorities may have found easier to supervise and regulate. Whatever their reasoning, the women's resistance reminds us that the intended consequences of sanitary reform could be at variance with established working-class spatial practices and preferences.

Conclusion

It has been argued here that the reports penned by G. T. Clark – and by implication those written by the other superintending inspectors – were far from objective accounts of the built environment of the mid-Victorian town. This runs contrary to Clark's own public pronouncements about his duties as an inspector. As we have seen, he was keen to describe himself as a mere collector of facts. That he was. Yet there are good reasons to suppose that the facts which he chose to include in his final documents were the ones which confirmed many of his preconceptions, preconceptions which had been arrived at long before he entered any of the slums. Indeed, the act of observation was itself shaped by such preconceptions. Thus, when Clark entered the rookeries he was *looking* for the stereotypical drunken Irishmen and women. Little wonder that those who stumbled across his path also found themselves represented in his reports. Contrariwise, the drunks of other ethnic origins – and we can be sure there were many – were not commented upon. Similarly, where the cultural habits of the working class defied bourgeois sanitary logic, Clark had a tendency either to overlook or misunderstand them. The pronouncements of the older inhabitants of Brynmawr were to be laughed at, not taken seriously.

If Clark's prejudices surface in his reports at times, it is also important to note the extent to which his predetermined conclusions played their part in influencing his reports. As has been shown, there is ample evidence of Clark's commitment to the 'Sanitary Idea'. In matters of urban hygiene he was a disciple of Chadwick. He actively preached the sanitary message on his tours, sought out supporters of the Public Health Act and privately castigated opponents. Firmly convinced of the need for sanitary reform, his reports should best be seen as arguments in favour of those reforms. They were certainly not the work of an impartial observer. In every town he inspected the argument was essentially the same; ineffective institutions of local government were populated by inept public officials who needed to be replaced; landlords needed to be made aware of their responsibilities and of the benefits that would accrue to them as a result; manufacturers should be left alone to work out their own solutions to industrial pollution; but the 'naturally' clean working class – and even the 'naturally' dirty Irish – needed help from their social betters if they were to survive life in the miasma-filled slums.

The above observations should make us cautious about praising Clark for his objectivity. To all intents and purposes he had written the key aspects of his reports – most notably the argument for reform – before setting eyes on a town. Yet those reports are still revealing documents. It has not been suggested that Clark manufactured evidence. Conditions in the mid-Victorian town and city were appalling, and the work of the superintending inspectors did much to publicize some of the worst horrors. Whilst Clark's experience of the slums and the slum dwellers, and his representations of them, were shaped by his own preconceptions and prejudices (how could they not be?), that is not to argue that the slums did not exist. His reports are still extremely valuable sources for the urban historian. We just need to exercise great care in teasing out their particular insights. Moreover, those reports provide us with a window into the thought-world of an individual who was to the fore in one of the great reforming movements of the nineteenth century. Clark believed that he could make a difference, that he could help to civilize the dark spaces of 'the urban', and that he could improve the lot of the working class in the process. We have seen how he conceived of sanitary reform as God's work, and was convinced of the need to urge members of his own class to action. He was no radical, and did not advocate revolutionary methods to solve the problems of urban life in capitalist Britain. Yet we should not doubt the depth of his concern for the working class. Certainly he feared the social disorder which might follow if reforms were not introduced. However, unlike many of his contemporaries he did not feel the need to blame the lower orders for the squalor of the rookeries. Such squalor he saw as the result of forces outside the control of the working class. And to that extent at least it would seem that this cultural outsider had succeeded in thinking himself into the mind-set of many of the slum dwellers themselves.

Acknowledgements

I would like to thank the following for their detailed and helpful comments on earlier drafts of this chapter: Chris Evans, Brian James, Bill Jones, Rhona Maclean, Chris Williams, Marian Williams and Neil Wynn.

Notes

[1] *Merthyr Express*, 5 February 1898.
[2] The phrase 'folk heroes' is S. E. Finer's. See his *The Life and Times of Edwin Chadwick* (London, Methuen, 1970 edn.), 439.
[3] See, for instance, Anthony S. Wohl, *Endangered Lives: Public Health in Victorian Britain* (London, Dent, 1983), 149. For a provocative approach to the nineteenth-century public health movement written from a neo-Foucauldian perspective, see Thomas Osborne, 'Security and vitality: drains, liberalism and power in the nineteenth century', in Andrew Barry, Thomas Osborne and Nikolas Rose (eds.), *Foucault and Political Reason: Liberalism, Neo-Liberalism and Rationalities of Government* (London, UCL Press, 1996).
[4] Clark, 'Sanitary reform', *British Quarterly Review*, 9 (February 1849), 41–70.
[5] National Library of Wales, AC 908 C59, 'Essays and reports G. T. C.' I am grateful to Brian James for this reference.
[6] PRO (MH5/1), General Board of Health, Minutes 24 November 1848.
[7] Clark's contribution compares well with most of the other inspectors. For example, Robert Rawlinson penned over fifty reports for the Board of Health; Edward Cresy, sixteen; Alfred Dickens, seventeen; James Smith, four. William Ranger, with over ninety reports to his name, tops the list.
[8] We can be sure that Clark was familiar with the instructions. In a letter written to the secretary of the Board of Health at the start of his inquiries he noted how 'They let me have a copy of the "Instructions" by return of Post – I read them once only and wish to read them again, as they will in some points govern my operations . . .' PRO (MH13/212), Clark to Henry Austin, 4 December 1848. For 'Instructions to Superintendent Inspectors', see *Report by the General Board of Health on the Measures Adopted . . . up to July 1849*, *PP* 1849 [1115] xxiv, 129–35.

[9] Henry Mayhew, *London Labour and the London Poor* (London, Penguin Books, 1985). Gertrude Himmelfarb discusses Mayhew's work in her *The Idea of Poverty: England in the Early Industrial Age* (London, Faber, 1985), 307–70. For an interesting discussion of late Victorian 'slum-land' literature see Alan Mayne, *The Imagined Slum: Newspaper Representation in Three Cities 1870–1914* (Leicester, Leicester University Press, 1993).

[10] G. T. Clark, *Report to the General Board of Health on a Preliminary Inquiry into the Sewerage, Drainage, and Supply of Water, and the Sanitary Condition of the Inhabitants of Beverley* (London, 1850), 18. Hereafter the titles of the various reports – all of which follow the same formula – will be shortened.

[11] For more on this, see M. J. Cullen, *The Statistical Movement in Early Victorian Britain: The Foundations of Empirical Social Research* (Hassocks, Harvester Press, 1975); Lawrence Goldman, 'The origins of British "social science": political economy, natural science and statistics, 1830–1835', *Historical Journal*, 26, 3 (1983), 587–616; Karl H. Metz, 'Social thought and social statistics in the early nineteenth century: the case of sanitary statistics in England', *International Review of Social History*, 29, 2 (1984), 254–73.

[12] See, for example, Thomas Laycock, *Report on the State of York* (1844), cited in M. Durey, *The First Spasmodic Cholera Epidemic in York, 1832* (York, St Anthony's Press, 1974), 16.

[13] *Preston Guardian*, 2 June 1849.

[14] *Bristol Gazette*, 21 February 1850.

[15] *Kendal Mercury*, 24 February 1849.

[16] *Bristol Gazette*, 21 February 1850.

[17] A number of historians have utilized the reports as a means of gleaning information about the environment of the mid-Victorian town. See, for example, Keith Strange's 'The condition of the working classes in Merthyr Tydfil, *c.*1840–1850' (Ph.D. thesis, University of Wales, 1982), a detailed study which makes good use of the report penned by T. W. Rammell. Also see J. D. Marshall, 'Colonisation as a factor in the planting of towns in north-west England', in H. J. Dyos (ed.), *The Study of Urban History* (London, Edward Arnold, 1968), 229.

[18] See Ieuan Gwynedd Jones, *Communities: Essays in the Social History of Victorian Wales* (Llandysul, Gomer Press, 1987), 335. In another context he has remarked that with the reports written by the inspectors 'we have left the windy area of rhetoric and ideals and holy moralities and have entered a world of ascertainable facts'. This was because the inspectors 'had to develop techniques of objective investigation': *Mid-Victorian Wales: The Observers and the Observed* (Cardiff, University of Wales Press, 1992), 8.

[19] *Taunton Courier*, 21 February 1849.

[20] *Penzance Gazette*, 17 January 1849.

[21] *Kendal Mercury*, 24 February 1849.

[23] *Taunton Courier*, 21 February 1849.

[23] *Bristol Times*, 23 February 1850.

[24] For a discussion of the fascination and horror evoked by Manchester, the paradigmatic 'shock' city, see Asa Briggs, *Victorian Cities* (London, Penguin Books, 1990), ch. 3.

[25] As late as 1901 11.4% of the urban population of England and Wales were living in towns with a population under 10,000. See P. J. Waller, *Town, City and Nation: England 1850–1914* (Oxford, Oxford University Press, 1983), 6.

[26] G. T. Clark, *Report . . . into . . . the Sanitary Condition of . . . Worcester* (London, 1849), 47.

[27] Ibid., 4, 11, 14, 19.

[28] G. T. Clark, *Report . . . into . . . the Sanitary Condition of . . . Bodmin* (London, 1850), 13.

[29] Ibid., 11.

[30] Finer, *Life and Times*, 442–3.
[31] Clark, 'Sanitary reform', 60.
[32] Ibid., 69.
[33] Ibid., 69–70.
[34] G. T. Clark, *Report . . . into . . . the Sanitary Condition of . . . Bristol* (London, 1850), 176.
[35] Clark, 'Sanitary reform', 70.
[36] PRO (MH13/143) Clark to General Board of Health, 26 September 1849.
[37] In every town Clark visited the conclusion was always the same, namely that the Act should be applied.
[38] PRO (MH13/156) Clark to Edwin Chadwick, 13 December 1848.
[39] PRO (MH13/66) Clark to Henry Austin, 30 October 1849. Henry Austin was an engineer, who was appointed secretary of the Health of Towns Association in 1844, and became secretary of the General Board of Health. In addition to being a close associate of Edwin Chadwick, Austin also had the distinction of being Charles Dickens's brother-in-law.
[40] PRO (MH13/66) Clark to Henry Austin, 14 November 1849.
[41] PRO (MH13/143) Clark to Henry Austin, 26 September 1849; PRO (MH13/212) Clark to Edwin Chadwick, 11 December 1848.
[42] Clark, 'Sanitary reform', 44.
[43] He was obviously heartened by the Public Health Act, 'which we accept as an instalment of something more efficient in future' (Clark, 'Sanitary reform', 68).
[44] G. T. Clark, *Report . . . into . . . the Sanitary Condition of . . . Wrexham* (London, 1849), 5–6.
[45] Clark, *Bristol*, 174.
[46] See Clark, *Wrexham*, 17.
[47] See Wohl, *Endangered Lives*, ch. 8, for a consideration of the atmospheric pollution caused by all manner of industrial concerns during the Victorian period.
[48] Clark, *Bristol*, 83.
[49] Clark, *Wrexham*, 13, 15.
[50] For a discussion of the manner in which Chadwick represented the poor in his sanitary surveys, see Joseph W. Childers, 'Observation and representation: Mr Chadwick writes the poor', *Victorian Studies*, 37, 3 (1994), 405–32.
[51] Clark, *Beverley*, 25.
[52] Clark, *Worcester*, 8.
[53] G. T. Clark, *Report . . . into . . . the Sanitary Condition of . . . Bridgend* (London, 1850), 13.
[54] G. T. Clark, *Report . . . into . . . the Sanitary Condition of . . . Brynmawr* (London, 1849), 8. It is worth noting that on other occasions Clark's sympathy for the working classes was noticeable by its absence. For his less than creditable role as chairman of the Merthyr Board of Guardians during the great strike of 1875 in south Wales see Tydfil Thomas, *Poor Relief in Merthyr Tydfil Union in Victorian Times* (Cardiff, Glamorgan Archive Service, 1992), 120–32.
[55] Clark, 'Sanitary reform', 49–50.
[56] Friedrich Engels, *The Condition of the Working Class in England* (London, 1984 edn.), 123–6.
[57] For more on these themes, see Alan O'Day, 'Varieties of anti-Irish behaviour in Britain, 1846–1922', in Panikos Panayi (ed.), *Racial Violence in Britain in the Nineteenth and Twentieth Centuries* (Leicester, Leicester University Press, 1996), 26–43; Paul O'Leary, 'Anti-Irish riots in Wales, 1826–1882', *Llafur*, 5, 2 (1991), 27–36, especially 31–3.
[58] An article which has much to say on this and other relevant themes is Mary Poovey, ' "Curing the social body" in 1832: James Phillips Kay and the Irish in Manchester', *Gender and History*, 5, 2 (1993), 196–211.

[59] See, for example, Clark, *Newport*, 22; *Kendal Mercury*, 24 February 1849.

[60] *Preston Guardian*, 26 May 1849.

[61] PRO (MH13/34) 'A Rate Payer' to the General Board of Health, 16 June 1851. Emphasis in the original.

[62] Some of the ways in which the working class related to their environment, and managed to confound the sanitary reformers in the process, are discussed in Michael Sigsworth and Michael Worboys, 'The public's view of public health in mid-Victorian Britain', *Urban History*, 21 pt. 2 (1994), 237–50.

[63] Clark, *Brynmawr*, 10.

[64] For more on spatial practices in the nineteenth-century town, see Andrew J. Croll, 'Civilizing the urban: popular culture, public space and urban meaning, Merthyr *c.*1870–1914' (Ph.D. thesis, University of Wales, 1997), especially ch. 3.

[65] Clark, *Wrexham*, 24.

[66] Ibid., 13. Evidence exists which suggests that some working-class inhabitants collected dung during the cholera epidemic of 1848–9 because they believed that its powerful odours would protect them against the disease. See Himmelfarb, *Idea of Poverty*, 336.

[67] G. T. Clark, *Report . . . into . . . the Sanitary Condition of . . . Penzance* (London, 1849), 8.

CHAPTER 3

Clark the Ironmaster

L. J. WILLIAMS

Until comparatively recently the significant part which G. T. Clark played in the nineteenth-century iron trade was obscured by two complementary considerations. The first was the natural attention directed at the period during which the world's outstanding ironworks was run by Lady Charlotte Guest. Apart from the somewhat inflated view of Lucy Thomas as the 'Mother of the Welsh Steam Coal Trade', it is difficult to think of any other woman who played a major role in the industrialization of south Wales. If Lady Charlotte has often been given credit for the transition of Dowlais after the negotiation of the new lease and the illness and death of Sir John Guest, most of the recognition for the successful continuation has been bestowed on the brilliant management by William Menelaus and E. P. Martin. This is a not unreasonable conclusion to be drawn from the nature of the material which is in the vast Dowlais archive in the Glamorgan Record Office. It is certainly the message of John Owen's historical survey of the Dowlais Iron Company (1977): Menelaus, especially, looms much larger than Clark, and so does E. P. Martin after his return to Dowlais just before the death of Menelaus in 1882. In seeking to shift the perspective by giving more explicit attention to the part played by Clark, this chapter does not deny the major contribution of these other Dowlais notables to Welsh iron-making in the second half of the nineteenth century.

Lady Charlotte had, over a period of twenty years from the mid-1830s, been actively involved with her husband in the business; she had taken an increasing responsibility for the works from around 1849 as her husband's health deteriorated;[1] and with John Evans, the long-established general manager, she effectively controlled the works from 1852 to 1855.[2] Although running an ironworks was far from romantic,[3] this involvement – certainly in retrospect – became resonant with romance which does little justice to her

48

real abilities. None the less, although Lady Charlotte had much of the necessary knowledge and experience, it is doubtful if her personal control could have been successfully sustained: she necessarily relied heavily on John Evans, whose life and attitudes were by then perhaps too deeply rooted in established Dowlais practices; and while she recognized the need for investment after the long run-down during the renegotiation of the lease and the protracted illness of Sir John Guest, the signs were that she would have baulked at the scale of investment needed because the risk attached to this use of capital clashed with her anxiety to amass 'such a fortune for the babies as to make them very well off hereafter' (most of the ten children were still very young in 1852).[4]

Be that as it may, Lady Charlotte's period of control was terminated by the prosaic consequence of an authentically romantic episode: that of her remarriage to the much younger Charles Schreiber, the tutor of one of her sons. Under the terms of Sir John's will the controlling power which she had been given at Dowlais was much diminished in the event of her remarriage.[5] In any case, as her interest in Charles Schreiber had flowed, her interest in Dowlais had ebbed.[6] Her powers in 1855 reverted to the two remaining trustees, H. A. Bruce[7] and G. T. Clark. During Lady Charlotte's reign there is little evidence that she much involved her co-trustees in the affairs of the ironworks and Clark himself claimed that he had been kept 'in utter darkness'.[8] Thereafter, with Bruce mostly in London pursuing a political career, Clark was left in control. The first point to grasp therefore is that from the mid-1850s the ultimate authority for running the Dowlais Iron Company rested with George Thomas Clark.

There were still two possible courses of challenge to Clark's position. Under the will the Guest sons could have been involved in management. Clark consistently opposed participation by any of the sons because he asserted that if it was known that one of them would 'be a partner, possibly a managing partner, my authority for good will be crippled'.[9] Lady Charlotte – initially reluctantly – accepted that the eldest son had no wish to take part and that 'Mr Clark has had a hard battle to assert and maintain his authority. And Ivor's presence might give him a great deal of trouble.'[10] Later she also decided not to use her powers to nominate the younger sons into the business.[11] The other challenge was that the works would be sold. This possibility, from time to time, was raised by the family – the actual owners – as an active policy. It was strongly mooted in 1855–6, 1863–4 and the early 1870s. On each occasion Clark successfully counselled against sale.

It is perhaps hazardous to speculate too much about Clark's motivation for these resistances, especially when the papers give specific reasons which are both solid and plausible. Family intervention *would* have weakened his position when a realistic strategy for the revitalization of Dowlais demanded decisive action. An early sale – after the decline in production and profit consequent on the uncertainty of lease renewal – *would* have realized less for the family, and Clark's strictures on the quality of management of joint-stock companies were widely shared at the time.[12] None the less it is difficult to stifle a strong impression from the correspondence that Clark enjoyed the exercise of power and was more than ready to provide the 'despotic management' which he said Dowlais required.[13] He backed his protests against these proposed incursions on his authority with the threats to resign: if these added force and effectiveness to his views they also reflected a general agreement about the nature and quality of his management.

Something of the nature of his management has already been indicated. Ultimately it involved single and undivided control. This was established at the outset. The authority derived from the provisions of Sir John Guest's will which gave the trustees powers to choose managers or to appoint themselves to carry on the business alone.[14] It was these provisions together with the withdrawal from direct participation, for different reasons, of his co-trustees – Lady Charlotte and H. A. Bruce – which gave Clark his unique position. One of his first acts was to consolidate this position by securing the retirement of John Evans, the long-serving works manager. This might have been a sensible move on its own terms, on the presumption that Evans's unavoidable association with a long period of stagnation and decline at Dowlais would make it difficult for him to readjust sufficiently to expansionist schemes. Indeed Clark later claimed that he had initially 'found the works in a state of rapid decay'[15] and blamed his early difficulties on 'J Evans's deficiencies and delinquencies in management' which were only corrected when 'we made up our minds contrary to advice to part with John Evans and change the system'.[16] But, as Bruce early observed, a new general manager 'would almost inevitably quarrel with John Evans',[17] and Clark later asked Bruce, rhetorically: 'If you and I had not forced our way with Evans where would the concern have been?'[18] A number of the other existing managerial and supervisory staff were also removed,[19] but Evans was the one person whose standing and famously autocratic bearing could have challenged Clark's judgements and decisions. Menelaus, despite his brilliant qualities and the fact that he was already employed at Dowlais before the advent of Clark, was clearly someone whose promotion to general manager was made by Clark: Clark's superior authority was manifest from the outset.

The nature of Clark's management was also largely defined by these early steps. He installed, or at least claimed that he had installed, a new team of more technically informed managers.[20] It is difficult to test this and, given his strictures on Evans's competence, it is not easy to reconcile it with the apparent fact that most of these new promotions had been trained at Dowlais. Of much greater significance was the overall management structure which he imposed and the way in which he used it. Its hierarchical nature was neither novel nor surprising: Clark himself was at the head, followed by Menelaus as general manager and then the various departmental heads each presiding over his own hierarchy. It was a pattern which was mirrored by the ranks they each held in the Dowlais Volunteer Force which was established in 1859.[21] What was more unusual was the use Clark made of this structure: each departmental head was required to submit regular (apparently monthly, though not enough have survived to be certain) reports on their achievements, problems and requirements. Although these were partly filtered to Clark through Menelaus there is no doubt that the system enabled Clark, without too much immersion in the details, to be fully aware of the broad position in the blast furnaces, the puddling furnaces, the rolling mills, the collieries and iron ore sectors. Clark's insistence on being kept abreast of 'everything important . . . concerning the business of the works'[22] was both necessary if he was to take an active part in the major aspects of decision-making, and is itself evidence that he did participate at this strategic level.

There are no obvious grounds for thinking that Clark had invented this system but his practice of it undoubtedly had elements of modernity: it is perhaps not too fanciful to make comparisons with Arnold (later Lord) Weinstock a century later, and on a grander scale, keeping control of the divisions of GEC for over a generation by similar means. For its time the Dowlais Iron Company, although its productive side had a single geographical location, was relatively of a size comparable to GEC. The playful parallel is pushed closer by another feature on which Clark placed great stress: the strongly statistical nature of the reports and information. He sought substance as well as embellishment, objectivity as well as opinion. The need to know was also embodied in his decision to be a resident manager who lived for a considerable time at Dowlais House which was, to all intents and purposes, part of the works. This again was a physical confirmation of his active role and reflected his assertion that 'a master who is not regularly resident cannot expect to know very much of what his agents do – although he may flatter himself to the contrary'.[23]

If these aspects give some impression of the nature and style of Clark's management, its quality is best assessed by looking at his part (so far as it can be positively known) in some of the major decisions which determined the trajectory of the company during the four decades of his stewardship. Given the much more visible role which Menelaus performed as the executive arm of

12 Dowlais House, photographed *c*.1860, with probably George and Ann Clark and their son. Dowlais House was the Clarks' main residence from the 1850s to the 1880s. *Glamorgan Record Office.*

the company, there are unavoidable doubts about the extent and significance of the contributions made by Clark as the non-executive arm. Some of these can be resolved by Clark's papers: others retain a greater element of ambiguity. The famous report on the 'General State of the Dowlais Works' in 1857 falls into the latter category. It was certainly written by Menelaus who also provided the basic analysis and proposals. But if as well as 'who wrote the report?' the prior question of 'why was it written?' is also posed, then it is more than plausible to see Clark's influence. Menelaus would have needed some authority to embark on such a large project and the natural source for this was Clark who had recently appointed him as general manager. It may also be germane that the much-quoted finale to the report toned in so smoothly with Clark's complaints on taking over about the inefficiencies and omissions under Evans's recent regime. 'Dowlais', concluded Menelaus, 'is standing still instead of taking the lead as from her size and position she ought and is quietly falling into the rear. To remedy this state of things a great effort is necessary and also a considerable outlay of capital.'[24]

Whether or no Clark played a facilitating role in the genesis of this key document, there is no doubt at all about his participation in some of the other

13 Lady Charlotte Schreiber (Guest) addressing the Dowlais school probably at the opening of the new buildings, designed by Sir Charles Barry, in September 1855. G. T. Clark and (probably) H. A. Bruce sit in the front row.
Glamorgan Record Office.

central issues. In one sense that is simply a truism since, at the very least, Clark's acquiescence was a necessary prerequisite for any significant expenditure. This authority clearly underpinned the single most crucial strategic decision which he took. By the time Clark took control, the broad options were: to sell the company; to continue the Lady Charlotte/John Evans approach of modest patching up; or to subscribe to the view that large-scale investment was now essential. The first option of sale was urged by 'Mr Evans the then manager . . . [who] informed Mr Bruce and myself that the work must ere long *be closed*'.[25] Whether or no his animus towards Evans influenced Clark's decision, he rejected this course on the reasonable grounds that the poor financial performance in recent years would depress the price. The second option was dismissed by Clark's insistence that Evans's policies had seriously reduced the relative competitive position of Dowlais: if continued it would have simply merged with option one – but now as a forced sale. Clark plumped for the third option of expansion through investment, arguing that costs could only be reduced by installing improved equipment while the spread of overheads over an increased output would also reduce costs per ton. This was the driving policy conclusion of the Menelaus report, but it is uncertain whether the report convinced Clark or Clark's conviction shaped the report. Clark's correspondence, both in 1855–7 and later, strongly suggests that he was always determined upon expansion.

By the mid-1860s Dowlais was again the leading Welsh ironworks; the strategy was thus hugely successful, but the success should not obscure the extent to which it had involved risks. The investment was obviously a long-term policy, but because of the accounting procedures[26] the investment programme could only be sustained if there were quick short-term benefits. There were no external sources of long-term capital for investment (the family was not – could not be – drawn upon, and there were no shareholders) so the funds for expansion were provided from revenue, from the operating surplus (or gross profit). At the outset Clark explained to the Dowlais bookkeepers that the annual final balance was essential

> . . . to show distinctly whether we have or have not any balance which we could carry over to the investment fund . . . If to enable us to carry on the works it be absolutely necessary in one year to spend say £20,000 on new works, and your books show £10,000 profit, there is really not only no £10,000 to be invested, but there is actually a deficit of £10,000 to be provided from some other source . . .[27]

It was thus important that the cost of production of a ton of iron which had been rising strongly in the early 1850s (from £6.68 to £7.86 between 1853 and 1856) on a fairly stagnant output of a little over 60,000 tons, fell sharply in the three succeeding years (to £5.31 by 1859) on a rapidly expanding output which reached 92,000 tons in 1858–9. It was also fortunate that the average selling price in the year beginning March 1856, at the start of the investment programme, rose by 15s. (75p) a ton.[28] Even so, the sharp fluctuations of the iron trade, a permanent source of anxiety, made for acute difficulties in these early years of Clark's reign. There was throughout the late 1850s a serious risk that trade depression would financially overwhelm the company. Resort was had to a variety of expedients: the circulating capital, essential for the day-to-day operation of the enterprise, was drawn upon (in itself a risky procedure); trade bills, a main source of liquid funds, were expensively discounted before their due date; negotiations with customers and creditors were conducted to ease the cash-flow problems; wages were reduced by 20 per cent in 1857; and the good name of both the Guests and Clark himself was used to secure bank loans in case of emergency.[29] None the less Clark clung to his belief that the 'only chance' for Dowlais to survive lay in aiming at high output at lower production costs.[30] His determination can be seen in the levels of expenditure on new works which in the three years up to March 1854 averaged £10,413, which in the next three years (marking Clark's period of control) averaged £30,745, and in the following three years up to March 1860 averaged £34,018. The last figure was achieved despite a substantial drop to £24,604 in 1858–9 when even Clark had to confine new expenditure to irreversible commitments for new coal pits.[31] It is quite possible to argue that it was easier for Clark to contemplate these risks because he was himself neither owner nor shareholder: if motives are debatable there is no doubt that substantial risks were involved, nor that Clark was willing to accept them.

The basic expansionary policy was thus largely Clark's direct responsibility. It would still be possible to represent this as a one-off decision, albeit with consequences which rippled outward but which Clark then left to the executive managers to deal with. The underlying implausibility of such an interpretation has already been implied by what was said above about his style of operation, requiring regular reports and information. It can be more explicitly refuted by looking at areas of decision-making which necessarily required more sustained involvement and in which Clark can be shown to have provided diagnosis and creative guidance, and not just financial control. These active ingredients can be seen in operation over the long-running efforts to economize in the use of coal for iron production and to stave off the looming inadequacy of the company's own supplies of coal.

The fact of an early 1850s shortage of coal is well documented,[32] as are the efforts to deal with it by contracting to buy in coal from Thomas Joseph.[33] The immediate problem of supply was largely solved with surprising speed, with Clark telling Bruce in mid-1857 that 'we are flush of coal'.[34] This was achieved by improved practices which allowed more economy in the use of fuel, the quick pay-off probably reflecting previous neglect. The expansion of iron output in itself improved coal efficiency per ton of finished iron while the use of small coal for coking and in engine boilers both acted as an additional source of supply and released more of the large bituminous coal for use in the furnaces.

All this would have been implemented, and probably initiated, by Menelaus and the departmental managers. But it did not, and could not, provide a full and permanent solution to the problem. One additional aspect of this was indicated by Bruce's rather dramatic declaration that 'the price of coal must be reduced or we die', which supplemented Clark's drier observation that increasing the make of iron would exhaust the coal in four decades and, well before that, make it excessively costly. More immediately he was concerned because, welcome as its more economical use was, it 'had been effected without any reduction in the cost of coal' and around the same time in 1857 warned Ivor Guest that 'coal is just now our great difficulty'.[35]

Clark thus identified, or accepted the identification of cost and increased supply as the two crucial aspects of the coal problem at Dowlais. He also showed a close and sustained interest in the steps taken towards their solution. Indeed, in several respects his managerial activity was crucial, perhaps even indispensable. This was certainly the case with two of the main approaches which were adopted to reduce the cost of coal-getting at Dowlais: reducing the sums paid in royalties and sinking new pits. A lower payment to the landlord for each ton of coal raised represented a very direct cost reduction, but it is doubtful if the authority to negotiate this with the agents of the Marquess of Bute could have been credibly conducted other than by the trustees themselves. The Dowlais lease when it was renewed in 1848 provided for a royalty of 9*d.* on coal used in the ironworks against 1*s.* on coal which was sold. At the time, Dowlais only used coal for iron-making but a decade later, when the possibility of entering the sale-coal trade emerged, Clark struggled to get these terms altered. He argued with Bute's representatives that reduction would be mutually beneficial by enabling Dowlais to sell large quantities, but that the absence of a reduction 'would place us out of all hope of competing with those much nearer to port than ourselves'.[36] No sooner had Clark secured, as a temporary measure, that the royalty on coal raised for sale would be the same as that for iron-making, than he was pressing for a further reduction on coal sales to 6*d.* This was partly on the grounds of depressed trade and partly on the grounds that its greater distance from the port made competition with Aberdare impossible. The latter argument was more specious since Merthyr had more railways competing for trade and wage levels were generally higher in the Aberdare than in Merthyr valley. None the less, the royalty on coal sales was reduced permanently to 9*d.* with a temporary fall to 6*d.*, a concession which was then also extended to coal used in iron-making.[37] These concessions gained by Clark and Bruce represented an important reduction in the cost of coal to Dowlais in the early 1860s before other measures had taken effect.

The time-lag of benefits was especially marked in relation to the policy of sinking new pits. Clark's control over capital expenditure obviously made his acquiescence an essential prerequisite for this approach. The existing pits were old, small and poorly equipped: Clark saw the need for new sinkings as much for cost reduction as for securing additional output. Indeed until the second half of the 1860s the main contribution of new workings was to enable the older expensive collieries to be closed or less intensively worked.

Finally, Dowlais coal costs were reduced by economies, both in production and use. Initially these were generally analysed and advocated in reports prepared by the works managers,[38] but Clark facilitated their introduction and monitored their progress. Perhaps the most significant economy in use was through the growing ability in the ironworks to substitute small for large coal. From 1860 onwards, Dowlais set out, as a matter of policy, to make greater use of small coal and devised means for this to be done not simply in the rolling mills and engines for steam power but also in the furnaces, mixed with large and using a fan blast. This had the double advantage of cutting the cost of the coal used in iron-making and, a new feature for Dowlais, releasing large coal for sale. From the annual Dowlais reports it is possible to calculate[39] that 180,000 tons less of large coal were used in 1868 than in 1860 for almost the same make of finished iron, largely because in the later year about 132,000 tons of small coal were being used. 'The small coal produced in working the large coal for sale, which in other collieries is comparatively useless, is to us worth 3*s*. per ton',[40] while Dowlais had the further advantage that no royalty had to be paid on the small coal they raised.

Clark also accepted Menelaus's proposals to install more powerful and efficient engines to enable compressed air to be used for haulage and pumping.[41] Similar improvements in the ironworks, in particular the greater use made of waste gases as a source of fuel, also reduced the cost of coal at Dowlais. There was, until the 1860s, an additional acute source of high cost for Dowlais coal. Most of the coal workings were situated to the dip of the colliery shafts. As a result the coal when cut had to be hauled against the gradient before it could be raised. Clark in his judgement that 'no really important saving can be expected until the bulk of the coal is hauled down-hill underground'[42] was again echoing Menelaus. The only practical solution to this problem was dependent upon a willingness to confront the second major coal issue mentioned above: that of increasing the supply.

Clark seems hardly to have hesitated in sanctioning the expenditure necessary for the sinking of new pits to increase output. As part of the same process the trustees also negotiated an extension of the mineral lease.[43] At this stage, in the late 1850s, the object seemed to be directed towards Clark's overall strategy of reviving Dowlais through the expansion and modernization of iron-making: it was only a little later that it was seen to fit in with the (for Dowlais) new activity of selling coal. Two new pits were sunk at Fochriw in the Cwmbargoed valley and extra levels were opened to work the Rhos Las seam. Sinking for coal, like the course of true love, rarely runs smooth: both the time and the money (£83,000 for the two Fochriw pits) far exceeded initial hopes. The significance of this for the present

14 Officers of the 2nd (Dowlais) Corps, Glamorganshire Rifle Volunteers, photographed in front of Dowlais House, *c.*1860. *From left to right*: Dr Burns, M. C. Harrison, Matthew Hirst, Wm. Jenkins, Edward Williams, George T. Clark, Matthew Truran, Wm. Menelaus, Dr Pearson Cresswell, George Martin, David James. *Glamorgan Record Office.*

purpose is that Clark kept up his support for the project, even to the extent at one stage when cash was particularly tight of deceiving (or, at least, misleading) London House (and Bruce) about the sums that would be used for colliery investment.

The other main source of relief for extra supplies of coal was more fortuitous. Early in 1859 the neighbouring Penydarren ironworks were in acute difficulties and the Forman brothers asked Clark to buy them. He jumped at the chance but it was immediately clear that the attraction was not the ironworks but the mineral field and the existing three large collieries which could already produce coal cheaper than Dowlais and could be improved.[44] Clark asked Menelaus to produce a detailed report which showed that the cheaper and better quality Penydarren coal would reduce the costs of iron-making at Dowlais and the extra supply would enable an expansion of iron production at Dowlais.

If it was its effects on the cost of iron production that was the initial driving force behind coal policy at Dowlais, the attractions of the direct selling of coal soon emerged. The impression from the papers is that Menelaus was prompt not only in seeing the possibility, but its acceptance.

15 G. T. Clark in uniform as lieutenant-colonel of
the Glamorganshire Rifle Volunteers,
photographed *c*.1860. *Cyfarthfa Castle Museum*
and *Stewart Williams, Publishers.*

Clark was briefly reluctant, perhaps exhibiting something of the great
ironmaster's disdain for the coal trade. Whether or not he was infected by
such industrial snobbery, it was more characteristic that Clark soon shed
any hesitancy in the face of the logic of the situation. Greater coal
production led to economies which reduced costs of iron production and
increased competitiveness in the coal market; coal sales could maintain
colliery activity when the iron trade was depressed; and, as Menelaus
emphasized, in a detailed report,[45] the coal trade offered an opportunity for
Dowlais to take advantage of colliers' wage rates in Merthyr being some 15
per cent below those of Aberdare. The revenue from coal soon became an
important source of liquid funds[46] and by 1868 more than a quarter of
profits came from coal.

This brief account of the way in which the problems of the cost and the
supply of coal were tackled in the 1850s and 1860s has been given to
demonstrate that Clark showed a sustained attention to such management

issues and that, at some stages, his decisions were crucial. It could be replicated around most of the basic developments at Dowlais over the four decades of Clark's managerial association. In the crucial process of bringing large-scale steel production to Dowlais, for example, it was the trustees – Clark *and* Bruce – who could be said to have played the key role. Indeed it seems that in this case their response preceded Menelaus's opinions: on the day after *The Times* reported Bessemer's paper to the British Association at Cheltenham Bruce was urging its possibilities on Clark and expressing a wish 'to hear what Menelaus says of it'.[47] Although Dowlais was the first to take out a licence there were many vicissitudes – legal, technical and financial – before Dowlais began steel production nearly a decade later in 1866. For present purposes the point to notice is that Clark played a decisive role at the beginning and the end of this decade – and, as Bessemer's autobiography[48] as well as Clark's papers confirm, he was in-between highly active. After some, as it turned out, too-hasty trials at Dowlais, Bruce and Clark decided less than a fortnight after the Cheltenham paper to call on Bessemer and, over a dinner, negotiated a licence. A decade later a final agreement was reached when Bessemer visited Clark and stayed overnight at Dowlais House.[49]

Significant functional aspects of the enterprise also captured Clark's attention. Transport was one of these – not surprisingly, when railway charges were costing Dowlais around £50,000 a year in the mid-1860s. Clark spent time both negotiating freight rates and pursuing the company's basic policy which was 'to encourage as many lines of railway as possible'.[50] A more continuous functional preoccupation was with marketing. Most of the selling was done through the company's London House (which also received the moneys and paid the bills). This left plenty of space for friction and policy differences between London House and the ironworks at Merthyr over such basic issues as: whether, in slack times, to produce for stock to keep the works going; whether the works were doing enough to cut costs; or whether the agents were sufficiently assiduous in getting orders. For example, one letter from London in reaction to receiving the latest cost sheet from Dowlais, began: 'Anxiety! Distress! Alarm! Horror!'[51] Clark bombarded London with letters on markets (and finance). Concerning coal sales, for example, he reorganized the sales structures when he became convinced that the needs of this new trade demanded that more independence should be given to agents at Cardiff and Liverpool while he also harangued the Navy (and Bruce to use his influence as an MP) until Dowlais coal was successfully on the prestigious Admiralty list.[52] A subtext in all this was that Clark aimed at, and succeeded in, establishing his as the ultimate authority in London as in Merthyr. This was symbolized when he, early on, insisted –

despite the obvious reluctance of Bruce at the London end – on the dismissal of George Kitson who, like John Evans at the works, had over a period of years established a strong position at the London House.[53]

Two last areas will be mentioned to indicate that on the central issues Clark continued to have a decisive say and influence. These concerned the securing of iron ore supplies, and the momentous decision effectively to shift steel production from Dowlais to a new works to be built adjacent to the docks in Cardiff. Local ores were already inadequate, both in quantity and quality, by the mid-century so that Dowlais, like other Welsh ironworks, was buying in supplies from England and abroad. Putting aside the long years of negotiating for supplies, the key decision was to form (along with the Consett Iron Company, Krupps of Germany and the landowning Ybarra family of Spain) the Orconera Iron Ore Company in 1873. Although the detailed negotiations seem to have been conducted by Menelaus, Clark first produced a careful analysis of the problem and then had the task of persuading Sir Ivor Guest that this was the most effective way of ensuring high-quality, low-cost ores for Dowlais.[54] In the case of the move to Cardiff, the indications are that the major part was played by Menelaus's successor, E. P. Martin, to whom Clark even left the conduct of the leasing negotiations with the trustee for the Bute interest, the formidable W. T. Lewis (later Lord Merthyr). Indeed the Clark MSS suggest that, in this as other Dowlais matters, he was playing a less pro-active part. There is a letter of appreciation in 1890 to W. T. Lewis,[55] but at that time Clark was eighty-one, and had been approaching eighty when the lease was signed at the end of 1887.

These episodes, or issues, have been dealt with summarily because the object of this chapter is not to give a full and detailed account of George Clark's association with the Dowlais ironworks. It is hoped that enough has been said to demonstrate that, over a period spanning more than three decades, he was crucially and creatively involved in the fortunes of the company. All this has long been known in a vague general sense, but it has been insufficiently recognized and acknowledged. In justice, Clark needs to be seen as a maker, as well as a recorder of Welsh history. It would be disingenuous to imagine that the sort of control which Clark exercised over a major enterprise could be entirely conducted by benevolence and sweetness. He was, for example, quite relentless and ruthless in getting rid of John Evans at Dowlais and George Kitson from the London House. There were strong objective reasons for doing so – especially in the case of John Evans – but there is no doubt that Clark was also concerned because these two stalwarts of the previous regime could be seen as rival figures of authority. In addition, he was ready enough to listen to expert advice, and wise enough to ask for evidence, but once he had decided a policy he was determined to have his decision accepted and implemented. On several occasions he used the threat of resignation to bring the waverers (members of the Guest family, Bruce, or worried men at London House) into line. It is interesting, but futile, to speculate on whether he would have resigned: he clearly enjoyed the power and was understandably proud of his achievement in turning the company round. Nor was he excessively diffident about his worth, but quite properly pressed for his remuneration to increase with his responsibilities and achievements.

None of this is meant to detract from the significance of others. Clark was especially fortunate in the quality of his lieutenants, first Menelaus and then Martin. These were men of exceptional ability. It is obvious, too, that much of the information and some of the judgements embodied in Clark's letters come from the various managers at the works. To a considerable degree, of course, this simply represents the efficiency and shrewdness of Clark's system of management control through regular reports and statistics. But the scale of the flow of the letters, at least until the 1880s, also amply illustrates his close attention to the essentials of the business.

This is not the point to attempt to sum up the whole man. Some relevant aspects do, however, emerge. On the basis of his Dowlais experience he seems by nature to be something of a risk-taker, and the impression is that he enjoyed the excitement as well as the power which his position in the Dowlais Iron Company gave him. It would certainly be wildly inaccurate to describe him as unworldly. Any assessments of the relative significance of his work as an ironmaster against his other activities, both scholarly and practical, must depend on the values applied. In so doing some attention needs to be paid to the fact that Clark's management involved creativity; that it engaged his energies and abilities over a sustained period; and that, compared to his other activities, it certainly touched far more lives.

Notes

[1] See, for example, *Lady Charlotte Guest: Extracts from her Journal, 1833–1852* (London, John Murray, 1950), 224.

[2] Revel Guest and Angela V. John, *Lady Charlotte: A Biography of the Nineteenth Century* (London, Weidenfeld and Nicolson, 1989).

[3] Ibid., especially ch. 6.

[4] Ibid., 120.

[5] GRO, DIC Collection, D/D G/H1/165, Copy of will and codicils of Sir Josiah John Guest.

[6] Guest and John, *Lady Charlotte*, ch. 8.

[7] Later Lord Aberdare. Bruce was in fact only appointed in 1855 on the urging of Lady Charlotte and after her decision to withdraw. He replaced the original trustee, Edward Divett.

8 Clark MSS, 57/323, letter to Lady Huntly, 12 December 1857.

9 Clark MSS, 60/185–91, G. T. C. to F. T. Bircham, 30 April 1860.

10 *Lady Charlotte Schreiber: Extracts from her Journal, 1853–1891* (London, John Murray, 1952), 77–8.

11 Clark MSS, 59/164, Lady Charlotte to G. T. C., 26 March 1859.

12 NLW MS 15,028C, Section 2, G. T. C. to F. T. Bircham, 6 October 1863.

13 Ibid.

14 GRO, DIC Collection, D/D G/H1/165, Will, 1st codicil, clause 5.

15 Clark MSS, 58/201, G. T. C. to F. T. Bircham, 15 May 1858.

16 Clark MSS, No. 8, G. T. C. to H. A. Bruce, February 1857 and 57/343–6, G. T. C. to Sir Ivor Guest, 19 November 1857.

17 Clark MSS, 55/15, H. A. Bruce to G. T. C., 14 March 1855.

18 NLW MS 15,028C, f. 338, G. T. C. to H. A. Bruce, 2 June 1863.

19 Clark MSS, 60/185–91, G. T. C. to F. T. Bircham, 30 April 1860.

20 Ibid.

21 John A. Owen, *The History of the Dowlais Iron Works, 1759–1970* (Risca, Starling Press, 1977), 61.

22 Clark MSS, 65/555, W. Jenkins to G. T. C., 24 July 1865.

23 Clark MSS, 58/228, G. T. C. to H. A. Bruce, 30 November 1858.

24 GRO, DIC Collection, D/D G/C8/5, Report by W. Menelaus on the General State of the Dowlais Works, 14 November 1857.

25 Clark MSS, 58/201–7, G. T. C. to F. T. Bircham, 15 May 1858.

26 These are fully and helpfully explained in J. R. Edwards and C. Baber, 'Dowlais Iron Company: accounting policies and procedures for profit measurement and reporting purposes', *Accounting and Business Research*, 9 (1978–9), 139–51.

27 GRO, DIC Collection, D/D G/E2/14, G. T. C. to J. Walkinshaw, 5 March 1856.

28 Clark MSS, 60/450. Review of the operation of DIC since death of Sir John Guest, 26 July 1860.

29 These anxieties are a constant theme of the time and run, for example, throughout the extensive correspondence of 1857 and 1858 in Clark MSS.

30 See, for example, Clark MSS, 57/402 and 57/194, letters to H. A. Bruce, June and October 1857.

31 Clark MSS, 58/137, G. T. C. to H. A. Bruce, 23 April 1858, and 58/359, H. A. Bruce to Lady Charlotte Schreiber, 18 August 1858.

32 See, for example, Menelaus's General Report and GRO, DIC Collection, D/D G/C4/6 Comparative account of make, coal consumption, and ore consumption, 1857.

33 Initially, from January 1854, 100 tons a day of coking coal, raised in 1856 to 200 tons a day for five years. Thomas Joseph was the brother-in-law of Samuel Thomas, the father of D. A. Thomas, later Lord Rhondda.

34 Clark MSS, 57/402, G. T. C. to H. A. Bruce, 12 June 1857.

35 Clark MSS, 57/79, H. A. Bruce to G. T. C., 27 October 1855; 58/201–7, G. T. C. to F. T. Bircham, 15 May 1858; and 57/472–5, G. T. C. to Sir Ivor Guest, 11 July 1857.

36 NLW MS 15,027D, f. 229, G. T. C. to John Boyle, 6 June 1859, and f. 211, G. T. C. to W. S. Clark, 10 May 1859.

37 Clark MSS, 61/653, F. T. Bircham to G. T. C., 30 November 1861, and 62/10, John Boyle to G. T. C., 3 January 1862.

38 For example, Menelaus produced a detailed report on Dowlais coal problems and possibilities which he sent to Clark in November 1861, GRO, DIC Collection, D/D G/D1/8.

39 M. J. Lewis, 'G. T. Clark and the Dowlais Iron Company: An entrepreneurial study' (M.Sc. (Econ.) thesis, University of Wales, 1983).

40 NLW MS 15,028C, f. 350, G. T. C. to Sir Ivor Guest, 23 May 1863.

41 GRO, DIC Collection, D/D G/C8/5, Menelaus's Report on the General State of the Works; Clark MSS, 59/363–4, G. T. C. to H. A. Bruce, 22 January 1859.

[42] Clark MSS, 58/201–7, G. T. C. to F. T. Bircham, 15 May 1858.

[43] Idem; and 57/265–7, 27 October 1857.

[44] Clark MSS, 59/408, G. T. C. to Lady Charlotte, 30 January 1859.

[45] GRO, DIC Collection, D/D G/D1/8, Menelaus to G. T. C., 7 November 1861.

[46] Clark MSS, 61/94, G. T. C. to H. A. Bruce, 7 May 1861; and 61/126, G. T. C. to L. M. Rate, 18 May 1861.

[47] Clark MSS, 56/164, H. A. Bruce to G. T. C., 15 August 1856.

[48] Sir Henry Bessemer, *Sir Henry Bessemer, F.R.S.: An Autobiography* (London, 'Engineering', 1905).

[49] NLW MS 15,029C, f. 336, G. T. C. to Bessemer and Company, 1 January 1866 and GRO, DIC Collection, D/D G/C2, Bessemer to E. P. Martin, 4 April 1897.

[50] NLW MS 15,030C, f. 224, G. T. C. to C. R. M. Talbot, 23 October 1870.

[51] Clark MSS, 59/219, L. M. Rate to G. T. C., 23 April 1859.

[52] See, for example, various letters in NLW MS 15,027D, for 1859.

[53] See, especially, NLW MS 15,028C, f. 388, G. T. C. to H. A. Bruce, 2 June 1863 and Clark MSS, 63/312, H. A. Bruce to G. T. C., 5 June 1863.

[54] NLW MS 15,030C, f. 1, Memorandum by G. T. C., 2 December 1871; and f. 305, G. T. C. to Sir Ivor Guest, 25 July 1873.

[55] GRO, DIC Collection, D/D G/B1/24, 7 June 1890.

CHAPTER 4

Clark and Politics

IEUAN GWYNEDD JONES

When G. T. Clark and H. A. Bruce became trustees for the family of Sir John Guest, who had died in November 1852, they determined that they would 'secure to the Dowlais electors complete freedom of voting'. Sixteen years later they believed that that determination had 'ever since been maintained'.[1] It is not immediately clear why they should have bound themselves to such a policy. It is possible that it reflected the liberal views of two high-minded gentlemen who suddenly, and almost uniquely, found themselves, or believed themselves to be, possessed of the power to act in accordance with such high ideals. It was as if they were repudiating electioneering practices which had been common in the past but which were now to cease. Nor is the context of their agreement entirely clear. Were they thinking only in terms of parliamentary or constituency politics and of the franchise which belonged to properly qualified voters, or did the freedom they had in mind extend also to ratepayers with votes in the elections of Poor Law Guardians, for example? Nor, finally, is it clear to what extent they understood and accepted the underlying social realities which determined the shape of politics in the borough – in particular, the ways in which power was distributed among the various social classes involved in the making of political decisions, whether in the course of parliamentary elections, which were infrequent, or in the more pervasive and continuous business of local government. The two men would soon learn that the enormous power they now possessed was in fact limited in many ways, by custom, by convention and by the conflicting and changing 'moralities' of the communities of which they were a part.

Even more difficult to understand is their claim that complete electoral freedom had been subsequently maintained. Though the charge was often made, Merthyr Tydfil was by no means a 'pocket borough': there were simply too many pockets. The four ironmasters could rarely be brought to agree on joint policies, even regarding economic matters, such as wage rates and product prices, and the Guest hold on the seat was dependent upon the grudging acquiescence, in varying combinations at different times, of the Crawshays of Cyfarthfa and Hirwaun, the Homfrays of Penydarren, the Hills of Plymouth, as well as the ironmasters of the other half of the constituency in Aberdare, where the coal industry was flourishing, the ironworks holding their own, and population growing at an extraordinary pace. Nevertheless, it was an accepted fact of political life in the years immediately following the 1832 general election that the Guests and their Merthyr supporters could invariably carry the representation against the opposition of the other ironmasters in the constituency. This had been the case in 1835, when Crawshay, Thompson and Hill had opposed the re-election of Guest,[2] but in the mean time circumstances were changing. In particular, a loose organization of middle-class business people, led by the Unitarian lawyer J. W. James, was developing in the town, and this caucus was active in the constituency and exerting a profound influence on local affairs, including the political opinions and activities of Sir John Guest who, since his election in 1832, had moved in more radical directions in response to constituency pressures.[3] Guest, on his death-bed, was re-elected unopposed in 1852, but his death on 26 November was the signal for electioneering to begin. The following day, even before the corpse was cold, as some cynics gladly recorded, William Milbourne James, a barrister and first cousin to J. W. James, issued his Address.[4] Yet, on the eve of the election three weeks later, the opposition candidate having withdrawn,[5] Lady Charlotte felt sufficiently confident of the result to discuss with Bruce the question of his successor as stipendiary magistrate, and when, on the day of the election, she was told that a meeting of her workmen was to take place she instructed her agents 'to request all our people from being present', adding, very significantly, that 'if there were to be a contest it would be different, for then the men would be called upon to exercise a trust'.[6] In other words, to put the best complexion on the matter, she expected the men to obey her wishes in their capacity as her employees, but, as was constitutionally proper, to be free when they acted as voters in a contested election. What if it had been the intention of the workers simply to meet in order to put up their own candidate at the hustings, which they had a perfectly good constitutional right to do, or merely as a gesture of independence, as they had done in 1841 when they had 'voted' by acclamation for the Chartist Morgan Williams rather than Guest?[7]

Such were the electoral realities when Bruce and Clark became trustees for the family. It was an ideal combination. Clark was to be the managing trustee, working closely with Lady Charlotte in the day-to-day running of the business, becoming resident manager when Lady Charlotte withdrew from active participation on her marriage in 1855. His friend, Bruce, as Merthyr's MP, was mainly occupied with scrutinizing all legislation which affected the interests of the Company, while taking an active role in the unfolding of affairs in general. This was a period of great political change in Great Britain when legislation of tremendous importance was occupying the attention of Parliament and the country. Industrial relations, public health, Factory Acts, communications, education, were all issues which affected the iron industry intimately, and in Bruce Merthyr iron manufacturers had a representative in Parliament who was rapidly making his way in national politics. It was a moot point whether he was entirely reliable from the point of view of the ironmasters on some of their major concerns, such as industrial relations and the labour laws, and it was widely felt that his future as the member for Merthyr would increasingly be dependent on the support of Dowlais and of the rising Nonconformist caucuses in Merthyr and Aberdare.

While Clark remained as resident trustee, or managing director, there was no fear that this would diminish. He and Bruce were bosom friends with implicit faith in each other's judgement, and though they consulted each other on a great variety of topics, including politics, they never interfered in their respective spheres of activity and influence. It was, perhaps, fortunate for the former that Clark had no political ambitions, and took no notice of suggestions that he should stand for the borough. In 1857, for example, John Camplin Wolrige, one of the DIC agents, gave it as his opinion that Clark, rather than Bruce, was the most eligible person to represent Merthyr. Bruce, he wrote, was high-minded but his votes tended to make government nugatory, and he had lost the confidence of his constituents.[8] Ten years later Clark was being talked of, along with Richard Fothergill and Sir Ivor Guest, as a possible candidate in the critical year of 1867 which saw the passing of the Second Reform Bill,[9] and in 1868 Cardiff Liberals, led by the formidable John Batchelor, invited him to consider standing for Cardiff in the event of James Stuart losing the support of Lord Bute.[10] Nor would he entertain the idea of standing for Caernarfon, which is understandable enough.[11] And when Wolrige, writing from Taunton, told him that if he wanted a seat in the House of Commons the borough of Taunton would offer him a fair chance, he replied that he was much obliged, but that 'he preferred the outside to the inside of the House in question'.[12]

This did not imply that he was not active in politics. On the contrary, he fully realized that his position as resident trustee of the Dowlais Iron Company was a crucial factor in the political life of Merthyr and Aberdare, and that he possessed residual powers inferior only to those which Sir John

Guest had exercised so effectively. Like Sir John and the other ironmasters he understood the vital necessity of attending to local affairs. Here, the key institutions were the Poor Law Guardians and, from 1850, the Local Board of Health. Both were elected bodies, the franchise being confined to owners and ratepayers assessed at a minimum of £50, who could claim one vote, rising to those assessed at £250 and above, who could claim six votes.[13] This was a wider franchise than that for the unreformed Parliament, but the stringent property qualifications had the effect of restricting the vote to a minority of ratepayers, while plural voting virtually ensured that the social composition of the Guardians and of the Board of Health would be heavily weighted in favour of the owners of property in the town. It was vitally important that the interests of the ironmasters should be protected, for these were spending institutions funded out of the rates, and it would be imprudent, to say the least, to allow their radical opponents to assess their annual liability. Hence, it was invariably the case that these boards were chaired by one of the ironmasters, and that their agents and managers should be prominent members. Thus, Guest was elected chairman of the Board of Health in 1850,[14] with all four ironmasters returned as members, a clear indication that control over spending on the health of the people would be the prerogative of the main employers of labour and the major ratepayers. Clark became chairman in 1862; he had already been elected chairman of the Board of Guardians in 1859, a position he held until 1881, when he resigned.[15]

It was in elections to these boards that Clark was brought face to face with the realities of the exercise of power and of the necessity to maintain control over events at the lowest level of initiative. The Local Board of Health was a much smaller body than the Board of Guardians,[16] and its statutory duties concerning sanitation, the provision of water and other social conditions affecting the health of the community, were subject to strict and enforceable rules in accordance with a constantly growing body of legislation. Before 1850 public health and the care of the sick had been among the responsibilities of the Poor Law Guardians, but, largely in order to avoid spending money and raising the rates, these duties had been neglected, and only after successive epidemics, including typhus in 1847, smallpox in 1848 and cholera in 1849 (when 1,517 died) could the authorities be brought to accept the fact that the town should be brought under the 1848 Public Health Act. Clark, who had inspected and reported upon the sanitary state of a number of towns in south Wales (as well as England) for the General Board of Health, and who was consequently extremely well-informed and sympathetic to the work of the Board, was ideally equipped to guide the local board, but it is abundantly clear that he was faced with the implacable opposition of some of the ironmasters. It was due to such opposition, aided and abetted by some of the town's notorious cottage owners, that progress was criminally slow in the building of reservoirs, the provision of clean water, the cleansing of the streets and courts, the removal and disposal of sewage, and the availability of medical services.[17]

Sanitary reform, like the alleviation of poverty and industrial relations, involved politics, and it was in these areas of public life that Clark had to deal with opposing ideologies and social forces. On the one hand were the ironmasters who could exercise control over developments and frustrate the public good by manipulating the so-called democratic processes of local government. When they acted in concert, as they often did, they were irresistible because they could depend upon the support of the bulk of the ratepayers. As Sir Edwin Chadwick had put it, the local government being introduced by this social legislation would be 'the Local government of a Class . . . and that Class the well to do Class'.[18] Ordinary workmen, however intelligent and respectable and well-informed, would be excluded, as would their radical leaders, most of whom were themselves workmen or small tradesmen or craftsmen. Out of a total population of over 40,000 there were only 1,377 ratepayers, and these could be influenced and manipulated and intimidated to vote with the masters of industry. As one sarcastic ratepayer put it in a letter to the local board,

> The next time you send Voting Papers to Dowlais, please to leave them all at Dowlais Office, for it will spare you and them a great deal of trouble. For the Man that was distributing this time could not find out the Voters residences because he was a Stranger in the place. The Dowlais Agents had to call in every house to tell the voter who he was to vote for . . . Therefore I beg to call your attention to the above plan, for it will answer the same purpose, and save a great deal of useless bodily exercise to both parties, the time spent without doing any good. Which the late Renowned Benjamin Franklyn said was Money.[19]

Or, as the Dowlais grocer, John Jones, complained in a letter to the General Board of Health in London in April 1853,

> Sir, I can not rest happy under the flagrant abuse of authority we suffer in this place without making our complaint known to you, as a higher power, and I suppose with power to control our movements. Will you be so kind as to inform me whether it is legal for the Iron Masters or any other party to send their agents to follow the deliveries of the voting papers dictating to

the voters how to fill them for them – and not only that but to fill them for them, – *and cross the names of the other candidates out* – the abuse here has been very great plenty of evidence to prove it – ready and willing – your kind instructions on the subject will oblige your humble Servt and hundreds of voters.[20]

William Simons, the High Constable, was just as damning in a long and detailed letter addressed to Sir Benjamin Hall, the president of the Board of Health, in March 1855,

There is so great a dread of the ironmasters in this place, and their powers so extensive, and so sure to be hostilily [*sic*] applied; that public duty and christian obligations are alike forgotten. Disease sweeps away its thousands, without an effort to control the agencies that induce it; and the sufferings of the poor, induced by want of water, occasion less dread than the powers of an Ironmaster.[21]

There is no evidence either one way or the other as to Clark's attitude to such abuses of power, nor is it sensible to attempt to apportion blame. Lady Charlotte Guest, whom he greatly admired and whose judgement he respected, had been quite clear in her mind as to the responsibility of the ironmasters to improve the sanitary condition of the people. This is clear from her criticism of the other masters, especially Crawshay and Hill, who claimed to have vested rights over the water of the Taff and other streams.[22] Nor should one doubt the sincerity of his conviction that the nature of local politics was a fundamental cause of the deplorable sanitary state of the numerous towns which he had inspected for the General Board, for this was universally the case. All the Board of Health reports on Merthyr – De la Beche's in 1845,[23] Rammell's in 1850,[24] William Kay's in 1854,[25] and the annual series of local reports by Dr T. J. Dyke, Medical Officer of Health, which begin in 1866 – had been astonished that a town of over 40,000 inhabitants should be 'as destitute of civic government as the smallest rural village of the empire'. Dr Kay's report drew attention to another basic factor in the social structure of the town, which he analysed with a fair amount of detail, namely, the absence of men of independent means, not connected with the works, and residing in the town, people, that is to say, who could be independent of the ironmasters, set standards of behaviour, and stand between the common people, including tradespeople, artisans and craftsmen, and the industrialists. But even if such a class of people had existed, there was no forum for debate, no machinery of government which they could hope to control. Indeed, because the ironmasters ruled like princes within their own territories, which were 'like states in miniature',[26] and suffered no interference in their affairs from any of their competitors or by any other body (even statutory bodies like the Poor Law Commissioners[27]) the public good inevitably suffered. Politics in such a situation was the art of doing as little as possible, and of resisting rather than initiating change.

Clark occupied a position of great political influence, therefore, in the town and parish, and there is no doubt that he used this power in as benevolent a fashion as possible and within the limitations imposed upon him by the necessity to co-operate with the other ironmasters. In such a situation he could try to compensate for the appalling lack of social progress, which was the hallmark of Merthyr, and alleviate some of the more atrocious effects of the lack of governance by charitable means. He was by nature an extremely kind and charitable person, and all Dowlais chapels, and many others in the town and parish, benefited from his benevolence irrespective of denomination. Education was a major concern and the Dowlais schools continued to flourish under his control. When the Merthyr School Board was formed he was unanimously elected its chairman,[28] and invariably he came head of the poll in subsequent elections.[29] He was generous in the help he gave to promoters of education elsewhere in the district,[30] and gave his support to Bruce's efforts to remove pauper children from the 'polluting atmosphere' of the workhouse.[31] All this is to say that his rule in Dowlais, where there was no countervailing power to his, was paternalistic rather than despotic, and that in the affairs of the town he was a moderating influence on the activities of some of the other ironmasters, especially of those, like Hill, who believed that the business of government was to tax and to punish.

Nevertheless, it is important to bear in mind that, whether he acknowledged it or not, behind his benevolence there may have been a wider political intention, which took little account of the political aspirations of those of his dependants who believed that democracy was the prerequisite for social progress. Philanthropy was one of the weapons in the armoury of politicians, and constituents expected politicians to be generous in their support of good causes. Although Clark had no political aspirations for himself, it was still necessary to maintain the Guest ascendancy in Merthyr and its influence in the representation of the other Glamorgan constituencies.[32] Such was the charisma attaching to the name of Guest that, up to 1868, Merthyr Tydfil was contested only twice. The other ironmasters, as we have already noted, were reluctant or, perhaps, afraid to oppose Guest or any other candidate supported by Dowlais, but they were equally hostile to anyone else from outside attempting to do so. Even Bruce, in 1857, admitted that if Sir Ivor Guest, the heir of Sir John, decided to put himself forward he would have to stand down.[33] The only candidate to attempt it was C. M. Elderton, a London solicitor with rather vague local connections, who stood as a Liberal in 1859 against Bruce, but, lacking the support of the ironmasters, he polled only 106 votes to Bruce's 800.[34] It was vitally important to maintain this ascendancy, and it was Clark's main political function to do so.

This, however, was becoming increasingly difficult, and virtually impossible after the passing of the 1867 Reform Act. Up to that date the kind of representational dominance possessed by the Guest interest was based on a small, restricted and fairly easily managed electorate. In 1852, when Bruce was elected, there were only 938 voters in the whole of the constituency (including Aberdare), and still only 1,387 in 1865. The parliamentary franchise was vested in male ten-pound householders, that is, in householders rated at £10 and above. But the overwhelming majority of people in Merthyr lived in houses rented from the ironmasters or from cottage owners and were thus excluded from the lists of voters. Moreover, the social class of the voters was likely to be predominantly lower class. In 1847, for example, of the total of 822 voters no fewer than 431 occupied houses rated at between £10 and £15, i.e. the lowest category or stratum in the electoral body.[35] They were probably shopkeepers, small traders, and the élite among the working classes. It was extremely difficult for ordinary working-class men to gain the vote, however respectable and intelligent they might be. The franchise had been deliberately fenced around with a multitude of restrictions designed to exclude all but a small minority of the people. It was the Dowlais portion of this tiny electorate which had to be controlled by Clark on behalf of the Guest family, told how to vote, and brought to the polling booths to do so on those rare occasions when there was a contest. No wonder that the population of Merthyr included a large number of disgruntled men who saw it as their duty to agitate against such an unjust system.

They were given the opportunity to do so in the election of 1859, which was fought on the question of parliamentary reform. The year before, John Bright and some of his old Anti-Corn Law associates, including Edward Miall, the main inspiration behind the Liberation Society which was then active in Wales, set out to organize an agitation in the main provincial cities of England and Scotland to support the Reform Bill which Bright was to draw up and present to Parliament in the coming session. The agitation was not a success, and his old friend, Cobden, came to the conclusion that what was needed was 'some multitudinous demonstrations by the unenfranchised in favour of Parliamentary reform'.[36] The response in Merthyr was not very promising for the reformers. A poorly attended meeting of a newly formed Reform Association, chaired by J. W. James, a close associate of Clark, passed resolutions calling for the ballot, triennial parliaments, the re-distribution of seats, and household franchise.[37] A similar, though better attended meeting at Aberdare later in the month passed the same resolutions, and shortly afterwards the two associations set up a joint committee to co-ordinate their tactics. Both these organizations were composed of moderate men, the towns' leading Liberals who were not disposed to extreme measures. Quite distinct from these two associations was an association of non-electors, consisting mainly of working-class men, and led and inspired by old Chartists.[38]

The existence of these political associations introduced new elements into the political life of the constituency. For the moment they were largely otiose for, except for the ballot, Bruce's platform was unimpeachably Liberal and the Reform Association could hardly oppose a man with whose ideas they agreed. There was disagreement only, and that mainly from the ironmasters rather than members of the Association, over Bruce's vote against Palmerston's policy on China in 1857.[39] Much more radical was the working-class organization of the unenfranchised, but they too were ineffective while the constitution remained unreformed. Given the vote they would have the capacity to challenge not only the Liberal élite but also the ironmasters themselves who controlled the political life of the borough. Democracy would destroy autocracy by sheer force of numbers.

Thereafter parliamentary reform moved into the centre of politics, both within Parliament and in the constituencies, and after February 1867 it was certain that a comprehensive measure of reform would be passed even though its details remained to be settled between the Conservative government under Lord Derby and the Liberal opposition led by Gladstone. The Merthyr and the Aberdare Reform Associations were active, and the two national societies, the National Reform League and the National Reform Union, were likewise building up a body of opinion in favour of an enlarged franchise. Of the two, the former was the more radical, and with the two Chartists, Mr Gould and Dr Jones, at the helm, they favoured household franchise, which would sweep away the property qualification of the ten-pound householder franchise of the 1832 Reform Act. The two Reform Associations preferred the stance of the Union, but in any case, this was a time of rising expectations and a sense that an old order was about to change.

It changed in unexpected but joyful ways when Disraeli, the architect of the Second Reform Bill, brought in the household franchise that the radical side of the Liberal Party in the country and the organization of the disenfranchised in Merthyr had been agitating for but which they scarcely hoped would come. The consequences of this change were enormous. At one stroke the numbers of electors grew from an estimated 1,400 to a massive 14,577. Of these, 13,135 were qualified as householders, and only 1,442 as ten-pounders, that is, 13,135 persons were voting for the first time.[40] In addition to these franchise changes Merthyr was given an additional member, thus becoming a two-member constituency in which each qualified elector had two votes which he could give to one candidate (plumping) or vote for two of the candidates. In this way the old political structures of the borough came to an end, and no one could foretell what new structures would emerge.

What soon became evident was that there would be powerful opposition to Bruce, not merely or only from those ironmasters who had long distrusted him, but also, and crucially, from the new working-class voters. For the past ten years relations between Bruce and the colliers had been worsening.[41] In the industrial relations pertaining during those years they thought that there was evidence that he was not the neutral observer and arbitrator that he claimed to be, but rather a spokesman for the masters. This had been the case in the long bitter strike of 1857 when he had lectured the Aberdare colliers on the economic realities of the market and the unreasonableness of their resistance to the wage reduction being imposed by the masters, and they believed that he could not be trusted to support the men in the current depression which was affecting the coal and the iron trades equally.

The new class of voters had other grievances too. Bruce had not fairly put the colliers' case during the debates on the Mines Inspection Act, but had rather supported the objections of the masters to the colliers' demand that assistant inspectors who were experienced colliers should be appointed. In addition, they had evidence – or believed that they had evidence – that Bruce supported the coalowners in their attempt to impose the Double Shift system in their collieries.[42] These were matters of the highest importance to the workmen, and they could no longer be ignored. They were now organized, had their own leadership, acted independently of the official parties, held their own meetings, used the press in a highly sophisticated manner, published a bilingual pamphlet on their grievances, *The Double and Single Shift Compared*,[43] and they had petitioned Parliament. They called Bruce to meet a committee of twenty representatives in Cwmaman, where he was mercilessly and expertly cross-examined by members of their executive. This was a turning-point in the election, and Bruce now faced the reality of defeat.

Above all, these new voters, already organized on these industrial issues, were also being persuaded to vote as Nonconformists. The constituency was a stronghold of Nonconformity, and the chapels, under the influence of the Liberation Society, had developed into quasi-political institutions.[44] The organization was well-nigh perfect, and there was no doubt in any quarter that the Nonconformist vote could be delivered. Under the old, unreformed system in which the franchise was restricted to a very small fraction of the male population none of these objections to the candidature of Bruce, or even all of them together, would have made much difference. The combination of a small electorate effectively controlled by the ironmasters would have ensured his return, as in 1859, when 'They sent him to Parliament even when the great majority had told him by their vote at the hustings that they did not want him to go, and when he had told them that he would go in spite of them', or, as another newspaper more succinctly reported, 'You may hold up your dirty hands against me, but tomorrow I'll be member for Merthyr in spite of you'.[45]

None of this augured well for Bruce and his supporters. By midsummer, when the electioneering began in earnest, it was known that the seat would be contested by Bruce, Richard Fothergill and Henry Richard. Fothergill was the owner of the Abernant ironworks in Aberdare and had recently purchased the derelict Penydarren works which had been idle for some years. He also let it be known that he was interested in reopening the Plymouth ironworks. As an employer of labour, therefore, he ranked next to the Guests and Crawshays in the industrial hierarchy. He was a Liberal, a supporter of Gladstone in economic, financial and religious matters, including support for the Nonconformist policy of disestablishing the Irish Church. Crucially, he was in favour of the ballot. It was his misfortune to be heartily disliked and distrusted by the other ironmasters and coalowners. He tended to take an individual line in industrial relations,[46] and often he seemed to be easier on the men in times of depression and unrest than were the others. Of the ironmasters, only Crawshay came out in his support, but Bruce and Clark were not too perturbed, knowing that Robert Crawshay was liable to change his mind when it suited him.

The most formidable candidate was Henry Richard. He was the choice of the Nonconformists which, in effect, meant the choice of a majority of the electorate. Of the three candidates he was, in some respects, the most original, since he could present himself to the electors not only as one of the leading Nonconformists in Britain, but also as a man with no access to wealth or influence, who could be trusted to represent the ordinary folk of the constituency rather than the industrial interests of the place. In this respect he could stand alone, and electors who believed in the tradition of having as their member someone who had an intimate knowledge of the iron and coal industry, preferably as an ironmaster, could cast their second vote either for Fothergill or Bruce: he was careful, except by implication, not to identify himself with either one or the other. Above all, he was a Welshman, the only one of the candidates who could address the majority of his listeners in their own language. He made much of this: indeed, as the election drew to its conclusion it became a dominant theme, and Richard presented himself to the Welsh people generally and not only to the Merthyr Tydfil electorate, as the prospective member for Wales.[47]

That Richard would be returned, probably at the head of the poll, transformed the campaigns of the other two candidates. Bruce, who was in receipt of regular reports of developments in all parts of the constituency, began to think of ways to induce Fothergill to retire. It is clear from his letters to Clark that he distrusted and disliked Fothergill but at the same time feared him. To what extent was Fothergill honest in his political principles? Bruce was convinced that Fothergill was exerting unfair influence on his own workmen, and that he was spreading false information about Dowlais. It was widely known that Fothergill was in favour of lowering ironworkers' wages, and it was rumoured that he had shown a private letter to him from Menelaus, the manager of the DIC, indicating that it was likewise the intention of Dowlais to do so.[48] He rejoiced when Fothergill was given a hostile reception in Dowlais, wondered whether Menelaus could persuade him to retire, and was glad when Clark instructed him to try to do so.[49]

Then came the decision which was to prove fatal for Bruce and which was to stain the reputation of Dowlais. It seems to have been widely believed that all Bruce's leading friends were supporters of Fothergill, and this clearly injured him. Fothergill, Bruce was convinced, was doing all that money, beer and lies could do to win the election, even at the expense of debauching the morals of the electorate. It was essential that Clark should now come to his aid. 'His sub-lieutenants', he told his friend,

> hold their meetings in different public houses where beer flows without stint. Such practices deserve reprobation which, after your long neutrality would come weightily from you, and would not affect your support of Richard, whom you would uphold not so much for his own merits, as by way of protest agst. Fothergill. It would leave you free, on any other occasion, to support any Candidate you might prefer to Fothergill.

Clark responded immediately, and sent a draft of a letter to Bruce and his agent. The latter responded by praising the letter, saying that it would delight the Dowlais Richardites and produce a good effect elsewhere in the constituency,[50] and after further drafting by Bruce it was published in the

Cardiff and Merthyr Guardian, the largest newspaper to circulate in both parts of the constituency, from which it would be copied by all other weeklies. It was widely read. It certainly raised the political temperature, but it also contributed substantially to the defeat of the candidate it was designed to sustain. Such are the ironies of politics.

The letter was addressed to Frank James. In it Clark said that he hoped to see Bruce returned, but that until recently he had been completely indifferent as to the success either of Richard or Fothergill. The former was not sufficiently experienced, and the fact that he was a Dissenter did not constitute a sufficient reason for his return. As for Fothergill, Clark acknowledged that he was an able and industrious man, but though he was a large employer of labour he had never shown any inclination to support education, and, moreover, he had kept a truck-shop.[51] He went on to say that he had resisted certain appeals to allow Bruce and Fothergill to combine so as to exclude Richard, and he had remained neutral as between the latter two. In the mean time, however, circumstances had changed: Richard, with very little exertion of his own, had been welcomed by the vast majority of electors, and would head the poll. 'This reception, by those among whom I live, and with whom my relations are very friendly, of a man against whom I have nothing to allege, does, I think, cause me to . . . join with them.' He went on to describe the 'evil change in the conduct of those who advise and act for Fothergill'. Dishonest attacks are made on Bruce, creditable transactions involving him falsified and distorted, wrong reports printed and Bruce's corrections rejected, and meetings held in low public houses, 'and wherever workmen could be induced to congregate, to injure the character of our representative, and to debauch the morality of our representative'. Fothergill is ultimately responsible for all this, and for those reasons he could no longer be neutral, but would vote for Bruce and Richard.[52]

There were howls of rage from the Fothergill camp at this intervention. It was not difficult to show that Clark was factually wrong in certain particulars, and such errors of fact were widely publicized, especially in the *Merthyr Telegraph*, which was very hostile to Bruce. More seriously, it was used as evidence that Dowlais was not neutral, and that the letter amounted to, at best a suggestion, at worst a directive, to the Dowlais voters to vote with Mr Clark. Bribery and corruption were virtually unknown in elections in Merthyr, but undue influence, especially in the ironworks, was rampant. 2,500 votes for Bruce, which was the estimated number of voters in the employment of the DIC, would be that number of votes cast against Fothergill, but at the expense of coercing free men.[53] Fothergill immediately issued a statement to the effect that his men were utterly free, and that this latest move only went to show how real was the need for the ballot to protect the men.[54] Evidently, Clark himself realized that a great tactical error had been made, for shortly afterwards he called a meeting of all the Dowlais agents, under-agents, gaffers, and overmen to hear a statement by the management intended to 'disabuse the minds of the electors in the employ of the Works from any erroneous impression that undue influence would be exercised over them in favour or against either of the candidates'.[55] A statement was issued to that effect by Menelaus, and explicit instructions given to those present to adhere to them. This could be regarded as either an explication or as a retraction: either way, it scarcely freed Bruce from the imputation that without the ballot he and his type would not long survive the hustings.

Yet another intervention by the Dowlais works in favour of Bruce soon followed as it became ever clearer that he would be defeated. Very unwisely, Menelaus attended a meeting of Dowlais voters in which he seemed to imply that he was in favour of Fothergill, and that he wished his workmen to vote with him. This was a serious matter indeed, and Bruce's agent thought that only by making it known that he (Menelaus) was in favour of Bruce first could the harm it had done be counteracted. He also thought that Clark should now attend Bruce's committee meetings, and that Sir Ivor Guest should be asked to write a letter in favour of Bruce – either for Bruce alone or at least for Bruce first. This latter point was very timely because it was alleged that Fothergill was constantly saying that Sir Ivor had told him that he would support him against anyone but a Guest.[56] Crawshay was concurrently giving his agents the same kind of instruction. If one of his workmen would not vote for both Mr Bruce and Mr Fothergill, then he should be asked to vote at least for Bruce, 'and if he will not promise until the Voting Day his second vote, I certainly tell my agents to ask the man "if he does not wish to show some acknowledgement of kind feeling towards his employer"'.[57] This was the conventional way of influencing voters in Merthyr, and undoubtedly this is what Dowlais workmen believed was happening in their case also.

Thus, Clark came to be personally embroiled in the election, the cause being the increasingly precarious position of Bruce in Merthyr itself. If Dowlais appeared divided within itself there could be no hope, and the election was as good as lost: 'If Dowlais splits, we are lost.' As the day of the election approached, the panic in the Bruce camp grew, and evidently only a direct intervention by the resident trustee could save the day.

Polling day showed how badly Bruce and Clark had miscalculated. At the hustings, where a huge, well-conducted crowd, variously estimated at between ten and fifteen thousand, was present, Bruce was proposed by

Clark, but the speeches of neither could be heard above the roars of disapproval and cries of 'the screw'. Men carried placards showing an open hand with the words, 'Here we come with our dirty hands, free voters at last.' By contrast both Richard and Fothergill were cheered to the echo, and Richard's speech especially was listened to carefully as he expounded his political philosophy. The poll itself the following day gave Richard 11,565 votes, Fothergill 7,153 and Bruce 5,697. Richard had polled 46 per cent of the total votes cast in Merthyr, and 49 per cent in Aberdare. Fothergill and Bruce polled respectively 28 and 26 per cent in Merthyr, and in Aberdare 33 and 18 per cent.[58] It is, of course, impossible to say to what extent Clark's letter influenced the results, but there seems to be no doubt that the iron-works influence still predominated in Dowlais, and from being an aloof and distant man in public affairs the senior trustee had become very much a part of the political process.

In future, however, he assumed a position of masterly inactivity so far as parliamentary politics were concerned. Only when the restless Sir Ivor Guest, who still nursed a keen desire to represent his native county, was a candidate did Clark again become involved. This was in the election of 1874 when Sir Ivor stood as a Tory for Glamorgan in opposition to Vivian (who thought Guest more suited to the crimson benches than the green) and C. R. M. Talbot. Bruce, as ever, was very dismissive, thinking he had very little chance of success, and that his political opinions were guided by deference to his father-in-law, the Duke of Marlborough, and the prospect of a peerage. Clark strongly disagreed with that assessment, noting that Guest's political principles had been adopted long before his marriage, and were sincere and honest.[59] In the event Sir Ivor lost, and came away with the conviction that the county was now hopelessly Liberal, and that probably he would not stand again for Glamorgan and fling his money about.[60] Clark kept aloof also in the Merthyr election of 1874, when the ironworkers and colliers had a genuine working-class candidate in Thomas Halliday, and in the 1880 election, when both Sir Ivor and his brother, Arthur, were rumoured to be interested, and when W. T. Lewis (later Lord Merthyr of Senghennydd) stood in opposition to C. H. James, he remained in the background. William Menelaus, who was now managing the works, how-ever, was very active on the Tory side in both those elections. But in local politics, where it mattered, Clark remained active and purposeful until 1881 when he resigned from the Board of Guardians. He also continued to be active in the field of education, coming top of the poll in the elections to the School Board in 1880.[61] Otherwise, he seemed to be above politics, and Talygarn was a haven of peace from which he could view changing events as from a distance. All the while, his bounteous liberality continued to flow in and around Dowlais, and for this he would be remembered long after the tribulations of 1868 had been forgotten.

Notes

[1] Clark MSS, 68/827, H. A. Bruce to Clark, 8 November 1868. See also *Aberdare Times*.

[2] For this election, see Islwyn W. R. David, 'Political and electioneering activity in south-east Wales, 1820–1852' (University of Wales MA thesis, 1959), and see Gwyn A. Williams, 'The making of radical Merthyr', *Welsh History Review*, 1 (1960–3), 161–92.

[3] G. A. Williams, 'The making of radical Merthyr', and the same author's essay, 'The Merthyr of Dic Penderyn', in Glanmor Williams (ed.), *Merthyr Politics: The Making of a Working-class Tradition* (Cardiff, University of Wales Press, 1966), 25–6.

[4] These elections are described in Ieuan Gwynedd Jones, *Communities: Essays in the Social History of Victorian Wales* (Llandysul, Gomer Press, 1987), 292–3.

[5] James withdrew on 6 December, the day Bruce published his Address. In the Address announcing his withdrawal James claimed to have been told by William Crawshay that 'there would be determined opposition to me on the part of the four ironworks, on the grounds that my return would give greater strength to that Independent Party, which had in parochial matters successfully opposed the Iron Masters'. This independent party, he declared, should organize their strength in order to 'use it to teach even Merthyr Iron Masters that property has its duties as well as its rights'. See *Cardiff and Merthyr Guardian*, 11 December 1852.

[6] These events can be followed in the journals of Lady Charlotte Guest, NLW Lady Charlotte Guest MSS XV, ff. 266–71. The quotation is under 13 December 1852, f. 271.

[7] For this election, see *Lady Charlotte Guest: Extracts from her Journal, 1833–1852* (London, John Murray, 1950), 123–4.

[8] Clark MSS, 57/53, J. C. Wolrige to Clark, 14 March 1857.

[9] Clark MSS, 67/351, William Jenkins (DIC manager) reporting to Clark, 3 June 1867.

[10] Clark MSS, 68/494, J. Batchelor to Clark, 17 July 1868.

[11] Clark MSS, 68/730, C. H. James to Clark, 21 September 1868.

[12] Clark MSS, 72/724, Wolrige to Clark, 11 November 1872.

[13] These were the rates under the Poor Law Amendment Act of 1844. The original 1834 Act had been much more restrictive and exclusive, the minimum property qualification being set at £200.

[14] 'Public Health in Mid-Victorian Wales. Correspondence from the Principality to the General Board of Health & the Local Government Act Office 1848–71', transcribed and edited with an introduction by A. H. Williams (University of Wales, Board of Celtic Studies, 1983), 1010. This invaluable but unpublished work is available in the libraries of the constituent institutions of the University of Wales, the Wellcome Institute, and the University of London Institute of Historical Research.

[15] NLW MS 15,032C, f. 123.

[16] For these boards, see Tydfil Davies Jones, 'Poor Law administration in Merthyr Tydfil Union 1834–1894', *Morgannwg*, 8 (1964), 35–62.

[17] I. G. Jones, *Communities*, 239–62.

[18] Quoted in R. A. Lewis, *Edwin Chadwick and the Public Health Movement 1832–1854* (London, Longmans, 1952), 301.

[19] 'Public Health in Mid-Victorian Wales', 1017.

[20] Ibid., 1016.

[21] Ibid., 1035.

22 Ibid., 1036. This is discussed in 'Merthyr Tydfil: The politics of survival', in I. G. Jones, *Communities*, 258.

23 Sir Henry de la Beche, *Report on the State of . . . Merthyr Tydfil* (London, 1845).

24 T. W. Rammell, *Report to the General Board of Health . . . into the Sanitary Condition of . . . Merthyr Tydfil* (London, 1850).

25 William Kay, *Report of the Sanitary Condition of Merthyr Tydfil* (Merthyr Tydfil, Local Board of Health, 1854).

26 John C. Fowler, *The Characteristics and Civilization of South Wales* (Neath, 1873), 11–12. I owe this reference to Mr Neil Evans.

27 See Tydfil Davies Jones, 'Poor Law administration'.

28 Clark MSS, 74/201, Revd J. Thomas to Clark, 30 March 1874.

29 As in 1880; Clark MSS, 80/155, James to Clark, 10 March 1880.

30 Clark MSS, 68/790.

31 Tydfil Davies Jones, 'Poor Law administration', 56.

32 Clark was a consistent supporter of the Glamorgan county members, H. H. Vivian and C. R. M Talbot, on whose committees he sat in successive parliaments. He was also a solid supporter of L. Ll. Dilwyn, the member for the Swansea Boroughs from 1852 until 1886.

33 Clark MSS, 57/49, Bruce to Clark, 12 March 1857.

34 On this election, see I. G. Jones, *Communities*, 297.

35 *Return of the £10 Voters in Each Borough. PP* 1847 (751) xlvi, 345.

36 Quoted in F. B. Smith, *The Making of the Second Reform Bill* (Cambridge University Press, 1966), 40.

37 *Cardiff and Merthyr Guardian*, 1 January 1859.

38 Its secretary was William Davies, a puddler. See *Cardiff and Merthyr Guardian*, 23 April 1859.

39 Clark MSS, 57/49 and 57/52, Bruce to R. T. Crawshay, 12 March and 13 March 1857. 'If they bring forward Sir I. Guest I shall of course retire – for what can I do with Crawshay, Forman and Hill against me, and Dowlais more than divided. I have heard nothing of this from anyone but yourself.'

40 *Electors in Cities and Boroughs. PP* 1868–9 (419) l, 110.

41 For the industrial history of the period of the election see I. G. Jones, *Explorations and Explanations: Essays in the Social History of Victorian Wales* (Llandysul, Gomer Press, 1981), 204–7.

42 These matters are discussed in some detail in I. G. Jones, *Explorations*, 206–7, and in I. G. Jones, *Communities*, 310–11. Bruce told Clark that he would be happy to join Clark himself, Vivian and Nixon in forming a committee with regard to colliers' insurance and the Double Shift system: Clark MSS, 67/728, Bruce to Clark, 12 December 1867.

43 The 1st edn. was issued in Welsh: *Y Double a'r Single Shift yn y Dafol; sef Sylwadau ar y ddwy Drefn o Weithio, yn nghyd a Gwrthdystiad yn erbyn yr Ymgais Presenol o Ddwyn y Double Shift i Ymarferiad yn Neheudir Cymru*. See the review in *Seren Cymru*, 27 March 1868.

44 On this, see 'The Liberation Society and Welsh politics, 1844 to 1868', in I. G. Jones, *Explorations*, 236–68.

45 *Merthyr Telegraph*, 10 October 1868 and *Aberdare Times*, 17 October 1868.

46 For example, he did not agree that the large employers of labour should take united action against the impending Labour Commission, and seems to have persuaded Crawshay to agree with him. Clark MSS, 67/131, W. Jenkins to Clark, 23 February 1867; 67/155, Crawshay to Clark, 4 March 1867.

47 This election has been exhaustively studied in I. G. Jones, *Explorations*, and I. G. Jones, *Communities*.

48 Clark MSS, 68/735, Jenkins to Clark, 23 September 1868.

49 Clark MSS, 68/757, Bruce to Clark, 30 August 1868.

[50] Clark MSS, 68/777, James to Clark, 9 October 1868.

[51] A company shop in which employees could buy goods on credit, or (until prohibited by the Truck Act of 1831) could exchange vouchers and tokens for goods.

[52] *Cardiff and Merthyr Guardian*, 17 October 1868.

[53] *Seren Cymru*, 30 October 1868.

[54] *Aberdare Times*, 24 October 1868.

[55] Ibid., 31 October 1868.

[56] Clark MSS, 68/824 and 68/826, Frank James to Clark, 1 and 7 November 1868.

[57] NLW, Cyfarthfa Papers, vol. 6, no. 211 (letter marked 'Private'), Robert Crawshay to Mr Stephens, 5 November 1868.

[58] These are based on the Nonconformist Committee's hourly reports. See *Merthyr Express*, 21 November 1868.

[59] Clark MSS, 74/85, Lord Aberdare to Clark, 31 January 1874.

[60] Clark MSS, 74/122, Guest to Clark, 19 February and 13 March 1874.

[61] Clark MSS, 80/154, James to Clark, 10 March 1880.

CHAPTER 5

Castle Studies and G. T. Clark, with Particular Reference to Wales and the Marches

JOHN R. KENYON

Introduction

Until the publication of 'Castle' Clark's *Mediaeval Military Architecture in England* (2 vols, 1884), henceforth *MMA*,[1] the student of medieval castles in Britain lacked an academic textbook on this subject. The most useful volume was French in origin, being a translation of Viollet-le-Duc's treatise of 1854, *Essai sur l'architecture militaire du moyen âge*, issued by J. H. Parker, the architectural historian and publisher, and later keeper of the Ashmolean Museum in Oxford, in 1860.[2] Clark's compilation of his earlier writings was thus a landmark in castle studies, and laid the foundation for all future research and publication.

An examination of the bibliography of Clark's writings shows that he was the author of about 130 publications in this field of study, mainly periodical articles, and of these the majority were in the *Builder*, *Archaeologia Cambrensis* and the *Archaeological Journal*. There can be no denying that such an output makes Clark the founding father of castle studies, and his contribution to the subject cannot be overestimated, for little of real worth had been produced on the subject until Clark began his studies.

The studies are dominated by castles in England and Wales, but Clark did write on two Scottish sites (Borthwick and Urquhart) and a few in France. Some of the papers on specific castles are quite short, and a few, such as those on Caerphilly, Corfe and the Tower of London, are substantial. Included in the figure of around 130 are a number of 'duplicates'; for example, two of Clark's studies, those on Montgomery Castle and the moated mounds of the upper Severn, first appeared in *Montgomeryshire Collections* for 1877, but were reprinted in the 1880 issue of *Archaeologia Cambrensis*, while his paper in the *Builder* for 1873 on the motte of Ewias Harold was reprinted in the 1877 issue of *Arch. Camb.* All this made for greater circulation of his publications, for not everyone would have had easy access to journals such as the *Builder*.

Even allowing for the fact that a number of Clark's papers appeared in more than one publication, his output on castle studies was prodigious, especially when one remembers not only that he was publishing on a wide range of other topics, but also that his professional life must have imposed considerable limits on the time that he could devote to the subject. One should also remember the constraints on travel at that time, even in the age of the first railways. Many of his castle papers were collected within *MMA* and, as Clark reminds us in the preface to the book, the original papers were not written with a view to some future compilation, and so allowance should be made. For example, the study of Caerphilly was first drawn up fifty years before *MMA*, and the views held by Clark had changed over the years. As J. H. Round pointed out in his long review of *MMA*,[3] Clark by 1884 had accepted the dating of the keep of Newcastle upon Tyne as being late twelfth century, although originally he had assigned it to the late eleventh century which is how it is dated in *MMA*.

If one compares some of the original papers with the entries in *MMA*, it is possible to detect some minor changes in the latter. For example, in his article on Berkhamsted in the *Builder* for 18 July 1868 Clark writes that 'The mound was no doubt a Saxon castle', altered in *MMA* to 'The mound was no doubt an English burh'. The meaning is still the same, but one is left wondering about the alteration when the rest of the text is unchanged.[4] However, it is interesting to note that in his first article on Berkhamsted,[5] published in 1843, over twenty years earlier, Clark states that 'The mound may be of Norman date . . . There is however no reason stronger than general analogy for regarding this mound as Norman.' It would appear from the text that Clark thought that the motte could have been later; there is nothing in the paper to suggest a Saxon origin. More significantly, the entry in *MMA* on Cardiff, originally published in 1862, was updated, the most important addition (p. 340) being reference to the discovery of the timber piles for a bridge across the motte ditch and the foundations of a gateway at the foot of the motte.

The publication of *MMA* was important for two reasons. First, it brought together for the scholar the great majority of Clark's papers, an obvious advantage for anyone working in the field of castle studies. Second, the commercial publication of the book provided the layman with a firm grounding in the subject, with its introductory chapters followed by the series of 100 case studies, and no doubt this helped further encourage the pursuit of this subject. Included in the twelve chapters in the first volume of *MMA* were accounts of the first Norman castles, rectangular and shell keeps, castles of the early thirteenth century, and the castles of Edward I. Thus the main developments in castle building, to its apogee in the reign of Edward I, were discussed, and although general essays on the later medieval castles were not written, several of these buildings were included in the case studies, for example Bodiam in Sussex.

The introductory chapters were not just an examination of the development of military architecture, for two looked at the political value and influence of castles in the Norman period. These might be viewed as enlightened pieces of writing when one considers that since 1945 very few amongst the great wealth of publications on castles incorporate political and social considerations, most being purely architectural studies.

To write the definitive study of the contribution that Clark made to the study of medieval military architecture it would be necessary to spend a long time going through the extensive collection of his papers held in the Department of Manuscripts and Records at the National Library of Wales in Aberystwyth, and reading everything that he wrote – not an easy task as Clark's writing can be hard to decipher. An example from his notebooks is shown as figure 16, which is taken from Clark's survey of Skenfrith Castle in Monmouthshire. An examination of a number of his publications, together with some of his notebooks, does, however, allow us to make an assessment of the man and the role he played in making castle studies an academic discipline. Many questions remain, however, and one cannot help but be intrigued as to how Clark set about his castle studies: why only two Scottish sites, and those Borthwick and Urquhart? Why did he produce short studies of a number of relatively minor castles, such as Fillongley, but ignore others of arguably more significance? The answer may lie somewhere in the large Clark archive, but some of the lesser-known sites may have been written up simply because Clark happened to be in a particular area at a particular time, either for pleasure or on business, and used some of his time to look at a number and variety of sites.

To the student of castle studies, and particularly the history of such studies, Clark may be remembered mainly because he associated castle mottes with the Anglo-Saxons; and this association ran through much of his writings, together with the confusion over Saxon *burhs* in general. The criticism of this view was begun by Round in his 1894 review of *MMA*, and Mrs Ella Armitage was to write in 1912 a somewhat scathing attack on Clark's views on *burhs* and Saxon fortifications;[6] this has tended to cloud people's views of the man. Clark, by 1894 an old man, perhaps did not see the need to defend his views, for no reply to Round's criticisms is known. This should not influence us too much in an appreciation of Clark, since it is for his work on masonry castles of England and Wales that he is best remembered as far as castle studies are concerned, and some of his papers are reviewed below.

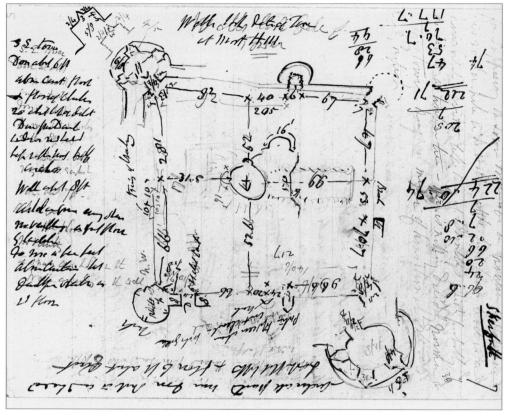

16 Part of G. T. Clark's survey of Skenfrith Castle, Monmouthshire, from one of his notebooks
(NLW MS 5192C).
National Library of Wales.

Castle studies before Clark

This is not the place to write the history of the study of military architecture
in Britain, but in order to assess Clark's place in this field, just a few words
are necessary. The greatest modern listing of castles in England and Wales is
David Cathcart King's *Castellarium Anglicanum*,[7] the culmination of work
from the late 1940s through to the 1980s, though some 450 years earlier
several hundred were mentioned by John Leland in his *Itinerary*. Both these
publications are purposely brief in their descriptions. Nor should we forget
James Moore's listing of over 500 castles in his *List of Principal Castles and
Monasteries in Great Britain* which was published in 1798.

Arguably the first proper studies of castle architecture were written by Edward King in papers in *Archaeologia*, 4 and 6 (1777 and 1782), and more particularly in his *Munimenta Antiqua* (1799–1805). King's publications have numerous engravings of plans and elevations of such castles as Conisbrough and Tonbridge, and his work has considerable merit. However, what was lacking was a general history of the subject. The earliest successful British attempt to produce such a book was Clark's *MMA*, and so in the development of castle studies we come to the first publications of G. T. Clark.

In the opening paragraphs of his review article of *MMA* in the *Quarterly Review*, Round makes a few general comments on Clark and castle studies that are worth repeating. Round begins with: 'The half-a-century of patient labour, of which the fruits have happily been collected in these two portly volumes, . . . has done much for a branch of study which had remained in a singularly backward state.' Further on, Round writes: 'It is necessary to realize the chaotic beliefs that had prevailed on the subject of our castles before we can justly estimate the work that Mr Clark has done, and appreciate the change he has wrought in our knowledge of military architecture.' What follows is an examination of some of Clark's writings and their place in castle studies.

Clark's early castle studies

It was the period from 1860 through to the late 1880s that saw the main output of Clark's castle studies, but his first foray into this field in fact goes back to the 1830s, with three articles on castles in Wales, all Glamorgan sites.[8] One can understand a castle such as Caerphilly attracting his attention, but it is surprising to find descriptions of the lesser-known Ogmore and Newcastle in Bridgend. The latter two are of interest because they are relatively minor castles of the twelfth and thirteenth centuries which underwent little or no alteration in later periods. It is possible that Clark came across various castles at a time when he was involved in some railway project or other professional duties, but at the time of his first publications on castles he was a surgeon at Clifton, Bristol. Clark's first two articles on castles appeared in the *Gentleman's Magazine* for 1835, being numbers I and II of a series on the castles of 'Gwent and Dyfed'. It is not known whether further studies in the series were intended, but certainly nothing further appeared other than these descriptions of Ogmore (figures 17–19) and Newcastle (figures 19–20). Clark was aware of the association of Ogmore with the de Londres family, that the family also became lords of Kidwelly,

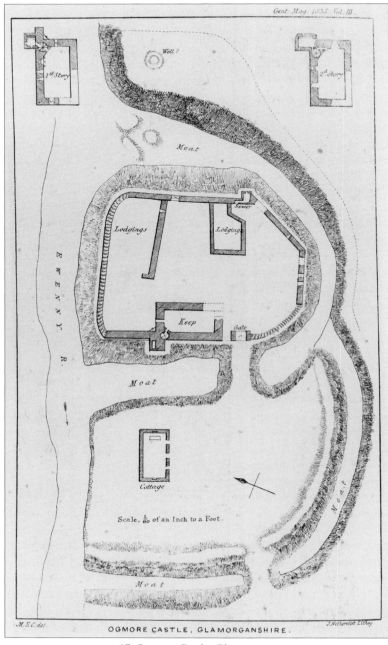

17 Ogmore Castle, Glamorgan.
Published in the *Gentleman's Magazine*, 1835.

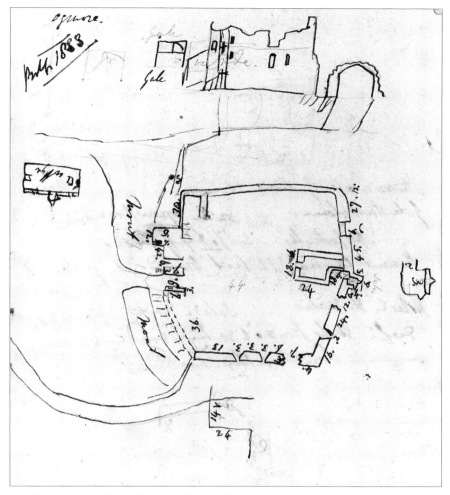

18 Plan and elevation of Ogmore Castle, Glamorgan, from one of G. T. Clark's notebooks (NLW MS 5197C). *National Library of Wales.*

and that Ogmore and Kidwelly later passed to the Duchy of Lancaster. The
entrance and the keep are described with some accuracy; he provided a
detailed description of the Norman main tower in spite of its interior being
choked with vegetation and occupied by a small hovel. Clark notes the series
of putlog holes, correctly stating that they supported the original scaffold-
ing. His date for the keep was Norman, although he thought that the latrine
turret that abutted it was also twelfth century when it is actually an addition
of the early thirteenth century. Little is said of the other buildings of the

89

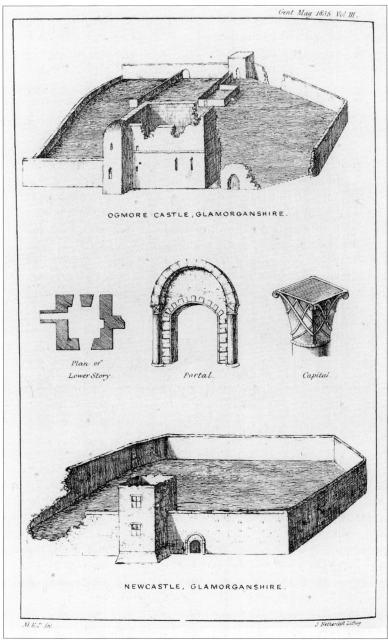

19 Bird's-eye views of Ogmore Castle and Newcastle, Bridgend.
Published in the *Gentleman's Magazine*, 1835.

inner ward other than that they were barely discernible and were probably lodgings. They appear in the bird's-eye view of Ogmore that accompanies the Newcastle article; the office range on the south side of the inner ward must have been buried totally in the 1830s, as Clark makes no mention of it.

The rectangular building in Ogmore's outer ward, known as the Court House and probably of late medieval date, is also described by Clark, who considers it Tudor. The Royal Commission on Ancient and Historical Monuments in Wales (RCAHMW) survey of Ogmore states that the identification of this building with the recorded court house 'is probable',[9] but Clark tells us that he was informed that here 'the court for the hundred is still held'. He also noted the existence of a fireplace at the west end; there is now no evidence for one at all, as the RCAHMW survey emphasizes.

In Clark's manuscript notes on Newcastle the remains of a rectangular or square keep are shown (figure 20), although in the bird's-eye view of the castle which accompanies his article in the *Gentleman's Magazine* (figure 19) there is no indication that a tower once stood within the curtain wall. It is this lost keep that confirms that the RCAHMW investigators were unaware of this article as they, quite naturally, use Clark's depiction of the keep in his field notebook as evidence that the remains were visible in 1834.[10] However, if we read Clark's account we learn that

> The *Keep*, which was in the middle of the enceinte, has now completely disappeared, no traces of it whatever remaining; its situation was, however, politely pointed out to us by the Rev. Incumbent, whose advanced age permitted his remembering the existence of portion of it. It is said to have been square.[11]

In the same year that his Ogmore and Newcastle articles appeared (1835) Clark published a four-part account of Caerphilly in a journal which he himself edited, the *West of England Journal*. It may be thought somewhat strange that Caerphilly should appear in a periodical with a seemingly west-of-England bias, but in fact its content is quite wide-ranging, with papers on the polders of Flanders, alluvial deposits in the Taff Valley, and remarks on the history of inventions, these possibly also being written by Clark. His study of this late thirteenth-century de Clare castle appeared four times in his lifetime. Part of his 1835 paper was used for the 1850 article in *Archae-ologia Cambrensis*, a piece of work with a number of small errors in it which might have been corrected if Clark had not been abroad at that time. Two years later, Clark's papers on Caerphilly, Kidwelly and Castell Coch were reprinted in book form, unaltered from the original articles in *Archaeologia*

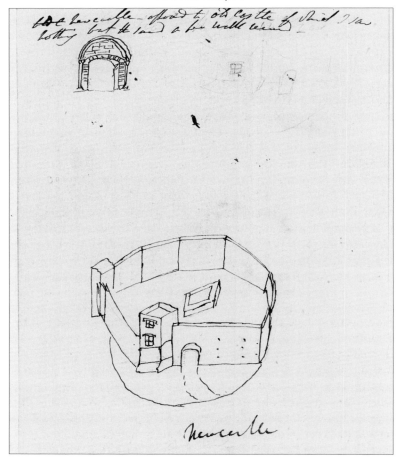

20 Clark's drawing of Newcastle, Bridgend, showing the position of the keep. From one of his notebooks (NLW MS 5197C). *National Library of Wales.*

Cambrensis; a note in the volume states that as Clark was still absent there had been no revisions. The Kidwelly paper was enhanced considerably with illustrations by H. Smyth and J. H. Le Keux[12] (see below and also figure 21), and these also appeared in *MMA*. Finally, an abridged version of Caerphilly appeared in *MMA*.

A paper which was not reprinted in *MMA* was a general essay on military architecture which was published in the first volume of the Royal Archaeological Institute's journal in 1845.[13] As Jonathan Coad has written, 'Many of his statements in that paper still remain valid, a tribute to Clark's scholarship and perseverance at a time when the railways had hardly begun

92

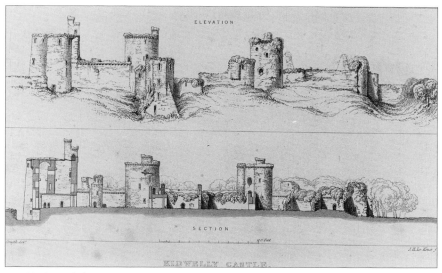

21 One of the Smyth/Le Keux illustrations for Clark's paper on Kidwelly Castle. Published in *Archaeologia Cambrensis*, 1852.

to revolutionise travel and, indirectly, archaeological fieldwork'.[14] The RAI paper presumably did not appear in *MMA* because the content was largely superseded by the general articles that he wrote at a later date. The form and content of the article are also very similar to the anonymous paper that is thought to have been written by Clark in the issue of the *West of England Journal of Science and Literature* for January 1836. This article gives us some idea of how serious Clark was as a young man in his early twenties in the pursuit of castle studies, for it is clear that he was familiar with the castle of Dinas in Breconshire, a stronghold situated on a hill that makes it one of the highest castles in either England or Wales. Clark had obviously visited the site, as he refers to the blocked cistern or well at Dinas, comparing it to the one still clearly to be seen at Morlais in Glamorgan, and an undated plan appears in his notebooks in the National Library of Wales.

In the 1835 paper on Caerphilly, Clark, in a footnote on p. 135, stated that 'Hitherto but little attention has been paid to ancient military architecture, the descriptions extant of castles and such buildings being deficient in critical information. It is hoped that many of the terms above introduced will be found useful in future descriptions.' We are thus at an important stage in the development of castle studies as an academic discipline. This article on Caerphilly is one of the earliest and most creditable studies of any major castle in the British Isles, all the more important because it describes the castle before the later nineteenth- and twentieth-century reconstructions.

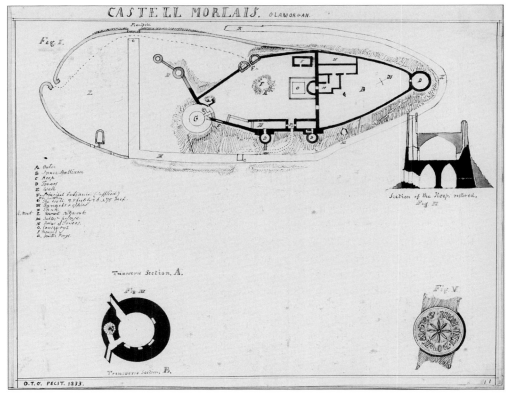

22 Clark's 1833 plan of Morlais Castle, Glamorgan. *National Museum of Wales.*

   A further example of a fine piece of writing, produced at the beginning of what turned out to be a constant flow of castle publications, is the paper on Kidwelly referred to above. It is well constructed, with twelve pages of description, prefaced by an account of the castle's setting, followed by eight pages of history. It is also one of the more profusely illustrated articles by Clark, for most of his papers, even the longer ones, usually only have one or two figures or plates, and for Chepstow (see below) only the one illustration (the plan) was provided, and that not by the author. There are six Smyth/Le Keux plates accompanying the Kidwelly text, and as Clark was abroad at the time of publication one wonders whether the officers of the Cambrian Archae-ological Association took it upon themselves to commission the illustrations; in the same issue of *Arch. Camb.* there are further Le Keux plates, in E. A. Freeman's account of the architectural antiquities of south Pembrokeshire. Neither author appears to refer in his text to the Le Keux illustrations.

One of the Kidwelly illustrations includes a general survey of the medieval town and castle, together with plans of the upper levels of both the castle's chapel and the great gate, so that Kidwelly is planned in more detail than were many other castles in the nineteenth century. The plates were certainly a boon to the present writer in the preparation of the current Cadw guidebook to the site.

Further evidence of Clark's early fieldwork in south Wales is contained in the third volume of the Traherne albums of 'illustrations of Glamorgan-shire' in the Department of Art, National Museum & Gallery, Cardiff. Included in this album is an original plan of Morlais Castle, drawn in ink, initialled and dated 'G. T. C. FECIT 1833' (figure 22). It appears to have been drawn for publication, but the present writer is unaware of a published version. Clark prepared a more accurate plan to accompany his 1859 article on Morlais in *Arch. Camb.*, a notable difference being that the spur wall on the 1833 plan to the west of the 'keep', at the southern end of the castle, is shown more accurately on the later plan as the site of the main curtain wall. It would seem from the 1859 article by Clark that his plan of 1833 was drawn in the same year as Lady Charlotte Guest's excavations at the castle; it is possible that he was there when the work was undertaken. Also in the Morlais paper (p. 101), Clark refers to the metal seal found near the castle, and this is depicted as 'Fig. V' on the 1833 plan.

Clark's later castle studies

Up until the later 1860s the majority of the castles studied by Clark were in Wales, but from 1866 he began a whole series of articles on castles in England and elsewhere for the *Builder*, a series which continued to 1883, the year before *MMA* was published. During this time, however, he continued to contribute numerous papers to *Archaeologia Cambrensis* and the *Archaeological Journal*; nor should we forget that a number of other studies appeared after *MMA* was published. A brief survey of his treatment of five castles in this period, both large and small, is given below.

Corfe Castle, Dorset
The core of this great castle, as with Chepstow, dates from the late eleventh century through to the late thirteenth century. The Royal Archaeological Institute visited Corfe in the summer of 1865, and the resultant publication by Clark serves as a reminder that he was not alone in the pursuit of learned studies of medieval military architecture. If one reads his description of Corfe in *MMA* and compares it with the paper in the *Archaeological*

Journal, the observant will note that the sentence 'visited by the Institute in August last' has been removed, understandably. One needs to refer to the journal itself to realize that Clark's account of the castle is really the second of a two-part feature on Corfe, with Thomas Bond contributing the other paper.[15] Although Clark's article is referred to as 'Description', there is much that is useful in Bond concerning the domestic arrangements of the castle, as well as an analysis of some of the building accounts, although of course this work has been superseded by more modern treatments of the architecture. It was Bond who also contributed an enlarged account of Corfe in the third edition of J. Hutchins's *History and Antiquities of Dorset* (1861–70). It is worth noting that an examination of the proceedings of the RAI's summer meeting based at Dorchester reveals that it was not Clark who took the members around the castle, as one might have thought, but J. H. Parker, the architectural historian and publisher.

The article suffers from the lack of a plan, which would have been a major undertaking anyway, although Bond includes a copy of Ralph Treswell's fine plan of 1586. Presumably Clark, writing from Dowlais, was basing his description on notes made during his visit, but he does make frequent mention of Bond's interpretations and dating evidence. His description is adequate for the time, and he avoids close dating of the fabric except where the building accounts assist in the matter. He refers to the great tower or keep as Norman, but Bond went further, and ascribed it to the reign of William I, although Parker in his tour of the castle begged to differ, and dated it to the reign of Henry I, a date that many would accept today. In fact, Clark's account of Corfe was surpassed in his own lifetime, for Bond published a book in 1883 which covered both the history and architecture of the castle in more detail than had hitherto been undertaken.[16]

Ludlow Castle, Shropshire
Ludlow is one of the finest castles in Britain, with a long history of occupation, through to the late seventeenth century as the headquarters of the Council in the Marches of Wales. Clark's paper of 1877 on Ludlow appeared in *Archaeologia Cambrensis*. The purpose of the article was to augment what others had already written, for in Clark's opinion the military aspect of the castle needed to be covered in more detail. For its day, and allowing for the then inaccessibility of parts of the castle, the treatment of the remains is competent, but was to be entirely surpassed by W. H. St John Hope's paper of 1908,[17] which still remains the most thorough survey of the whole castle, well illustrated with photographs and plans. It is worth noting that both authors mention features of the castle which are no longer to be seen.[18]

It is the general plan in Clark's article that does not do the description justice; it is somewhat crude, perhaps based on an earlier plan, although the two other illustrations, plans of the ground and first floors of the keep, are more professional. The Ludlow plan is in marked contrast to that of Coity which accompanies Clark's paper at the beginning of the same issue of the journal with which we are concerned; this is more professional, and the detail compares very favourably with the recent plan in the RCAHMW's volume on the early castles of Glamorgan.[19] It is not always clear whether the drawings that accompany Clark's papers are his work or another's, but the author is known to mention when a plan is the work of someone else: for example, a Mr Turnbull in connection with the plan of Caerphilly that appeared in 1835, this possibly being George Turnbull, Lord Bute's resident engineer on the construction of Cardiff docks.

Hopton Castle, Shropshire

This southern Shropshire castle was included in an article on Clun in 1877.[20] Although the account is a brief history and description, it has been included here as it shows what turned out to be Clark at his best. The rectangular tower of Hopton Castle has often been regarded as a Norman keep,[21] and to some extent this is understandable. In 1989 Peter Curnow published a masterly survey of the castle, describing it as a tower-house of the late thirteenth century.[22] If we examine the final paragraph of Clark's paper we read: 'Altogether this is a very peculiar building, much more like a Scottish than an English castle. It is all of one date, probably the work of Walter de Hopton, who died in 1304–5 . . .' If we accept Curnow's analysis, which we surely must, then Clark deserves a great deal of credit for his paper. The same applies to Clun, for Curnow mentions that the main residential block on the edge of the motte at this castle is the likely progenitor for Hopton. Although it also has been referred to as the keep of the castle, and it is in a fine defensive position, both Clark and Curnow suggest an early thirteenth-century date for this tower, the work of the first William Fitzalan of Clun. It is possible, however, that it is a late thirteenth-century building.[23]

Whittington Castle, Shropshire

We tend to forget today when studying castles what the condition of many of these monuments was like in the last and early part of this century. Clark could say little about the upper levels of Hopton due to the density of the brambles, and this is why one must treat some of the details on the plans in his articles with caution. To be fair, Clark often states in the text where vegetation got the better of him. Whittington in northern Shropshire is a case in point.[24] It now stands free of Mother Nature, and excavations in the early 1970s (largely unpublished) revealed further features on the motte summit, such as the remains of the keep. However, Clark must be right in his ascribing the revetment of the motte with its gatehouse to the reign of Henry III (1216–72), and he was also observant enough to recognize that the surrounding 'loose earth and thick vegetation' seemingly hid a number of mural towers that formed part of the thirteenth-century revetment. Allowing for the later discoveries, Clark's description of this castle still remains one of the most authoritative.

Chepstow Castle, Monmouthshire

More than once someone has remarked to the present writer that it is surprising that Clark never described one of the greatest of European castles, Chepstow, the evidence for this being that there is no entry for this castle in *MMA*. He did in fact publish a paper on Chepstow which must have been excluded from *MMA* because the article was not issued until it was too late to incorporate it.[25] The earliest part of the castle dates to the tenure of William fitz Osbern, Earl of Hereford (1067–71), with major additions made by the Marshal family in the first half of the thirteenth century, and by Roger Bigod, Earl of Norfolk, in the later thirteenth century.

The paper on Chepstow is accompanied by one of the best plans to be found in a Clark article, the work of A. S. Ellis and W. Frame in August 1865, although no attempt is made on the plan to show the various phases of architectural development. It is not known why Clark left it so late in his life to publish an account of the castle, for he was certainly familiar with it as early as the 1830s, as can be ascertained from a number of his papers. At least two sets of notes with drawings on the castle are to be found in the Clark papers, stemming from visits made in 1868 and 1875,[26] the earlier visit concentrating on the great tower, the one in 1875 paying particular attention to the barbican and Marten's Tower.

The description of Chepstow is not as detailed as one might expect; for example, a notable feature of the barbican is the framing of the wall-walk by both a parapet and a parados. Clark is wrong over the matter of the upper flooring of William fitz Osbern's great tower (1067/71), believing that it never existed, there simply being a gallery. He places this building in the twelfth century as opposed to the eleventh century, but then he was not alone in this theory for several twentieth-century writers have followed suit.[27] He certainly noted the reuse of Roman materials, however.

One of the buildings at Chepstow that has given rise to some difference of opinion in its interpretation is part of the late thirteenth-century range in the lower ward. Below and to the east of the hall is a handsomely lit room, built open to the roof. In recent times this has been referred to as the lesser hall,[28] but the current guidebook describes it as the kitchen,[29] which is logical, given its position in relation to the pantry and stores and to the staircase leading up into the hall. Clark had no hesitation in describing this room as the kitchen, and so we have come full circle.

Conclusion

Clark was interested in castles throughout his life. His last academic publication on the subject appeared in 1890, this being an article in *Archaeologia Cambrensis*, a journal to which he had made so many important contributions. It was on Cardiff Castle and highlighted some of the discoveries recently made on the Roman fort. On 28 January 1898, a few days before his death, he wrote further on the recent work at the castle in the *South Wales Echo*[30] – a student of castles to the end.

Let me end with a quotation.

> There were flaws in this imposing figure. His energy outran even his very respectable abilities . . . Accurate writers have been known to complain of his summary historical notes; and his beliefs as to the origin of mottes were thoroughly mistaken . . . It might have been better if he had not attempted so much; but his work on castles, at least, is founded on so great a bulk of shrewd observation and lucid exposition that his position of authority can hardly be questioned, even at the present.

So wrote that great figure of twentieth-century castle studies, David Cathcart King, in his introduction to *Castellarium Anglicanum*.[31] It is an accurate assessment. Our views on Clark should not be clouded by the issue of mottes, for his work involved so much more than the study of earthwork castles. All those who are involved in the study of masonry castles of England and Wales today ignore at their peril what Clark wrote more than a century ago. This is especially so since features recorded by him in any particular castle may no longer be apparent, although one has to be careful with regard to discrepancies that sometimes appear between text and illustrations.[32]

Castle studies have progressed enormously since the last century and although Clark's word may be the first on the subject of a particular castle, more likely than not it has not proved the last. If we take the main English and Welsh entries in *MMA*, out of some eighty castles only a handful have not been covered by some form of publication during this half of the twentieth century, whether monographs, guidebooks or periodical articles.[33] Our knowledge of the development of several of the major castles in Britain has often had to change as detailed studies are produced by such bodies as English Heritage and the various Royal Commissions on Ancient Monuments; all this is a continuation of what Clark began in the midnineteenth century. There can be no doubt that George Thomas Clark must be regarded as the founding father of castle studies. Michael Thompson has pointed out that the framework for the modern study of this subject was laid by people like Ella Armitage, John Horace Round, William St John Hope and Alexander Hamilton Thompson.[34] However, the foundation for that framework was laid by Clark and the scholars who followed him, and we today owe him a great debt.

Acknowledgements

I am indebted to Brian James for providing me with a copy of his bibliography of Clark's publications, without which the writing of this contribution would have been much harder, and for providing other information which has been incorporated into the text. My thanks also to Dr Derek Renn and my wife, Chris, for reading and commenting on a draft of this paper, and to the National Library of Wales for permission to reproduce material from the Clark Papers. I am indebted to the National Museum of Wales for allowing me to reproduce the 1833 plan of Morlais Castle, and I would also like to thank my colleague Juliet Carey of the Department of Art for showing me Mrs C. L. Traherne's albums, in the course of an examination of which I 'discovered' the Morlais drawing. As this volume includes Clark's bibliography, I have not always cited the full reference to a particular paper other than the date and the journal title.

Notes

[1] Brian James has informed me that there is evidence in the Clark papers that Clark had assembled *MMA* by 1881. In that year the publishers Macmillan rejected the book, unless the author was prepared to pay for its publication, as it was felt that there was too little interest in the subject to make the venture profitable. The delay in publication allowed Clark to include additional papers published in 1881 through to 1883, but for some reason he chose to omit Chepstow.

[2] E. Viollet-le-Duc, *An Essay on the Military Architecture of the Middle Ages* (Oxford and London, Parker, 1860). It is interesting to note, however, that at the end of this volume a number of architectural and archaeological works published by Parker were listed, including an item referred to as 'In the press'. This was a book by the Revd Charles Henry Hartshorne (d. 1865) entitled *An Historical and Architectural Account of English Castles*. In an obituary published in 1866 in the *Journal of the British Archaeological Association* (vol. 22, 322–5), the book is said to be 'now ready for the press'.

However, it seems that it was never published, for it does not appear in the BL collections and those of other major libraries, nor is it listed amongst Hartshorne's works with his entry in *DNB*. Sir James MacKenzie refers to various publications of Hartshorne in vol. I of his *The Castles of England: Their Story and Structure* (London, Heinemann, 1897), but no mention is made in the bibliography of the *Account of English Castles*.

3 Although J. H. Round's name does not actually appear as the author of the review, it is accepted that he wrote it. Published ten years after *MMA* came out, the review is in the *Quarterly Review*, 179 (1894), 27–57. It largely concentrates on Clark's interpretation of Norman castles as opposed to those of the thirteenth century and later.

4 'Berkhampstead Castle', *Builder*, 26 (1868), 529; *MMA*, i, 226.

5 'Description of Berkhampstead Castle', *Gent. Mag.*, NS 20 (1843), 36–8.

6 E. Armitage, *The Early Norman Castles of the British Isles* (London, John Murray, 1912), 19–20. Mrs Armitage's first assault on the *burh*/motte theory appeared in 1900, in the *Proceedings of the Society of Antiquaries of Scotland*. See also J. Counihan, 'Mrs Ella Armitage, John Horace Round, G. T. Clark and early Norman castles', in R. A. Brown (ed.), *Anglo-Norman Studies*, 8 (Woodbridge, Boydell Press, 1986), 73–87. For Clark's view of Saxon defences see his paper in the *Arch. J.*, 38 (1881), 21–41; it is also printed in *MMA*.

7 D. J. C. King, *Castellarium Anglicanum: An Index and Bibliography of the Castles in England, Wales and the Islands* (Millwood, NY, Kraus International, 1983), 2 vols.: pp. xi–xiv contain a brief but useful outline of the recording of English castles.

8 'Castles of Gwent and Dyfed. No. I. Castle of Ogmore', *Gent. Mag.*, NS 3 (1835), 243–6; 'Castles of Gwent and Dyfed. No. II. Newcastle', *Gent. Mag.*, NS 3 (1835), 489–90; 'Essay on Caerphilly Castle', *West of England Journal of Science and Literature*, 1 (1835–6), 62–71, 101–4, 135–43, 185–99. This latter journal was edited by Clark, and he may also have been the author of 'Observations on English castles', in its fifth number (217–28). In his notes on Newcastle, Bridgend, Clark wrote that 'we visited the place in 1834'.

9 Royal Commission on Ancient and Historical Monuments in Wales, *An Inventory of the Ancient Monuments in Glamorgan*, iii/1a, *Medieval Secular Monuments: The Early Castles from the Norman Conquest to 1217* (London, HMSO, 1991), 287. As will be shown when considering the paper on Newcastle, the RCAHMW seems to have been unaware that Clark had published accounts of both these castles, although use was made of Clark's notes on the two sites in NLW.

10 Ibid., 40, 336.

11 Clark on Newcastle, *Gent. Mag.*, NS 3 (1835), 489. The incumbent in question was the Revd Thomas Mansel Hancorne, vicar from 1798 until he died in 1838. I am indebted to the present incumbent of the parish, the Revd M. D. Witcombe, for this information.

12 The Library of the National Museum of Wales has recently acquired a copy of Clark's *A Description and History of the Castles of Kidwelly and Caerphilly, and of Castell Coch* (London, Pickering; Tenby, Mason, 1852), with annotations and corrections by William Douglas Simpson (1896–1968), the great Scottish castellologist.

13 'Military architecture', *Arch. J.*, 1 (1845), 93–107. This volume also contained an account by Charles Hartshorne (see n. 2) of Rockingham Castle, Northamptonshire.

14 J. Coad, 'Medieval fortifications and post-medieval artillery defences: Developments in post-war research and future trends', in B. Vyner (ed.), *Building on the Past: Papers Celebrating 150 Years of the Royal Archaeological Institute* (London, RAI, 1994), 215.

15 It is possible that the visit of the RAI to Dorset initiated Clark's first visit to Corfe as his notes are dated August 1865. See NLW MS 5197C.

16 T. Bond, *History and Description of Corfe Castle in the Isle of Purbeck, Dorset* (London, Stanford, 1883).

[17] 'The castle of Ludlow', *Archaeologia*, 61 (1908–9), 257–328.

[18] D. Renn, ' "Chastel de Dynan": The first phases of Ludlow', in J. R. Kenyon and R. Avent (eds.), *Castles in Wales and the Marches* (Cardiff, University of Wales Press, 1987), 63.

[19] RCAHMW, *Inventory*, iii/1a, 224.

[20] 'The castle and barony of Clun: Hopton Castle', *Builder*, 35 (1877), 1047–50.

[21] N. Pevsner, *Shropshire (The Buildings of England)* (Harmondsworth, Penguin, 1958), 153. Pevsner does mention, however, that the windows are fourteenth century.

[22] P. E. Curnow, 'The tower house of Hopton Castle and its affinities', in C. Harper-Bill, C. J. Holdsworth and J. L. Nelson (eds.), *Studies in Medieval History Presented to R. Allen Brown* (Woodbridge, Boydell Press, 1989), 81–102.

[23] [R. Morriss], *Clun Castle, Shropshire: An Interim Report* (Hereford Archaeology Series 176) (Hereford, City of Hereford Archaeology Unit, 1993).

[24] 'Oswestry and Whittington', *Arch. Camb.*, 4th ser. 9 (1878), 179–94.

[25] The article appeared in vol. 6 of the *Transactions of the Bristol and Gloucestershire Archaeological Society* which was issued for 1881–2.

[26] NLW MS 5197C and MS 5198E.

[27] See J. C. Perks, 'The architectural history of Chepstow Castle during the middle ages', *Transactions of the Bristol and Gloucestershire Archaeological Society*, 67 (1946–8), 307–46. On p. 326 Perks details those who have championed the various dating theories, he himself firmly coming down in favour of the earlier date.

[28] J. C. Perks, *Chepstow Castle, Monmouthshire*, 2nd edn. (London, HMSO, 1967). It is worth noting, however, that Perks in his article cited above and in the 1st edition of his Chepstow guidebook (London, 1955) described this building as the kitchen.

[29] J. K. Knight, *Chepstow Castle and Port Wall*, rev. edn. (Cardiff, Cadw: Welsh Historic Monuments, 1991).

[30] RCAHMW, *Inventory*, iii/1a, 173, citing *South Wales Echo*, 29 January 1898.

[31] King, *Castellarium*, p. xi.

[32] For example, Clark's measurements of Dolforwyn Castle in Montgomeryshire are given as yards instead of feet; see L. A. S. Butler, 'Dolforwyn Castle, Montgomery, Powys: First report', *Arch. Camb.*, 138 (1989), 83, n. 10. Derek Renn has informed me (pers. comm.) that in the article on St Leonard's Tower, West Malling in Kent, that appeared in the *Builder* for 27 November 1880, the plans (p. 641), which do not appear in *MMA*, are inconsistent with each other and with Clark's description.

[33] Publications written since 1945 are listed in the first three volumes of the present writer's *Castles, Town Defences, and Artillery Fortifications in Britain and Ireland: A Bibliography* (London, Council for British Archaeology, 1978–90). With the fourth volume under compilation, more recent publications are detailed each year in the *Castle Studies Group Newsletter*, the eleventh round-up (for 1997–8) appearing for the first time as a separate thirty-one page supplement to the newsletter.

[34] M. W. Thompson, 'The military interpretation of castles', *Arch. J.*, 151 (1994), 442.

I Talygarn: drawing-room door, by Cortelazzo. *David Williams*

II   Talygarn: wooden panels, by Biraghi.
A. M. Banbury

III   Talygarn: wooden panels, by Biraghi.
A. M. Banbury

IV   Talygarn: drawing-room overmantel, by Cortelazzo.   *David Williams*

V   Talygarn: ceiling in the gallery.   *David Williams*

VI   Talygarn: drawing-room ceiling, the 'Veronese'.   *David Williams*

VII   Talygarn: ceiling in the gallery.   *David Williams*

VIII   Talygarn: heads of Clark and Layard, carved by Biraghi.   *A. M. Banbury*

IX   Talygarn: the Clark and Lewis arms set within the Clark
family cipher.   *A. M. Banbury*

X   44 Berkeley Square: watercolour by Adrian Daintrey of the façade.
By courtesy of Mark Birley

XI   44 Berkeley Square: watercolour by Adrian Daintrey of the staircase.
By courtesy of Mark Birley

XII Talygarn Church: the Torcello mosaic as it appeared in 1986 before its removal from the wall. *Peter Leech*

CHAPTER 6

Clark's Cartae

BRIAN LL. JAMES

Geographic Thomas Clark gave his great printed collection of historical documents relating to Glamorgan the grandiloquent title: *Cartae et alia Munimenta quae ad Dominium de Glamorgan Pertinent* (Charters and other documents which relate to the lordship of Glamorgan). The four volumes, printed between 1885 and 1893, contained nearly 2,300 pages; it was one of the most munificent publishing phenomena in late nineteenth-century Wales. (The word 'publication' had best be avoided, since the work was printed for private circulation at the expense of the compiler, and was never 'published' in the strict sense.) Preceding the appearance of the first volume in 1885 there was a long gestation, and the story was not complete until 1910, the year in which Godfrey Lewis Clark, George Thomas's son, issued the second, revised and enlarged edition, in six volumes, having the slightly variant title – *Cartae et alia Munimenta quae ad Dominium de Glamorgancia Pertinent*.

By the 1830s, when Clark first began contributing to the periodical press, the editing and printing of historical texts and records of various kinds already had a long established tradition, going back at least to Dugdale's *Monasticon Anglicanum* in the mid-seventeenth century.[1] In the 1830s developments both facilitated and reflected a growing interest in historical documents, as shown for instance by the rapidly increasing use made of the reading rooms of the British Museum, where the Harleian and Cottonian collections of manuscripts and charters had found their permanent home.[2] The texts and calendars published since 1802 by the Record Commissioners had already done something to make known the incomparable riches of the national archives. But until 1838, when the Public Record Office was established, initiating the gradual process of centralizing these archives under one roof and under competent management, consultation of original public records was fraught with difficulty and was somewhat infrequently attempted.[3] In the 1830s also the Surtees Society, the English Historical Society, the Welsh Manuscripts Society and the Camden Society were founded with the express purpose of printing significant texts which had hitherto languished in manuscript, paying particular attention to medieval chronicles, historical narratives and monastic cartularies. Thus that decade saw a very major advance in the preserving, publishing and study of historical documents. The 1840s saw a further extension of these activities as new antiquarian societies – as yet there was no clear separation of the spheres of interest of antiquarians, archaeologists and historians[4] – were set up both in London and in the provinces, most of them welcoming transcripts of individual documents or even collections of documents, as well as historical texts, for inclusion in their transactions. Among these new societies were two with which G. T. Clark was long associated, namely the (Royal) Archaeological Institute (which published the *Archaeological Journal*), and the Cambrian Archaeological Association (whose journal was *Archaeologia Cambrensis*).

In Glamorgan itself a number of antiquaries were beginning to interest themselves in the editing of manuscripts and records. Of these the two most productive and significant were the Revd John Montgomery Traherne of Coedriglan (1788–1860) and George Grant Francis of Swansea (1814–82). The former printed four Margam Abbey charters, the property of his brother-in-law, C. R. M. Talbot, and the text of the *Stradling Correspondence* (1840), amongst other things, while the latter was amassing his highly important collection of original documents which were to form one of the major elements in the *Cartae*. In 1845 Grant Francis printed a limited edition of *Original Charters and Materials for a History of Neath and its Abbey*, gathered from many sources, including the British Museum, various branches of the nascent Public Record Office, the Corporation of Neath and private collections, notably his own. This was the most ambitious venture into record printing before Clark appeared on the local scene.[5]

Not long after moving from Surrey to Dowlais in 1856, Clark began to publish occasional articles incorporating miscellaneous records, pedigrees, monumental inscriptions and the like in the columns of a weekly newspaper, the *Cardiff and Merthyr Guardian*. By 1864 he was well advanced on a more systematic exploration of the primary sources for the history of Glamorgan in the British Museum and the Public Record Office, and he was borrowing original charters from his acquaintances in the county, most notably George Grant Francis. Over ten years, from 1864 to 1873, he published a series of charters and surveys in *Archaeologia Cambrensis* and the *Archaeological Journal*, and as early as 16 July 1864 he was seeking Grant Francis's permission 'to print several of your charters with those of Aberavan & several others of early date, in a private volume, which I think will be a very useful contribution to the future County History'.[6] He returned to this idea in other letters to Grant Francis in 1864 and 1865 but, although he had many of the charters printed in Cardiff by the *Guardian* in the form of proofs ('slips' he called them[7]), the great project for a substantial volume was allowed to hang fire while Clark focused his energies upon castle studies in the late 1860s and through the 1870s.

It was essential to Clark's success in the rarified world of medieval charters that he made friends with, first, William Floyd, and then with Walter de Gray Birch. They guided him to relevant documents in the London repositories, and their palaeographical expertise was invaluable. William Floyd (1809–99) was a Londoner who had spent some years around 1850 at Cardiff employed in the Bute Docks office; between 1870 and 1882 he sometimes gave the London Institution in Finsbury Circus as his address, but he does not appear to have held any official position there. He was, or at least became in later life, a man of substantial private means, and he lived for the last ten years or so of his life at 39 Russell Square, close to the British Museum. Although little is known about Floyd, it is clear that for the greater part of his long life he had made extensive notes from medieval documents, especially those of the Norman period, relating to all parts of England and Wales. These notes now make a very large collection at the National Library of Wales[8] and they demonstrate that he had given particular attention to medieval Glamorgan.[9] The high opinion he entertained of the *Antiquities of Shropshire*, by the Revd Robert William Eyton, published in twelve volumes 1854–60, suggests he might have aimed to do something of the same kind and on the same scale for Glamorgan. Eyton's work was arranged by hundred and parish; it was strictly document-based, and it concentrated upon the two centuries and a half following the Norman Conquest.[10] Among the Floyd MSS are two volumes of notes collected towards a history of Glamorgan and arranged by hundred and parish.[11] Nothing like this ever appeared in print, though there do exist proofs of the first thirty-two pages of 'An account of the principal Norman families of the lordship of Glamorgan'.[12] The only thing that Floyd is known to have published is a paper on the 'Conquest of south Wales', read at the meeting of the Royal Archaeological Institute in Cardiff in the summer of 1871.[13] Clark paid him generous tribute in *The Land of Morgan* (1883) and *Cartae*, vol. iv (1893), and in a letter he told Floyd that

> no man has brought anything approaching to your industry and accuracy to the study of our county records – and no man is, or ever has been, or I fear is ever likely to be so well acquainted with them – especially as they exist in the Record Office & the B. Museum.[14]

It was quite possibly Floyd who pointed out to Clark the Margam Abbey charters in the Harleian Collection at the British Museum. These had been given by the first Lord Mansel (1667–1723) to his friend and political ally, Robert Harley, Earl of Oxford.[15] Surprised and disappointed that Henry Richards Luard had not even mentioned these valuable charters in his edition of the Annals of Margam in the Rolls Series,[16] Clark had them copied – presumably by a record agent[17] – collected other documents relating to the Abbey from printed sources and published an extensively annotated 'Contribution towards a cartulary of Margam'.[18] This was a major advance in the historiography of Margam, though it is not clear why Clark selected only 46 of the 176 Harleian charters for inclusion; they were almost all eventually put into the *Cartae*.[19]

Ten of the Harleian charters were also included in an appendix to his article on 'The lords of Avan of the blood of Jestyn',[20] with five from George Grant Francis's collection and three belonging to Henry Hussey Vivian, later the first Lord Swansea. The last were especially interesting because they were borough charters granted by Welsh lords.[21]

In the early 1870s Clark printed a number of other documents, such as the borough charters of Kenfig and Llantrisant, several documents belonging to Robert Oliver Jones of Fonmon Castle and J. W. Nicholl-Carne of St Donats Castle, and a valuable extent of Glamorgan in 1262, brought to his notice by his friend, Joseph Burtt (1818–76), an assistant keeper at the Public Record Office and editor of the *Archaeological Journal*.

If Floyd projected a work on medieval Glamorgan inspired by the example of R. W. Eyton, then Clark at least partially realized it. His *Land of Morgan* was a critical, document-based history of the lordship of Glamorgan from the Norman Conquest down to the death of Gilbert de Clare in 1314. Of course, by itself, it was not on the same scale as Eyton's dozen volumes on Shropshire, but add to it the four volumes of documents – the *Cartae* – then the scale begins to match, allowing for the greater size of Shropshire and its richer documentation.[22] And although the *Cartae* contains documents from the early Middle Ages to the eighteenth century, it is important to appreciate that there is a decided bias in favour of the twelfth, thirteenth and fourteenth centuries. In fact, more than 70 per cent of the charters printed in the first edition are from those three centuries and one might hazard that, for that period, Clark succeeded in gathering a large proportion of the surviving documents. For the subsequent centuries the proportion of charters included in the *Cartae* must fall steeply, and it is in this context that the comments of a reviewer in 1893–4 need to be reappraised. Edward Owen (1853–1943) noted several classes of documents in the Public Record Office that Clark had not included in the *Cartae*, and

TABLE. Dates of Charters in the First Edition of the *Cartae* (1885–93)

	vol. i	vol. ii	vol. iii	vol. iv	Total
pre 1100			32		32
12th cent.	61		116	18	195
13th cent.	154		406	29	589
14th cent.	62	37		159	258
15th cent.		92		78	170
16th cent.		75		97	172
17th cent.		27		10	37
18th cent.		2			2
	277	233	554	391	1455

commented that these would 'go far to vitalise and vivify many of the dry and uninteresting leases, conveyances, and quit-claims, that are contained in Mr Clark's . . . volumes'.[23] He had in mind manorial surveys (such as those preserved among the Duchy of Lancaster's records) and the voluminous records of the Court of Wards and Liveries; he might have mentioned many other classes, and there is no denying that the number of documents from the Public Record Office included in the *Cartae* is small.[24] The paucity of this harvest reflects the fact that Glamorgan was not under royal control during the Middle Ages, except during minorities of the marcher lords. Furthermore, there were important private archives to which Clark had not had access – those of the Marquess of Bute and Lord Windsor, for instance.[25] But the overwhelming bulk of the Glamorgan material contained in these PRO classes and private collections – whether more lively than the title-deeds printed in the *Cartae* is open to question – would have been later than the fourteenth century. There is no reason to think that Clark had ever set himself the goal of comprehensiveness, except possibly for the early centuries.

Having neglected Glamorgan charters for some ten or fifteen years, Clark turned back to them in the 1880s. It is tempting to think that R. W. Eyton's example again had an influence, for in 1881 appeared the first instalment of what he evidently planned should become a major, coherent collection of early documents relating to Staffordshire, entitled 'The Staffordshire Chartulary', published in a new record series to which G. T. Clark was a subscriber.[26] In the event Eyton died in that year, and the 'Chartulary' never developed as he intended, but that is not the point here; the first instalment may have spurred Clark to revive the plan that he had mentioned to Grant Francis in 1864.

The first volume of the *Cartae* was printed in 1885 on a private press that Clark had set up in the Guest Memorial Library at Dowlais.[27] It seems possible that the press had been bought specifically to print the *Cartae*, and the printing there of *Some Account of Sir Robert Mansel . . . and of Admiral Sir Thomas Button* in 1883 was perhaps intended as a relatively easy trial run. Little is known of this press and nothing else in Clark's bibliography can be identified as having been printed on it. Clark made use of many of his circle as proof-readers – R. O. Jones of Fonmon, William Floyd and Henry Dicey were among those pressed into service. Numerous (mostly minor) errors, however, remained, and perhaps it was the difficulty of accurate typesetting in Latin that persuaded Clark to abandon the private press and to have the later volumes printed by an experienced commercial printer in Cardiff, William Lewis of Duke Street. Volume i of the *Cartae* has a slight air of the experimental; volume ii established the definitive style of the whole series – a style that was retained for the second edition. In it each charter was given an English heading which summarized the content or type of document (in volume i there were brief Latin headings), and many charters were annotated, whereas in volume i there were very few notes.

Walter de Gray Birch (1842–1924) became Clark's main coadjutor with the *Cartae*. Clark first mentioned him in the preface to volume ii, printed in 1890, for having brought many of the British Museum charters to his attention, and for his help with correcting proofs. Appointed to the Department of Manuscripts of the British Museum in 1864, Birch continued there until 1902 and became one of the great authorities of his day on charters and seals. Although his principal published works were the *Cartularium Saxonicum* (1885–99) and the *Catalogue of Seals* (1893–1900), his contacts with Clark and with Miss Talbot of Margam brought him into close connection with Glamorgan. The fruits of that connection with the county were his *Descriptive Catalogue of the Penrice and Margam Abbey Manuscripts* (1893–1905), *A History of Margam Abbey* (1897), *A History of Neath Abbey* (1902) and *Memorials of the See and Cathedral of Llandaff* (1912). From 1902 to 1914 he was librarian and curator to the Marquess of Bute.

More problematical is his part in bringing out both the first and second editions of the *Cartae*. He appears to be acknowledged a little grudgingly in the prefaces, and yet research and reflection suggest that his role must have been important, even crucial.[28] Take, for example, a letter from Birch to G. T. Clark, dated 17 March 1893, as volume iv was nearing completion:

My dear Sir,

        I am sending you the Latin copy of the Subsidy Roll of co. Glam. which you wanted from the Record Office, and return your English translation of it. The whole of the county is not copied but only the part which corresponds with your paper . . .

    I am also sending you some copies and descriptions of the Hen.8. charters found among the later series of Penrice Charters. There are still a few more to go through. One of the enclosures is a correct copy of an important charter of John to Margam which should take the place of No LXIV in your series, which is apparently from an incorrect text.

> Believe me
> Yours very truly,
> W. de Gray Birch.[29]

This letter – and several others like it – demonstrates that Birch was at the very heart of the activity and bustle which produced the first edition of the *Cartae*.

It seems likely that it was Birch who was invited to survey the Penrice and Margam archive by Emily Charlotte Talbot (1840–1918), soon after she inherited the estate from her father in January 1890. C. R. M. Talbot had rarely allowed access, other than to members of his family; the Revd John David Davies (1831–1911), who had been permitted to 'peruse the splendid collection of ancient documents preserved at Penrice Castle' for *The History of West Gower* (1877–94), appears to have been uniquely favoured.[30] Thus the policy of the new owner represented a change of enormous significance to students of medieval Glamorgan, for – taken together with the documents that had passed into the Harleian Collection – virtually the whole archive in the possession of the Abbey at the dissolution, with the exception of account rolls and court rolls, had survived.[31] Added to these were the extensive muniments of the Gower lands of the Mansels and their predecessors, beginning in the thirteenth century. Birch was employed to catalogue the documents at Penrice (including those of the Mansels who acquired the Abbey's property in the 1540s), and the texts which Birch transcribed were passed on – with Miss Talbot's approval, of course – for inclusion in the third and fourth volumes of the *Cartae*. Clark says in his enthusiastic preface to volume iii 'that circumstances placed within my reach a very large collection of deeds relating chiefly to the Cistercian Abbey of Margam'. These made the third volume, which would have been printed anyway, into the largest of the set, and they made necessary a fourth volume. Nearly 600 charters and other documents from Penrice and Margam were printed in those two volumes, in addition to some 150

Margam Abbey charters from the British Museum. This is a precise measure of the dominance of this single provenance: it accounted for just over half the documents in the four-volume set.[32]

G. T. Clark died in 1898. By 1901 his son, Godfrey Lewis Clark, was actively engaged on a new edition of the *Cartae*. In the preface of 1910 he expressed his gratitude to Walter de Gray Birch 'for the invaluable assistance he has given in arranging these Charters'. It would seem that Birch did more than 'assist' and 'arrange'. Edward Owen, reviewing his *Neath Abbey* in 1902, understood that Dr Birch had undertaken a new edition of the *Cartae*; and H. J. Randall of Bridgend (1877–1964), the distinguished amateur historian, made a point of citing Birch as the editor of the 1910 edition.[33] It was G. L. Clark's name that appeared on the title-pages as editor, and correspondence survives to show that he did indeed co-ordinate the work on the edition.[34] Also, the whole work, in six generous volumes, was printed by William Lewis of Cardiff at G. L. Clark's expense.

What, exactly, was Birch's contribution to it? To assess this we must enumerate the improvements and additions in the new *Cartae*. The charters have been rearranged and renumbered in a single chronological sequence (apart from 117 in an appendix); the dates and captions have been amended, as necessary; additional notes have been appended to some of the charters; the texts have been corrected; a slight amount of duplication has been eliminated; about 220 charters have been included for the first time, and a consolidated index has been compiled. Preceding the texts of the charters is a short memoir of G. T. Clark, together with his essay on the history of Glamorgan prepared originally for the British Association's *Handbook* in 1891.

Of all the changes in the second edition of the *Cartae*, it is only the memoir of his father that is likely to have been the sole responsibility of G. L. Clark. Birch alone would have been capable of establishing a new chronological arrangement of the charters, many of which had been very erratically placed within the several sequences of the first edition, though even he found a large number of the Penrice and Margam charters undatable.[35]

Lengthy annotation in the second edition is in part carried across from the first (in which long notes occurred with increasing frequency in the later volumes) and is partly new. Birch supplied much information, but certainly some commentary was sent to G. L. Clark by John Stuart Corbett, solicitor to the Bute Estate. Corbett was one of the best of G. T. Clark's immediate successors in the study of the history of medieval Glamorgan.[36] Again, it is not impossible that some notes were written by G. L. Clark.

On the point of correction of the texts, it is clear that Birch took the responsibility. He was, after all, the great authority of his day on charters. Although the transcription of documents for the first edition had been very competently done[37] – by Floyd, by record agents, and by G. T. Clark and Birch themselves – the checking for the second edition seems to have been thorough, as far as the original documents were within Birch's reach. To facilitate the checking of Grant Francis's charters, which Clark himself had copied in the 1860s, the Royal Institution of South Wales agreed to deposit the whole collection temporarily in the British Museum.[38] The changes made to the texts by Birch were mostly quite minor, though some more significant amendments, to the spelling of proper names for example, do occur. The generally high standard of the *Cartae* has been widely accepted, and where later editions of particular charters have been published – by R. B. Patterson and David Crouch, among others[39] – the differences are slight, and chiefly arise from changing conventions of transcription.

The 220 (or so) additional charters in the new edition mostly owed their presence to Birch since three-quarters of them were Penrice and Margam MSS. There were more than a hundred new charters of the twelfth and thirteenth centuries, and more than fifty of the sixteenth century. A few documents were contributed by two men who were closely linked to Margam: Thomas Franklen,[40] the nephew of C. R. M. Talbot, and Robert William Llewellyn of Baglan, head of a family that had provided the chief agents of the Margam Estate for more than a century. The five documents the property of the Marquess of Bute were perhaps sent to G. L. Clark by J. S. Corbett, though Birch had been 'librarian and curator' to the Marquess since his retirement from the Museum, and he may have had access to the Bute muniments; of course, these five were an inconsiderable portion of what might have been contributed to the *Cartae* from that source.

The compiler of the index printed in volume vi of the second edition is not named. It may have been Birch himself, or someone working under his expert direction; certainly a competent, professional job was done. It was however less full than the individual indexes in each of the four volumes of the first edition, which were quite possibly by G. T. Clark himself. Those, too, were compiled by someone who had a good idea of how to overcome the problems of indexing medieval names, but he was less consistent than the 1910 indexer.

If it is not possible to attribute exactly to G. L. Clark and Walter de Gray Birch their respective parts in the production of the new *Cartae*, there is a very clear balance of probability that the intellectual force behind the edition was Birch's. There can be no doubt that he provided more than 'assistance', 'invaluable' though G. L. Clark judged it. It may be that Birch was being paid for his work on the *Cartae* and would on that account not have been entitled to more generous acknowledgement. It may never be possible to determine the compass of G. L. Clark's editorial role, and the extent to which he shared and continued his father's antiquarian interests also seems a matter for conjecture.

Clark's *Cartae* is one of those great works that underlie the historical study of medieval Glamorgan. Citations of the *Cartae* (and, indeed of Clark's other major works) are frequent, and a glance at the notes to chapters 1–7 of the *Glamorgan County History*, vol. iii (1971), will show how fundamental is the debt of historians to this pioneering collection of documents.[41] The printing of reliable texts of so many primary sources for the history of medieval Glamorgan entirely revolutionized the subject and provided the basis for an alternative view of the county's past to that which prevailed in the mid-nineteenth century.

The traditional narrative was still dominated by the story of the conquest of Glamorgan by Robert Fitzhamon and his twelve knights, and the sharing out among the conquerors of the manors of the Vale of Glamorgan. Clark described the story as 'an article of faith' in south Wales. It was 'a legendary tale, very neat and round, very circumstantial, but as deficient in evidence as though it had proceeded from the pen of Geoffrey himself'.[42] The story, and the account of the descendants of the twelve knights, had been related by Sir Edward Stradling and, in fuller form, by Rice Merrick in the sixteenth century, and it had been retold and amplified by Edward Williams (Iolo Morganwg) at the turn of the eighteenth century.[43] The veracity of the traditional story was elaborately defended in the 1870s by Dafydd Morganwg, Thomas Nicholas and John Roland Phillips, all of them being aware that its truth had 'come to be questioned by certain writers'.[44] It was still related in school textbooks[45] in the first decade of the twentieth century and its influence has persisted in oral tradition.[46]

Clark's critical approach to the sources of history was the sovereign antidote to these fantasies of old tradition and of more recent romanticism. Unfortunately, his work appealed to a limited readership, which delayed the spread of its influence. His *Land of Morgan*, his articles on particular parishes in the Vale and his descriptions of castles were austerely scholarly. He disdained the anecdotes and purple passages that the reading public so much enjoyed in the writings of earlier antiquarians and of Marie Trevelyan and Owen Rhoscomyl – to mention just two of slightly later date.[47] The charters themselves were presented in their original Latin, which Clark did not deign to translate since the educated people who were the recipients of the volumes of the *Cartae* had no need of a crib. In this respect Clark's work contrasted with the Revd J. D. Davies's *History of West Gower* in which the author provided English versions of the numerous Latin documents quoted.

A new kind of local history, distinguished by its critical use of documentary sources, did emerge in Glamorgan. Clark, Grant Francis, J. D. Davies and Birch were its pioneers; John Stuart Corbett (1845–1921) worthily carried on the work of G. T. Clark.[48] A generation of talented amateur historians born in the 1860s confirmed the new tradition: D. Rhys Phillips, D. R. Paterson, Clarence A. Seyler, Lewis D. Nicholl are representative. Their published work, which mostly appeared between the two wars, may not in every respect have worn well, but in their books and articles the critical principle was established that local history should be based upon the close study of primary sources. From then on the tradition was carried forward mainly by academically trained historians, whose citations of the *Cartae* have already been noted. Some words of L. D. Nicholl's can stand as a statement of that generation's regard for and indebtedness to G. T. Clark and the *Cartae*: 'I usually refer to him as I would refer to a great man, such as Shakespeare; not as "Mr" Shakespeare, not as "Mr" Clark, but as Clark.'[49]

Notes

[1] Sir William Dugdale, *Monasticon Anglicanum* (London, 1655–73). Clark used the edition of this prime collection of monastic charters published in the nineteenth century by John Caley and others, the edition often referred to as the *New Monasticon*.

[2] Edward Miller, *That Noble Cabinet* (London, André Deutsch, 1973), 146.

[3] John D. Cantwell, *The Public Record Office 1838–1958* (London, HMSO, 1991), ch. 1.

[4] On the general context of antiquarianism in this period, see Philippa Levine, *The Amateur and the Professional: Antiquarians, Historians and Archaeologists in Victorian England, 1838–1886* (Cambridge, Cambridge University Press, 1986).

[5] On Francis, see Sandra Thomas, *George Grant Francis of Swansea 1814–1882* (Swansea, West Glamorgan County Archive Service, 1993). He continued to edit documents long after 1845; ibid., 49–50.

[6] University of Wales Swansea Library, George Grant Francis Collection 24, General correspondence.

[7] These are almost certainly the 'proofs' preserved by R. O. Jones of Fonmon, now GRO D/D F V/13–70. The settings of type are different from the *Cartae*.

[8] NLW MS 3641–4252.

[9] See especially NLW MS 3739–40D.

[10] C. R. J. Currie and C. P. Lewis (eds.), *A Guide to English County Histories* (Stroud, Sutton Publishing, 1994), 341–2.

[11] NLW MS 3739–40D.

[12] NLW MS 3753C.

[13] *Arch. J.*, 28 (1871), 293–304. His paper on the Hawey and Stradling families was also read at this meeting, but was not printed in the *Journal*.

[14] NLW MS 3763C. Letter from G. T. Clark to Floyd, 18 May 1895.

[15] *The Diary of Humfrey Wanley 1715–1726*, ed. C. E. Wright and R. C. Wright (London, Bibliographical Society, 1966), vol. i, lix, 176.

[16] *Annales Monastici*, vol. i (London, 1864), pp. xiii–xv, 1–40.

[17] He made considerable use of the services of Clarence Hopper (1817–68). Submitting his 'Christmas account' in 1866, Hopper asked Clark if he would like to have a 'perfect *Calendar of Inquisitions Post Mortem* relative to the county continued from Hen.VII to Car.I.' NLW MS 5203E.

[18] *Arch. Camb.*, 3rd ser. 13/14 (1867), 311–34; (1868), 24–59, 182–96, 345–84.

[19] W. de Gray Birch, *A History of Margam Abbey* (London, 1897), 280; Edward Owen, *A Catalogue of the Manuscripts Relating to Wales in the British Museum*, part iii (London, 1908), 549–75.

[20] *Arch. Camb.*, 3rd ser. 13 (1867), 1–44.

[21] The earliest of the borough charters of Aberafan, granted by Lleision ap Morgan *c*.1307, is now in the WGRO.

[22] Of course, the arrangement by hundred and parish of Eyton's *Shropshire* – there was no general treatment of the county – was quite different from anything that Clark ever published. But among his MSS are seven volumes (NLW MS 5209–5215E) into which he collected notes and documents under names of manors rather than of parishes.

[23] *Arch. Camb.*, 5th ser. 10/11 (1893), 266–7; (1894), 73–4. These are the only reviews of the *Cartae* that have been discovered.

[24] Only 99, not counting documents that Clark reprinted from various texts and calendars published by the Record Commissioners and the Public Record Office.

[25] GRO has a copy of *Limbus Patrum* containing a holograph letter from Clark to the Hon. and Revd G. T. O. Bridgeman, dated 3 February 1886, stating that he had had no help from Lord Bute, Lord Windsor, Lord Tredegar or C. R. M. Talbot. I am grateful to Mrs M. P. Moore for information about this letter.

[26] *Collections for a History of Staffordshire*, ed. the Wm. Salt Archaeological Society, vol. ii, part i (1881), 178–276.

[27] *Western Mail*, 29 November 1883, p. 3. I owe this reference to Dr T. F. Holley.

[28] F. G. Cowley, 'Walter de Gray Birch, 1842–1924: a tribute', *Gower*, 47 (1996), 79.

[29] NLW MS 5218B.

[30] F. G. Cowley, 'Revd John David Davies', *Morgannwg*, 38 (1994), 34–5.

[31] Birch, *Margam Abbey*, 280.

[32] Ten Penrice and Margam charters had already been included in vols. i and ii. A further 160 were provided by Birch for the 2nd edn., making a grand total of about 914.

[33] *Arch. Camb.*, 6th ser. ii (1902), 295; H. J. Randall, *Bridgend: the Story of a Market Town* (Newport, R. H. Johns, 1955), p. xiii.

[34] NLW MS 5177E.

[35] Even today many can only be dated approximately, or within broad limits; cf. Matthew Griffiths, 'Native society on the Anglo-Norman frontier: The evidence of the Margam charters', *Welsh History Review*, 14 (1988–9), 179–216; also K. L. Maund, *Handlist of the Acts of Native Welsh Rulers 1132–1283* (Cardiff, University of Wales Press, 1996), 16–33. Birch has, however, introduced an error by his misdating of the accounts of John Giffard of Brimpsfield to 1281 instead of 1316; in the 1st edn. Clark had correctly assigned this important document to 9 Edward II rather than 9 Edward I.

[36] J. S. Corbett, *Glamorgan: Papers and Notes on the Lordship and its Members* (Cardiff, William Lewis, 1925), 12; letters in NLW MS 5177E.

[37] There are exceptions, as for example CCCVII (in the 1st edn.), MLXIX (in the 2nd edn.), an inquisition post mortem of 1395. Whoever had made the original copy had made numerous mistakes in the proper names and in the expansion of the contractions.

[38] NLW MS 5177E. Letter from C. H. Glascodine to G. L. Clark, 19 April 1901. A few of the Grant Francis MSS were apparently already missing, and several of those lent for

the new edition of the *Cartae* were never returned to Swansea. These are now in NLW Miscellaneous I, Wyndham D. Clark Deeds 1–3 and possibly 5. The bulk of the Grant Francis MSS are now in the Library of the University of Wales Swansea.

[39] R. B. Patterson, *Earldom of Gloucester Charters* (Oxford, Clarendon Press, 1973); David Crouch, *Llandaff Episcopal Acta 1140–1287* (Cardiff, South Wales Record Society, 1988).

[40] Sir Thomas Mansel Franklen (1840–1928), clerk of the Peace for Glamorgan.

[41] T. B. Pugh (ed.), *Glamorgan County History*, iii (Cardiff, University of Wales Press, 1971), 583–649. The *Cartae* is cited in 220 footnotes out of 1,642.

[42] *The Land of Morgan* (London, 1883), 18.

[43] Rice Merrick, *Morganiae Archaiographia* (Barry, South Wales Record Society, 1983), 15–27, 52–62, 150–64. Iolo Morganwg composed what is known as 'Brut Aberpergwm', in which the amplified story of Fitzhamon finds its chronological place, and printed it in *The Myvyrian Archaiology of Wales*, ii (London, 1801), 524–6. 'Brut Aberpergwm' was re-edited (with a translation) for the Cambrian Archaeological Association as *Brut y Tywysogion: The Gwentian Chronicle of Caradoc of Llancarvan* (London, 1863), the relevant pages 68–75.

[44] D. W. Jones (Dafydd Morganwg), *Hanes Morganwg* (Aberdar, 1874), 88–91; Thomas Nicholas, *The History and Antiquities of Glamorganshire* (London, 1874), 30–9; J. R. Phillips, *An Attempt at a Concise History of Glamorgan* (London, 1879), 28–32.

[45] Abraham Morris, *Glamorgan* (Newport, 1907), 257–63; C. J. Evans, *The Story of Glamorgan* (Cardiff, 1908), 286–9.

[46] Sir Cennydd Traherne (1910–95) said that he learned the story 'from my mother's knee, as have Glamorgan children since, I believe, the thirteenth century'; *Arch. Camb.*, 133 (1984), 2.

[47] Emma Mary Paslieu (Marie Trevelyan), a native of Llantwit Major, was the author of several popular works published in the 1890s that mixed history, legend and folk-tales. Owen Rhoscomyl (pseudonym of Robert Scourfield Mills, otherwise known as Arthur Owen Vaughan) published his best-known book, *Flamebearers of Welsh History*, in 1905.

[48] Sir John Ballinger, in J. S. Corbett, *Glamorgan*, 12.

[49] L. D. Nicholl, *The Normans in Glamorgan, Gower and Kidweli* (Cardiff, William Lewis, 1936), p. vii.

CHAPTER 7

Limbus Patrum

J. BARRY DAVIES

In 1886 George T. Clark published a volume of pedigrees with the impressive title *Limbus Patrum Morganiae et Glamorganiae. Being the Genealogies of the Older Families of the Lordships of Morgan and Glamorgan. Now, for the first time, collected, collated, and printed by George T. Clark, of Talygarn, F.A.S.* This closely printed volume of 620 pages has in the intervening years established itself as one of the indispensable reference works of Glamorgan which every historian of the county must seek to acquire for his or her library. No other county of Wales has had such comprehensive treatment lavished upon its gentry. Convention required that the eighteenth-century county historians should include pedigrees of the major families and this they invariably did in full measure, but rarely, if ever, did they trouble to extend the lines beyond the late seventeenth century where the herald scribes generally left off. And even more rarely did they include the pedigrees of the lesser gentry and yeomanry as Clark has done. The product of some thirty years of well-spent leisure time, *Limbus Patrum* deservedly stands amongst the major monuments to its author's remarkable industry.

Its first appearance provoked a strong reaction in one of Clark's antiquarian contemporaries. David Jones of Wallington, writing in the autumn of 1888, referred to the great work as 'that tantalising, bewildering and distracting book, . . . compiled mainly for the glorification of the Lewis's'. This comment was made in the context of noting that Richard Williams of the town of Llantrisant, carpenter and shopkeeper, was omitted from a 'hop, skip and jump' treatment of the Williamses of Parc in Llanilltern, a family Clark was 'obliged to mention . . . because the Lewis's of Greenmeadow represent them and inherit their wealth'. Jones concluded that this selective pedigree of Clark's wife's maternal ancestors stemmed from his having found 'their pedigree too high not for his ideas but for his nose'.[1]

The description of Richard Williams the carpenter as a 'reputed magician who in his time caused the great bell at Llantrissent to be raised by art' was not the only peg which David Jones found in the pages of William Thomas's Diary upon which to hang vitriolic criticism of Clark's work. Another was the case of

> Jenkin Llewellin the Gingerbread Maker of Eglwysilan [who] is not a person to be sneezed at by the proud and lofty for he actually has a place in Mr Clark's wonderfully exclusive *'Genealogies of Glamorgan'* where only the very bluest blood of Glamorganshire aristocracy can comfortably find admission.[2]

David Jones (1834–90) was a maltster's son born in Llanblethian. After working in several parts of England he was able to retire in 1879 and settled at Wallington in Surrey. His remaining years were devoted to antiquarian pursuits in the British Museum, the Public Record Office and local Diocesan Registries in many parts of the country. The result, a large collection of notebooks now mostly in the Cardiff Central Library, reveals him as a leading authority on the early modern history of his native county but he did not live to publish the results of his research. The year before *Limbus Patrum* appeared Jones had had the temerity to present himself at Talygarn, without appointment, to consult Clark on a genealogical problem relating to the Morgan family. For this 'impertinence' he was treated to a sharp dressing down.[3] No doubt the memory of this brusque reception at Talygarn was still rankling with the critic when he wrote the above assessments, causing him perhaps to overlook the opening sentence of the Preface which refers to the 'Genealogies of the families, gentry *and yeomanry*, of the County of Glamorgan'. Indeed, Jones could not have perused the work very thoroughly if he imagined that the gingerbread-maker was an isolated example of less than blue blood.

However, the criticism deserves to be taken seriously and it falls into two parts; first, that Clark was a snob since the whole work was compiled to the glorification of his wife's family, and secondly, that it was lacking in sound scholarship, if we might so interpret the terms 'tantalising, bewildering and distracting'. Certainly this description has struck a chord with many users of this standard work of reference over the past century, but if Jones meant to impute lack of scholarship he was well wide of the mark. Tantalizing the work certainly is, if only because of its almost total lack of references; bewildering because, in common with its various sources, it contains contradictory versions in so many cases; and distracting because, like any good reference book, it tempts the reader down fascinating byways. But does the charge of snobbishness stand, and is it fair to assert that the work was all to the glorification of his wife's family? These are questions worthy of consideration since the motivation behind such a remarkable project is of interest.

No doubt, by modern standards, Clark was a 'snob' but what member of his social class in 1886 was not? He was proud of his wife's ancestry, probably because he was proud of her; after all, he rebuilt Talygarn church in her memory. He was also proud of his own forefathers who, although of gentle stock, were professionals and not members of the landowning class, a family having more in common, perhaps, with his wife's Price ancestors, the family of the philosopher Richard Price – or was the latter too radical for his liking? The Lewises, scions of a long line of landowners who, apart from their brief and profitable flirtation with iron-making, were squires with few apparent interests beyond the hunting field, would have seemed dull, to say the least, to most of Clark's learned ancestors. Could mastery of the ramifications of Welsh genealogy have been this strange, scholarly man's entrée to the social milieu into which he had married? Perhaps it was a way that came more easily to him than competing in various rural sports to earn their respect.

There is some reason to suppose that Clark's interest in the subject was first engaged by *Glamorganshire Pedigrees*, a collection printed by Sir Thomas Phillipps[4] in 1845. In a letter to Phillipps in 1859,[5] in search of more information about pedigree sources, he wrote: 'The basis of my knowledge of the Glam. Pedigrees is the thin[?] volume printed by you & which I have amused[?] myself in correcting & collating & when I could in adding to.' This was a man who was interested in all that surrounded him. Coming face to face with the Lewis pedigree would have stimulated his curiosity, raised questions in his mind that his restless intelligence would not have allowed to go unanswered. In the Phillipps publication he would have found a context for his wife's background that raised even more serious questions. We may well imagine that the occupation of bringing some of the old pedigrees down to his own days was one that amused him and if the Lewises were, perhaps, given more comprehensive treatment than others, why should he not have devoted more effort to his wife's family? It is important to remember that the pedigrees had originally been published as entertaining contributions to the columns of the *Cardiff and Merthyr Guardian* and it was not until some twenty years after their first transient appearance that their author brought them together in a permanent form. Such a history surely confirms Clark's own claim that his interest was in the nature of an intellectual recreation.

The charge of allowing his 'snobbish' instincts to influence editorial decisions on inclusion or exclusion could only apply in relation to David

Jones's specific accusation regarding the carpenter/shopkeeper maternal ancestor of the Williamses of Parc. But since there is no reason to suppose that Clark ever saw the diary of William Thomas he would have been quite unaware of Richard Williams of Llantrisant's status in life. Therefore, while his offhand treatment of the Williams pedigree does raise some general questions, the accusation of snobbery does not arise.

Versions of the Williams pedigree appear in several of Clark's manuscripts and he had taken the trouble to expand it, making use of the memorial inscription evidence in Capel Llanilltern church.[6] Why was this not included in the final work? There is no obvious answer to that question but it was not necessarily for reasons of personal snobbery because there is a great deal of material in the manuscript pedigree books, as well, indeed, as in the original *Merthyr Guardian* publications, that has been omitted. Some of the excluded material would have added immeasurably to the book's usefulness without greatly increasing its bulk. A striking example, but others could be quoted, is the family of Herbert of Cogan Pill and the Cardiff Friary[7] which is allowed to tail away into obscurity without explanation. Yet the version published twenty years earlier in the *Merthyr Guardian* had a detailed descent showing how the estate came to be divided between the Hursts of Gabalfa and Calvert Jones of Swansea.[8]

The complaint most often made of *Limbus Patrum* is that it lacks references. In his preface, the author lists the general sources of the original newspaper publications as including the Harleian Collection in the British Museum, the Golden Grove Book and manuscripts from the Isaac Heard Collection bequeathed to the College of Arms. That such reliable primary sources were the basis of the work is evident from its general structure and should be enough to satisfy us of the book's academic credentials. So why are these sources not specifically cited? The omission is all the more surprising when examination of his working library of sumptuously bound manuscripts,[9] mostly in his own hand, reveals extensive lists of references on almost every page. From these volumes it is possible to trace the use that has been made of the major primary sources as well as to identify some of the 'local collections, of which there exist three or four of the age of Elizabeth or James I, in private hands, unprinted, and but little known'.[10] These included several books in the Baglan Collection now in the Cardiff Library, *Llyfr Baglan*, subsequently published by Bradney, amongst them. There is also an 'Ewenny Book', now in the Glamorgan Record Office,[11] transcribed almost in full, but more impressive still is the fact that almost all the Glamorgan pages of Golden Grove, then in the Public Record Office, were copied by this busy man, as also were lengthy sections of several Harley MSS and much else. One example of an interesting local source, not copied and yet to be tracked down, is variously described as the 'Lanelay Roll' or the 'Lanelay Book 1678' attributed by Clark to Cradock Wells of Cardiff and said to be 'now at Rheola'. This appears to have been the source of some details in the Basset of Miskin pedigree, such as the information that Edmund, eldest son of William Basset, was hanged for murdering his wife.[12]

Whatever minor criticisms we may level at it, the plan of *Limbus Patrum* betrays a mature understanding of Welsh genealogical sources. Clark follows the classification of Welsh families derived from the tribal patriarchs as perfected by generations of scholar-heralds beginning with George Owen of Henllys and culminating in the work of David Edwardes of Rhyd-y-gors as updated by Hugh Thomas, which, for Glamorgan, is preserved in the Golden Grove copy. He was not conversant with the history of this material and he had no means of determining the relative reliability of the various conflicting sources, but he clearly understood the general principles. Sir Thomas Phillipps's *Glamorganshire Pedigrees* may have been 'the basis of his knowledge', but through his attempts at correction and collation he would have come to realize that that was not a classified collection as could be found elsewhere, in more reliable sources.

His own arrangement of pedigrees follows the classified tradition and begins with descents from the patriarchs, followed by the Norman and English blood lines grouped as the *Advenae*. The patriarchal families native to Glamorgan are thoroughly treated: Mathew, Lewis of the Van, the descendants of Iestyn ap Gwrgan and of Einion ap Gollwyn. On the question of patriarchs, he saw that there must have been more than one Gwaithfoed, but, lacking the guidance of Dr Bartrum, the thicket of confusion was impenetrable to him and he has derived the Mathew family and his wife's, the Lewises, from the same ancestor. Had he been able to distinguish between Gwaithfoed of Gwynfe, considered by Dr Bartrum likely to have been the Lewis ancestor, and Gwaithfoed of Gwent, the probable Mathew ancestor,[13] would he still have placed the former at the beginning of the book? It seems odd to give any Gwaithfoed precedence over Iestyn ap Gwrgan in a genealogy of Glamorgan. Was that something David Jones had noticed as glorifying the Lewises? Maybe so, but it is only in its introductory essay that the Lewis family is more extensively served than the other Glamorgan lines.

Also very well represented is the Monmouthshire family of Morgan (probably taken wholesale from Thomas Wakeman, as acknowledged in the preface) and the Herberts, widespread throughout Wales. Two Breconshire families with branches established in Glamorgan, the Vaughans and the descendants of Maenyrch, are well covered, but one striking blemish is the shabby treatment given to the family of the county's premier historian, Rice

Merrick. Instead of being presented as a patriarchal line from Rhys Goch, or, as might have been done, from Caradog Freichfras, it is tucked away under Miscellaneous Welsh Pedigrees as 'Meyrick of Cotterell'[14] and the position of Rice Merrick himself sadly muddled.

These miscellaneous Welsh pedigrees gathered at the end form the weakest part of the book. Given time, no doubt, Clark would have sorted some of them out but as they stand they seem to represent the rag-bag of odds and ends he had not by that time identified. The unsatisfactory treatment of Cottrell is typical of this section, but it is the harder to forgive when we find in his manuscript pedigrees[15] two or three broadly accurate versions, including one from Golden Grove. And yet he used one taken from a Francis MS[16] in which a transcription error, probably by himself not Francis, omitted a crucial generation, that of Rice Merrick's father. Consequently, Clark failed to realize that the Rhys given as second son of Thomas Powell of Porth Andrew, whose children and their marriages are related in detail, was really Rice Merrick.

In addition to the standard manuscript pedigree sources already noted, numerous eighteenth-century genealogical publications were consulted, including such esoteric volumes as Benjamin Buckler's *Stemmata Chichele-ana: or a Genealogical Account of Some of the Families Derived from Thomas Chichele, of Higham Ferrers* (Oxford, 1765). From one of several histories of the baronetage, a four-volume epic by William Betham, comes the remarkable history of the Thomas family of Wenvoe, descended from the Harpways of Simonstown in Herefordshire,[17] which appears under the *Advenae*. (In one of his 'bewildering' moods, Clark had another version of the Wenvoe baronets under Miscellaneous Welsh Pedigrees, but this omitted the Harpways.[18]) Surprisingly, he failed to spot that Simonstown was Tresimon or Bonvilston, besides which the whole pedigree looks suspiciously like a sixteenth- or seventeenth-century forgery drawn up to order by some local bard. The culprit may very likely have been the author of a manuscript pedigree book collected by Angharad Llwyd and now in the National Library.[19] This contains a broadly similar pedigree of the Harpway origin, though placing 'Simonstown', under its Welsh name as being near Wenvoe and not as the Herefordshire home of the Harpways. In fairness it must be said that this manuscript has much convincing detail of the sixteenth- and seventeenth-century generations not seen elsewhere and we might leave open the possibility of an immigrant family from Herefordshire who, having gone native, abandoned but did not forget their surname, especially as the name John ap Thomas Harpway can be found in several local deeds.[20]

The Welsh pedigree sources are naturally very thin when it comes to the *Advenae* and here is where Clark has had to rely almost entirely on his own researches. The outline sketches of pedigrees for the early Norman families may seem to be wanting but, apart from reference to possible reworking of some of the evidence by W. de Gray Birch in footnotes to the second edition of the *Cartae,* or in the *History of Margam Abbey,* we are unlikely to be able to improve much on an area where Clark was so knowledgeable. Indeed, where he has preferred Golden Grove or other sources to his own the result is generally unhappy, as his Fleming pedigrees show.[21] It is impossible to make sense of the first five generations which Clark himself described as exceedingly doubtful. It omits all the historic Flemings such as Walter and Philip whom he identified as belonging to the thirteenth century, yet in his introduction to the pedigree he gives us a convincing descent back to 1315 which is quite at odds with the Golden Grove travesty.

Despite the intelligent understanding that runs so clearly through all Clark's work there is one area where he appears to have misunderstood, or at least not to have taken account of, the nature of Welsh genealogy before 1540 and this has long tended to mislead many of us who should know better. Being constrained by a pedigree layout that assumes primogeniture and demands a precise knowledge of the precedence of younger sons where branches occur, Clark tells us time and time again that this or that branch stems from the second, third or fourth son of a particular man when in fact, as P. C. Bartrum points out, 'in most cases the true order is unknown'.[22] That this precision is dictated by the format seems to be confirmed by Clark's own admission, in the Introduction that 'although the manuscripts agree in the main, they often differ as to the wives and as to the order and names of the younger children'.[23] But he seems rarely to have been in doubt as to the eldest son, although often enough the 'hendre' might have been inherited by the youngest, whose line has subsequently been elevated to seniority by unwitting copyists.

Another problem with the principal source material is the use of place-names. The earliest authorities rarely put them in and when, a little later, they do appear it is often unclear to which generation the 'family seat' is first attributed. Clark recognized the great importance that the inclusion of place-names has for local studies and his index is a model of its kind in making such information available, notwithstanding the occasional errors and omissions. His treatment of the family of Powell of Llandow[24] illustrates an Anglocentric attitude to primogeniture, but in seeming to imply the family's descent from Rhys Goch ap Richard of Glyn Nedd in the senior male line he has no support in the pedigree sources and is probably misleading us. More importantly, in so doing, he has omitted the family homestead named in Golden Grove and other sources, which may have been their 'hendre'. The first Powell of Llandow, David ap Hywel, married the Nerber heiress and thus established a lowland gentry line with a fixed surname. Most of the sources seem to say that he established a branch and that one of his brothers inherited Cwrt Llanfigelydd, a place-name attributed to David's father by Dafydd Benwyn[25] and to the brother's descendants by Golden Grove. Few may know where Cwrt Llanfigelydd is or was – Bartrum puts it in Margam – but to local historians such omissions are unfortunate and one of the beauties of *Limbus Patrum* is that they are rare.

But worse than omission is error, and in one instance at least generations of readers have been misled by the invention of one Jevan Eos of Gelligaer.[26] Golden Grove has this written quite clearly as 'Gelly Vawr'[27] but Clark seems to have preferred a misreading from some other, unidentified, source. Gelli Fawr is in fact a farm in Llanwynno and the 1570 Survey of Glynrhondda shows that its freeholder then was Thomas David ap Jevan Eos. Any regular user of *Limbus Patrum* will be aware of the numerous errors with which it is littered. Many of these are obviously typographical and the only conclusion to be drawn is that Clark did no serious proof-reading at all. But how many were his own mistakes in the first place? It is noticeable that where he gives the dates of sheriffs, he is almost invariably wrong. It can hardly be always down to the printer. An example of an error which is not his can be seen in his treatment of the Prichards of Collenna,[28] which, by his own admission, is inadequate, though he lays the blame upon the family for failing to preserve their own history properly. In fact, this version was taken from Sir Thomas Phillipps's *Glamorganshire Pedigrees* which, as we have seen, was, initially, the basis of his knowledge and where it appears as 'PREES, of COLENNE'. In correcting this and putting the pedigree in its proper place in the overall classification, Clark reveals, as ever, his good grasp of the subject. But his usual sound instinct let him down on the detail, for he accepted the last two generations at face value as two generations more than in the Golden Grove version. As it happens this was a transcription error by Sir Isaac Heard, as we can see by comparing his manuscript, now in the Cardiff Library,[29] with the original now in the National Library.[30] Sir Isaac misread a sixteenth-century cadet branch, clearly distinguished in the original, as a continuation of the main line and Clark adopted this without question despite the difficulty it gave him in trying to link up with such later generations as he had managed to trace.

It is all too easy to compile a catalogue of shortcomings which tends to overemphasize the blemishes in what remains a major undertaking. Faced with such an ambitious project from the pen of a man whose output of scholarly publication was so vast and varied, it is natural that many should have wondered, over the years, just how much work Clark himself put into

Limbus Patrum and to what extent he relied upon record agents. From his correspondence it is clear that his principal collaborator in this project was his friend R. O. Jones of Fonmon, upon whose local knowledge and family muniments he drew extensively. He had evidently approached the Revd John Montgomery Traherne and been stimulated by tantalizing glimpses of that noted local antiquarian's books of pedigrees. Unfortunately he was a little too late here and by 1859 he wrote, 'Mr Traherne has, of late years, been so infirm in body, that I have not cared to trouble him on what at one time so much delighted him.'[31] Indeed, had he had access to Traherne's library he would no doubt have made copies of the pedigree books, amongst which he would have found an accurate Collenna pedigree extending to the late eighteenth century which would have saved him from compounding Isaac Heard's error, noted above.

The shadowy William Floyd who spent so many years of his life in the British Museum and Public Record Office has often been the speculative source of much of *Limbus Patrum*, but there is no evidence in Clark's papers to suggest that Floyd was any more than a consultant, though one in whose knowledge and judgement Clark placed the greatest confidence. It is likely that to a great extent the educated understanding of Welsh pedigrees that informs the work throughout owed much to conversations with Floyd, but the pedigree compilation itself was Clark's alone and the evidence of his manuscripts is eloquent of the many hours he too had spent in the British Museum and the Public Record Office. Indeed, we have the testimony of David Jones by way of confirmation. Jones wrote:

> Mr Clark is on the point of bringing out a work on which he has expended much time – a volume of pedigrees of Glamorganshire families . . . It is already printed . . . and a complete index is now being compiled by Mr Clark himself. Hence the delay in publication. He has had, I believe, entrusted to him the registers of every parish in the county for examination.[32]

Perhaps the most important aspect of *Limbus Patrum* is the extent to which the pedigrees from the standard sources have been amplified, corrected and extended from the end of the seventeenth century, where Hugh Thomas, the last of the scholar-heralds, left off and, in many cases, brought down to the mid or late nineteenth century. Clark scoured many sources to corroborate and elaborate the later pedigrees of the more important families which he had obtained by personal contact or through the good offices of his friends. It was, however, a disappointment to him, and a matter of frustration, that he had had no co-operation from the great families of the County.

I had no help from Lord Bute or Lord Windsor or Lord Tredegar – Lord Bute's people always say they have no papers of any consequence, which is not likely to be true . . . Talbot has immense numbers of early charters, part of the spoil of Margam, but he will not allow any copies to be made . . . So I have worked at a great disadvantage & hope that my shortcomings will be favourably dealt with.[33]

Much of the later material came to him in complete pedigree form and, where it concerned the minor gentry, has generally been passed on to us without amendment. The source of this minor gentry and yeomanry material is of particular interest. It has long been recognized that much interesting, if sometimes doubtful, detail of eighteenth-century descents is derived from pedigrees collected, compiled or added to by Thomas Truman of Pantylliwydd in Llansannor (*c*.1713–86). The bulk of this, including Truman's own family connections with the Herberts, Mathews and Powells, can be seen to come from the Isaac Heard MS, now in the Cardiff Library, which was copied from the seventeenth-century pedigree book that had belonged to Anthony Powell of Maesteg and which has extensive additions in Truman's hand,[34] all faithfully copied by Sir Isaac Heard and printed by Sir Thomas Phillipps in 1845.

However, *Limbus Patrum* contains other Truman additions, notably the later generations of Mathew of Maesmawr in Llantwit Fardre, which are not in the Heard MS. Many sources already mentioned, Harleian MSS, Golden Grove, the Ewenny Book, Baglan MSS, G. G. Francis MSS and others, more or less readily identifiable, are extensively copied out in Clark's books, in his own hand. But one source which crops up time and time again in Clark's references he does not appear to have copied. This is a five-volume collection of pedigrees which he calls the 'Perkins MSS'. These contained the Truman pedigrees as well as a number of other individual family trees found in minor gentry possession in the eighteenth and early nineteenth centuries. For example, the pedigree of Evans, a branch from Thomas of Dyffryn Ffrwd,[35] is taken from Perkins III, 'copied by him from a pedigree at Abertridwr in Eglwysilan, late in the possession of Mr Evans, 1798'. So now we know where Clark learned about the gingerbread-maker whose inclusion so intrigued David Jones.

These Perkins MSS are the most important source for *Limbus Patrum* not immediately identifiable. Where are the five volumes now and who was Perkins? As to the second question, the most likely candidate is William Perkins of Croesgêd in Llantwit Fardre, best remembered in some quarters as a sportsman who kept a noted pack of hounds, but in others as the hard-nosed stipendiary magistrate in Merthyr Tydfil, a capacity in which he would have been known to Clark. For the first question, they may have descended to Miss Alexander of Monkton Combe, near Bath, and failed to escape the 1967 bonfire of her effects, from which the diary of John Perkins of Llantrithyd was rescued.[36] Apart from the liberal sprinkling of references throughout the manuscript pedigree books, our only direct clue to their provenance is provided by a letter of May 1861[37] to Clark from his friend R. O. Jones of Fonmon. Jones writes:

> I have got from Perkins some books [?] of Pedigrees which belonged to Howells of Rhiwvelin – I suspect they are mainly copies of the Truman book or Sir Thomas Philips [*sic*] printed book. I give you on the back of this what the pedigrees contained which will enable you to guess.

And on the back is written Jones's reading of the book's past author/ownership as: 'This book was written by Williams bach yr Llsgualuyd written in a pocket book of 1769'.

This attribution, together with the list of contents, proves beyond doubt that the book in question was one of the three originals from which William Mathew of Fairwater had copied his pedigree book now in the Glamorgan Record Office.[38] It is the one which Mathew described as the book of 'William bach yr ysqualail'd'. Who else could this be but 'William bach ysgolhaig', the diminutive schoolmaster and diarist, William Thomas of Michaelston super Ely? If this were one of the Perkins MSS, what were the other four? The idea that the five volumes might have been a uniform collection of conventional pedigrees copied by or for Mr Perkins is dispelled. More likely they were five disparate volumes of various dates and provenance which had been lately collected by their putative owner.

It is also clear that their inferred content is not entirely that of a conventional pedigree book. The family of Evans/Thomas/Williams of Dyffryn Ffrwd, for instance, with or without the gingerbread-maker, is by no means one of Glamorgan's bluest blood nor is the respectable family of estate agents known as the Thomases of Eglwys Nunydd. The latter, described in one of Clark's pedigree books[39] as the 'Cory Family of Pyle' by reason of their maternal descent from the Revd James Cory, a seventeenth-century incumbent of Penarth, Llandough, Leckwith, etc., appears in *Limbus Patrum* with the *Advenae*.[40] Neither of these families finds a place in any of the traditional pedigree sources. Clark's reference for the Cory family is to Perkins MS V and his page reference matches that in the William Mathew of Fairwater MS, betraying the fact that this particular pedigree comes from the book of a certain Thomas Morgan, glazier of Cardiff. Matching other Perkins references proves that Perkins V is certainly the William Mathew of

Fairwater MS or, more likely perhaps, a page-by-page copy thereof since the original was presumably always in Mathew family possession.

As well as copying parts at least of the Thomas Morgan and William bach books, William Mathew made a few extracts of his family's pedigrees from a volume he described as 'Mr Truman's Old Book', together with a full index of the latter's contents. Again in one of Clark's manuscripts[41] we find twenty pages of Mathew pedigree, in a professional writer's hand, which includes all the eighteenth-century additions to the standard pedigree sources, not only those taken from the Thomas Phillipps printed book, but also, not in the latter, the Maesmawr Mathews with a colourful catalogue of local Llantrisant and Llantwit Fardre connections that has all the hallmarks of Thomas Truman. The only other known source for this is again the Fairwater MS and once more Clark's reference is Perkins V, and the copy incorporates the pagination of its source document, a pagination that exactly matches the William Mathew copy of the index to 'Mr Truman's Old Book'.

We are thus able to identify three of the five Perkins volumes as: (a) the William Mathew of Fairwater MS; (b) the William bach ysgolhaig MS, part copied in (a); and (c) 'Mr Truman's Old Book', also part copied in (a). No progress has yet been made in identifying the other two, but what is clear is that they had all passed through the hands of what seems to have been almost a 'school of Glamorgan genealogists' devoted to continuing Thomas Truman's work. These worthies may have included Richard Howell of Rhiwfelin in Llantrisant, a prosperous freeholder and land agent who seems to have owned the books before Perkins, the obscure Cardiff glazier, Thomas Morgan and perhaps, later, William Perkins himself.

At this stage we might pause to consider what contribution Thomas Truman made to Glamorgan genealogy. While his work was evidently well known to R. O. Jones, nowhere does G. T. Clark acknowledge his or our debt to Iolo Morganwg's mentor. Nor, surprisingly, despite having copied what must have been one of his books, does William Thomas even mention his death. Yet we know that Truman's contribution amounted to much more than just collecting old manuscripts. Several important so-called Pantylliwydd MSS that once belonged to him survive in the National Library, including the Anthony Powell pedigree book copied by Sir Isaac Heard and a couple that have survived amongst Iolo Morganwg's papers. These have been much used by scholars, including J. Hobson Matthews,[42] and they received the careful attention of the late Professor G. J. Williams.[43] But the most important manuscript for understanding the nature of his contribution is a small octavo notebook described as 'Thomas Truman's Pedigree Book, 1783'.[44] This is a copy of most of the pedigrees describing descents from his Herbert ancestors that are to be found in all the other surviving Truman books. The focus, however, is upon Maud, the daughter of Thomas ap William ap Howel of Betws, who married Evan Bevan Meyrick of Lan in the parish of Llantwit Fardre, gentleman. She appears, without further detail, in *Limbus Patrum* as Ann who married Evan ap Evan Bevan Meyrick of Llantwit Fardre,[45] but the little Truman book brings their descendants down to the year 1779 with various gaps left and the note: 'When this comes to the Hands of Mr Evans I desire of him to Fill up the vacancies as above and continue his Pedigree down to himself and return to me. Yours Thomas Truman.' And sure enough further details are added in another hand, presumably that of Mr Evans of Lan, details which appear nowhere else and certainly not in *Limbus Patrum*. From this we may deduce that the volume was not returned to Truman, a suspicion confirmed by the fact that it was donated to the National Library by a Colonel Edward de Winton Bradley of Chippenham, clearly a descendant of Mr Evans's sister and heiress who married Cann de Winton. All of which gives us an indication of Truman's *modus operandi* and explains the provenance of the lively touches that pepper later generations in *Limbus Patrum* such as 'William [younger son of Thomas Powell of Llandow] m. Ann, d. of Edward Roberts of St. Mary Hill, Llantrissant [*sic*], and had Edward, aged 9 in 1771, when he was the sole male of the Powels of Llandow'.

What the Perkins source seems to suggest is that Truman MSS were still circulating and being copied and added to right down to the mid-nineteenth century by minor gentry keen to identify that grandmother or great-grand-mother of pedigree stock. Then G. T. Clark and R. O. Jones began to take an active interest and Clark's invaluable contribution in this instance was to have saved some of the fruits of Truman's industry that would otherwise have been lost to us. Indeed, although he might well regard the company as far beneath his dignity, we could argue that Clark himself was a follower in Truman's footsteps, as much as the latter was, for Glamorgan, a humble disciple of George Owen, David Edwardes and other leading Welsh heralds. In such company Clark must rank with the greatest.

At the risk of appearing to do him less than justice, we might sum up the value of *Limbus Patrum* in Clark's own words: 'The collection has at least this merit, that it stands alone. There was not, and even now there is not, any other printed collection of Glamorgan Pedigrees, excepting the meagre and very scarce folio of Sir Thomas Phillipps.'[46] More than a century on this merit still stands and although his further claim that 'many omissions have been made good, many errors corrected, and here and there a redundancy cut off' rings a little hollow we cannot but applaud this publishing endeav-our in which Clark had scarcely anywhere to turn for guidance apart from William Floyd. The scholarly attention of Major Francis Jones, Dr P. C. Bartrum and Dr Michael Siddons and others had yet to be turned upon this field of study. And this thought, in itself, goes far to explain the lack of references. For many years *Limbus Patrum* has been consulted and cited by academics, but what academic market was there for a book of pedigrees in 1886? There is no doubt that the purpose in publishing this work was no more than to re-edit, expand upon and reprint what had appeared in the columns of the *Merthyr Guardian*. It was a task he had undertaken for his own amusement and the intended readership was the county gentry who, Clark rightly supposed, would appreciate a thorough index but be indifferent to an apparatus of references.

There is just the one charge of carelessness against which the great man has no defence. We can only say that Clark was a genius with a powerful, restless intelligence, who was temperamentally unfitted for the tasks of proof-reading[47] and editing. We may be thankful that, oblivious to these failings, he persevered with his hobby to leave us a monument of scholarship the strengths of which far outweigh the petty flaws.

APPENDIX: Pedigree working books and collections amongst the Clark MSS in NLW

First amongst the large collection of Clark's papers preserved in NLW, all extravagantly guarded in large leather-bound volumes, is a group of four pedigree books. The first of these, MS 5171F, is an unfinished 'fair copy' which was evidently intended to bring together a final version of his life-long collection. This volume has references added to most of the pedigrees, but, apart from the descendants of Iestyn ap Gwrgan with which it opens, it is not organized in patriarchal form as is *Limbus Patrum*. The pedigrees in this volume run to 98 pages in tabular format.

The second pedigree book, MS 5172F, contains working copies of tabular pedigrees with many additions and alterations. It is interleaved with the chart pedigree 'pull-outs' from *Limbus Patrum* and while mainly in Clark's hand includes many pages from his correspondents. There is a lengthy index of places and families and the references are much more copious.

The third and fourth volumes, MSS 5173D and 5174E, comprise pasted-in cuttings from the *Merthyr Guardian* with many additions and corrections but few references. These appear to be working drafts for *Limbus Patrum*.

Other pedigree MSS are mainly composite volumes of transcripts, notebooks and odd scraps of paper. They lack continuous pagination, and include:

- Two unscheduled volumes which were part of the W. D. Clark donation in 1955–6 and described in the Annual Report for that year as 'a draft of G. T. C.'s *Limbus Patrum*'. Certainly they are entitled *Limbus Patrum* but they are, in fact mainly a fairly complete transcript of the Glamorgan pedigrees in the Golden Grove Book and of an 'Ewenny Book' which is now in the Glamorgan Record Office as D/D E 439/440.
- MS 5178E. This is a collection of transcripts from several sources including the Edwards MS which belonged to Edward Priest Richards. This was 'Copied from Mr E. P. Richards' collated copy of the Llandaff or Edwards MS Book. Dowlais Nov. 1860. G. T. C.' This had evidently come from E. P. Richards's grandfather Thomas Edwards the lawyer of Llandaff, and is probably the large folio which William Thomas of Michaelston super Ely claimed to have seen.

  > December 1794: . . . [Thomas Edwards] a very good historian the last years of his life he made his clerk at spare times as he gave him scripts to write the History of the County of Glamorgan from the earliest times with the Pedigree of all the Antient families with their Coat of Arms in a large folio for I have seen it.

  Also in this volume are transcripts from Harley and Baglan MSS.
- MS 5179E. This has transcripts from Jones's *Brecknockshire*, a fair copy of the Edwards MS in MS 5178E, Baglan MSS, G. G. Francis MSS, and others.
- MS 5181E, draft pedigrees, notes and evidences on various families, followed by another copy of Mr E. P. Richards's book. This volume contains a draft of the *Limbus Patrum* version of that part of the Mathew pedigree which seems to come from 'Mr Truman's old book' as copied by William Mathew of Fairwater.
- MS 5185E. A slim volume comprising a draft and printed (?page proof) table of Lewis family ancestors. It seems to be intended as a 'complete wheel'.

Notes

[1] Cardiff MS 4.877. David Jones's transcript of the William Thomas Diary.
[2] T. J. Hopkins, 'David Jones of Wallington: his work as a genealogist', in Stewart Williams (ed.), *Glamorgan Historian*, vii (Cowbridge, D. Brown and Sons, 1971), 51.
[3] T. J. Hopkins, 'David Jones of Wallington: An introduction to his life and work', in Stewart Williams (ed.), *Glamorgan Historian*, iv (Cowbridge, D. Brown and Sons, 1967), 87–8.
[4] Sir Thomas Phillipps (ed.), *Glamorganshire Pedigrees from the MSS. of Sir Isaac Heard, Knt.* (Worcester, 1845).
[5] Bodleian Library MS Phillipps-Robinson d.170, ff. 32–3. I am grateful to Brian Ll. James for this reference.
[6] NLW MS 5171F, 40; MS 5172F, 387–8; MS 5178E.
[7] G. T. Clark, *Limbus Patrum* (London, 1886), 286–7.

[8] NLW MS 5173D.

[9] Now in the National Library of Wales. See Appendix in this chapter.

[10] *Limbus Patrum*, 1.

[11] GRO D/D E 439–40.

[12] *Limbus Patrum*, 354.

[13] P. C. Bartrum, 'Pedigrees of the Welsh tribal patriarchs', *NLWJ*, xiii (1963–4), 126–7.

[14] *Limbus Patrum*, 540–4.

[15] NLW unscheduled G. T. Clark MS '*Limbus Patrum*', 2; NLW MS 5178E, 29–274.

[16] NLW MS 5179E, copied by Clark from a MS of George Grant Francis (1814–82), the Swansea businessman and antiquary.

[17] *Limbus Patrum*, 444–6.

[18] Ibid., 558–9.

[19] NLW Kinmel Park MS 1598D.

[20] GRO CL/BRA 247/47, 31 January 1522/3.

[21] *Limbus Patrum*, 383.

[22] P. C. Bartrum, *Welsh Genealogies 300–1400* (Cardiff, University of Wales Press, 1974), i, 8; id., 'Notes on the Welsh genealogical manuscripts', *THSC*, 1968, 66.

[23] *Limbus Patrum*, 4.

[24] Ibid., 181–3.

[25] P. C. Bartrum, *Welsh Genealogies 1400–1500* (Aberystwyth, National Library of Wales, 1983), iv, 580; Carmarthenshire RO, Golden Grove MS, Glam., 86; Cardiff MS 2.1.

[26] *Limbus Patrum*, 134.

[27] Golden Grove MS, Glam., 48.

[28] *Limbus Patrum*, 136–7.

[29] Cardiff MS 3.1.

[30] NLW MSS 7A and 8A.

[31] Bodleian Library MS Phillipps-Robinson d.170, ff. 32–3.

[32] Cardiff MS 1.640, vol. 5; T. J. Hopkins, *Glamorgan Historian*, iv, 90.

[33] Letter from Clark to the Hon. and Revd G. T. O. Bridgeman (1823–95), author of *History of the Princes of South Wales* (1876), in a copy of *Limbus Patrum* having Bridgeman's bookplate, in the Glamorgan Record Office Reference Library (G/2a). I am indebted to Mrs Patricia Moore for drawing my attention to this.

[34] NLW MS 7A.

[35] *Limbus Patrum*, 519; NLW MS 5172F, 95.

[36] William Linnard, 'John Perkins of Llantrithyd', *Morgannwg*, 31 (1987), 9.

[37] NLW MS 5203E. I am indebted to Brian Ll. James for drawing my attention to this.

[38] GRO D/D Mat 57A.

[39] NLW MS 5171F, 24.

[40] *Limbus Patrum*, 379.

[41] NLW MS 5181E.

[42] J. Hobson Matthews (ed.), *Cardiff Records*, iv (Cardiff, 1903), 23.

[43] G. J. Williams, *Traddodiad Llenyddol Morgannwg* (Caerdydd, Gwasg Prifysgol Cymru, 1948), 3n., 172n., 201n., 216–17, 220, 224n.

[44] NLW MS 15,596A.

[45] *Limbus Patrum*, 89.

[46] Ibid., 1.

[47] Clark admitted that he was 'not a very accurate corrector' of proofs in a letter to Charles Octavius Swinnerton Morgan of Newport, 4 July 1885, now among the tract collection in the Library of the Society of Antiquaries of London.

CHAPTER 8

The Clark Family Portraits

DONALD MOORE

In Talygarn House today portraits of eight members of the Clark family appear on seven canvases hanging in the lofty 'billiard room', unremarked by the patients who attend the Talygarn Rehabilitation Centre for treatment. These pictures make a powerful statement about a gentry family which George Thomas Clark founded in Glamorgan, but which has since ceased to live in his chosen abode.

Every gentry house has, or had, its collection of family portraits, often accumulated over several centuries. They present a visible record of the descent of the owners – a pedigree in pictures. The sitters' costumes highlight the roles played in society by members of the family. But more than this, the portraits are a reminder of inheritances which have brought land and other wealth to the present generation. Marriage alliances are often signalled by additional portraits bearing other family names. Such pictures are normally painted in oils, a durable and impressive medium; oil paintings can be exposed indefinitely to daylight, unlike fragile watercolours or miniatures, which need protection from the ultra-violet rays of the sun. Pictures are not the only means of commemorating individuals. Sculptures can be made in durable marble or fragile plaster, or sometimes carved in wood. The final apotheosis of a portrait can even be in stained glass, but in a domestic setting this medium is more usually favoured for coats of arms and emblems.

At first sight one might assume that the Clark portraits now at Talygarn had been there continuously since G. T. Clark's time, but that is not so. They were kept there for a long period – until 1922, when the family put Talygarn up for sale and auctioned most of its contents. Then, it seems, they were removed to London, where the family owned a town house in the West End, 44 Berkeley Square. Photographs of that house, in the collection of English Heritage, record the interior, apparently in the late 1950s, and show

23 George Thomas Clark. Bust by Joseph Edwards, 1874.
East Glamorgan NHS Trust.

that at least six out of the seven canvases were hanging there. The family sold that property in about 1960, and had to find somewhere else to put the portraits. During a visit to south Wales not long before his death in 1961, Wyndham Damer Clark had the idea of sending the portraits back to their old home at Talygarn, which had in the mean time been turned into a convalescent home for miners, and he arranged for them to be transferred.[1]

In the old days, the portraits had been displayed variously throughout the house. Photographs now in the Glamorgan Record Office show some of the rooms as then furnished, with pictures on the walls. Mrs Clark's portrait, for example, hung in G. T. Clark's library. It was not practicable to repeat the original arrangement, since under the new ownership the functions, furnishings and names of the various rooms had been changed to suit new requirements. On their return, all the portraits were hung in one room. Their size demanded a wide and lofty space, and the room chosen was the former lounge, now serving as the billiard room. Today the collection gains from having been brought together, but unfortunately the lighting, designed for the billiard-playing, does little for oil paintings hung high on the walls. There were other portraits; at least nine oil paintings depicting members of the family were listed in the sale catalogue of 1922, and others may survive unknown. In addition, various portraits of G. T. Clark and of other members of the family have appeared in printed form.

Today's visitor to Talygarn is greeted by a splendid marble bust of G. T. Clark in a dramatic position at the end of the entrance hall. This is not its original location, for in 1922 it stood in the old Hall. Its present position is more effective since it draws attention immediately to the genius who once presided over the place. Clark could be taken for a Roman senator, his shoulders draped in a sculpted toga, were it not for his bushy moustache and side-whiskers, which instantly place him in the late nineteenth century. Clark could only have worn the toga in his imagination, but sculptors used it as the hallmark of high status, culture and influence; Clark's broad face and short neck were ideally suited to that garment.

The bust was sculpted in 1874 by Joseph Edwards (1814–82). Edwards was born at Ynys-gau, Merthyr Tydfil, the son of a stonecutter.[2] His artistic talent became evident at an early age, and when seventeen years old he chanced to see the famous collection of classical sculptures at Margam, Glamorgan, which had been collected in Italy by Thomas Mansel Talbot while on the Grand Tour (the only sculpture surviving at Margam today is a statue of the Roman emperor Lucius Verus, inside the Orangery at the west end).

The visit to Margam was a turning-point in Edwards's career. He was inspired to become a sculptor himself and began in a modest way by working for a monumental mason in Swansea. Then, with help, he secured an art training in London, becoming a student in the Royal Academy Schools in December 1835. His early promise was fulfilled and his reputation grew. He became known for his allegorical pieces – personifications of abstract virtues – a favourite genre of the Victorians. He received numerous commissions for funerary monuments and portrait busts. So in this roundabout way the tradition of classical sculpture was adopted by a talented Welsh exponent, whose creations found their way to many houses and public places in England and Wales. Edwards's sitters included members of the foremost families of south Wales: Beaufort, Guest, Raglan and Crawshay, as well as famous literary figures such as Taliesin Williams (ab Iolo) and Thomas Stephens. It was therefore not surprising that Edwards should have been commissioned to make a bust of Clark.

There is a closely similar marble bust, also in Roman style, now displayed in Cyfarthfa Castle Museum, Merthyr Tydfil. It is incised *verso* G. T. CLARK

ESQRE., F.S.A. etc.; he had been elected Fellow of the Society of Antiquaries of London in 1866, and this was counted a distinction of note. The sculptor was indicated by a carved inscription JOSEPH EDWARDS, SCULPTOR, LONDON, 1872. The bust was presented to Clark by the Merthyr Tydfil Board of Guardians, of which he had been elected chairman on 21 April 1860.[3] It is almost the same size as the Talygarn version, done two years later; then F.R.G.S. was added after his name, representing another fellowship, this time of the Royal Geographical Society.

At Talygarn there are two small wooden carvings of Clark's head, installed between 1885 and 1895 by G. Biraghi, an Italian craftsman commissioned by Clark to create much of the interior woodwork. One is located in what was originally the billiard room, carved in high relief, in a small panel, well above the fireplace at the west end of the room. Biraghi placed a carved head of himself in a similar position at the east end – but in low relief.

In the main corridor at Talygarn there are miniature heads of five individuals carved in low relief on wooden panels about 31 cm square; one (on the south side) shows Clark himself, with an inscription above his head INDUSTRIAL CELEBRITIES. The use of the plural is curious, and it would seem to stem from the title accompanying a printed portrait which appeared in the *British Trade Journal* to illustrate an article on Clark, which was the tenth of a series.[4] Coincidentally – or perhaps not – this carved portrait was in the tenth panel from the corridor door. Presumably the relevant page had been shown to the Italian carver, who saw the title and simply transcribed it as it was. Exactly opposite on the other side of the corridor is a carved head of Clark's great friend, Sir Henry Layard. Biraghi also included his own head in this series.

Individuals of means who want a portrait of themselves to hang in their own home usually wait for a 'defining moment' at the height of their career, to commission an artist of their choice who will produce the desired interpretation. Sitters who have to rely on public subscription may suffer from being painted before their ideal image has evolved, or, more likely, when old age has taken its toll of their features.

Clark's defining image emerged at the age of fifty-six. An entry in his diary for Tuesday 7 November 1865, states 'Phillips began my picture'.[5] This was a reference to Henry Wyndham Phillips, who had been invited to stay with the Clarks. Phillips arrived on the 6th and departed on Thursday the 16th, having had ten days to make sketch portraits from life, which he would have taken back to his studio to prepare a finished painting in oils.[6] Exactly when the final canvas was completed is not clear, but it must be dated 1865/6.

The portrait shows Clark clad in a dark brown coat, blue waistcoat and grey trousers, sitting at ease in a wooden armchair, and holding a letter in his left hand, visibly addressed to 'G. T. Clark, Esq.'. Two large volumes rest upright against a large chest beside his chair, suggesting perhaps some ongoing antiquarian research. He wears a white shirt with high wing-collar and a large black cravat tied in a bow. His bushy side-whiskers and slightly tousled hair set off a strong but kindly face; the upper lip and chin are shaven, creating a mature but homely image – in short, a fresh-faced country gentleman (see frontispiece).

Clark had reason to feel pleased with himself. After managing the Dowlais ironworks for ten years, he had succeeded in turning the business around and in bringing it to a pre-eminent position in terms of output and technical innovation. He had just purchased a property in the country at Talygarn, which he was renovating and extending, with the intention of providing a fitting residence for himself and his family. On 11 October 1865 he states that he slept at Talygarn for the first time.[7] The portrait sittings must have taken place at Dowlais House, which was his home, office – and military headquarters.

The choice of artist is interesting. Henry Wyndham Phillips (1820–68) was a prominent and fashionable painter of public celebrities.[8] He had an example to emulate in his father, Thomas Phillips, RA (1770–1845), the celebrated society painter. Portrait painters know that a person's face is at its most characteristic when just about to speak or just having spoken, so they naturally engage their sitter in conversation while they pursue their work. In the case of Clark, an interest in military matters might have furnished common ground, since Henry Phillips was a captain in the Artists' Volunteer Corps, while Clark was active in the Glamorgan Rifle Volunteers.

Another sitter of Henry Phillips was Sir Henry Layard, explorer and archaeologist, and a close friend of Clark. Layard's expeditions to Nineveh and Babylon in the Near East (1845–51) had made him a well-known public figure, and Phillips's likeness of him received a wide circulation in a mezzotint print by Samuel W. Reynolds. Phillips was no stranger to the Clark household. In a summary of events for 1860, bound in with G. T. Clark's diaries, an entry for 16 December states 'H. W. Phillips at Dowlais to paint the 2 children'. The artist stayed until 22 December.[9] Blanch was then nine years old, and Godfrey five. The present location of the picture (or pictures) is not known.

Phillips's portrait of Clark may be compared with a rather grainy photograph, preserved in the National Library of Wales, which shows Clark attired in 'country clothes', leaning back in an armchair. His sideboards are clearly visible and his upper lip and chin are shaven. The photograph seems to have been taken out-of-doors in bright sunlight (an important requirement in early photography); this, however, caused the sitter to half-close his eyes, creating an unflattering effect. The photograph is inscribed *verso* 'taken by Pendarves Vivian at Cambridge, one of the earliest specimens of the imperfect art' (i.e. photography). There is another copy of this photograph in a family album of the Guests, now in the possession of Stephen Rowson of Cardiff, identified as 'George Clark' and dated 1854, which would fit into Pendarves Vivian's time as an undergraduate at Cambridge, 1852–5. This is a young-looking, relaxed Clark, eleven years before being painted in oils.

There is a full-face portrait of Clark in the form of a large lithograph (now in the Glamorgan Record Office) which formerly belonged to the family. The sitter's signature was appended, as was frequently the practice on printed portraits, with his coat of arms. The print shows signs of having been framed and hung, as do a number of other large printed portraits presented by the family to the Record Office at the same time.

The same image was used as the frontispiece of Clark's *Cartae* (1910 edition), and also to illustrate *The History of Lewis' School, Pengam*, by Arthur Wright (plate VII there). A portrait of Clark was recorded as hanging in the school when the *History* was published in 1929, and it may have been a copy of the large lithograph described above. Clark wears a cravat tied in a bow, a high wing-collar, a coat and waistcoat. The face here displays a bushy moustache in addition to the side-whiskers; the chin remains shaven. This resulted in a more avuncular image, as befitted a benefactor of the school and its first Chairman of Governors when its ancient constitution was reorganized.

A similar portrait, but facing right, appeared in the form of a lithograph bearing the signature, Geo. T. Clark, published in the *British Trade Journal*, already cited. It illustrated an article on Clark in a series entitled 'Industrial Celebrities', and, as already mentioned, it must have served as the pattern for the carved portrait in the corridor at Talygarn. The article itself was reprinted in the *Merthyr Express*.[10]

There exist two photographs which show Clark in another role, not unexpected for his status and position. He raised and commanded the 2nd (Dowlais) Corps, Glamorgan Rifle Volunteers; the headquarters of the Corps was at Dowlais House, then his home. He was no stranger to the military environment, since he had spent his boyhood at the Royal Military Asylum and seen his father buried there with military honours.[11] At Dowlais he was first a captain, then promoted lieutenant-colonel in 1861. His second-in-command in this unit – as well as in the ironworks – was William Menelaus. Clark cleverly integrated his military and civilian activities. He devised tactical exercises for his unit, based on the castles which he knew so well. In 1863 a mock attack and defence of Caerphilly Castle was mounted, and in 1862 a similar exercise on the ancient fortifications of Caerau.[12]

The first photograph is a 'studio portrait' of Clark, seated in full uniform, cutting an impressive figure, with ornate cuffs, belt, high boots and spurs. His sword rests across his knees, and his plumed shako stands on a sideboard. His side-whiskers are bushier than ever, obviously an important part of the image which he wished to cultivate. The second photograph shows Clark with his military staff, outside the porch of Dowlais House. It was elaborately posed to create the impression that some grand manœuvre was being planned on the map spread out before them. He sits at an octagonal table of quality, no doubt brought out of the house as a 'prop' for the photograph. Clark had himself designed the uniform for the Dowlais Rifle Corps: 'a tunic and trousers of dark grey cloth with red facings, a shako with a plume to match, a waist belt with frog and two pouches'. For this he had to secure the approval of the lord-lieutenant of Glamorgan.[13]

When Mrs Clark's portrait was painted is not known; it is not dated or signed. She was born Ann Price Lewis, and shown by Clark in his *Limbus* to belong to the Greenmeadow branch of the Lewis family of the Van, Caerphilly. She was actually born and brought up at Parc, Capel Llanilltern (a few miles west of Tongwynlais, where Greenmeadow was situated). Her own name, Ann, could well have referred back to the daughter of Sir William Morgan of Pencoyd, Monmouthshire, who married the first of the family to adopt the surname Lewis in the sixteenth century. Clark was very conscious of this historic family link, which secured his position among the *uchelwyr* of south Wales.

Mrs Clark is seated, full-face, in an armchair, beside an occasional table on which stands a bowl of roses. She is wearing a white lace cap and black dress with white lace cuffs and collar, the latter decorated at the front with a brooch. She makes no great display of jewellery – simply a pair of eardrops. No rings are visible on her fingers and no bracelets on her wrists. A buckle at her waist completes her adornments. Her face has been delicately painted. She gives the impression that she has been interrupted in some task and is looking up at the artist. In fact, she is holding knitting needles in her hands, and the right hand is poised above a ball of white wool, as she 'casts-on' to start knitting. Her upper eyelids appear strangely heavy, perhaps some inherited physical trait. To modern eyes she presents a sad and long-suffering image, but too much could be read into such an appearance, for ladies were expected to appear modest and domestically inclined. There exists in the Glamorgan Record Office an oval, undated drawing of Mrs Clark in charcoal and white chalk, signed 'Helen Shaw'. It resembles the oil portrait, especially in the apparent age of the sitter, but it cannot be proved that either is derived from the other.

Surprisingly little has emerged regarding Mrs Clark's private or public life, though her housekeeping books, now in the National Library of Wales,

24 Ann Price Clark (née Lewis), wife of G. T. Clark. Painting,
artist and date unknown. *National Library of Wales.*

would undoubtedly reveal more about her activities, if analysed. Contemporary references show that she supported her husband in public activities. She also organized a small works hospital at Dowlais, though it must
be admitted that this project was viewed with suspicion by the work-force.[14]

The Clarks had one daughter, Blanch (sometimes spelled 'Blanche')
Lancaster, born in 1851. She married Clarence Francis Forestier-Walker in
1891, when she was forty years of age, and went to live at Castleton between
Cardiff and Newport. He died in 1907, while she lived on until 1933; there
were no children. Her portrait at Talygarn is not dated, but her age appears
to be about twenty, implying a date for the picture of about 1871. In her
portrait Blanch Clark is shown seated, full-face, wearing a low-cut, square-
necked dress, light blue in colour, with half sleeves, generously trimmed with

139

25 Blanch Lancaster Clark, G. T. Clark's daughter. Painting by
Desiré Laugée, *c.*1871. *National Library of Wales.*

lace, as also is the neck. The waist of the dress is decorated with a bow in front. Around her right wrist is a black band. Her long hair is parted at the front and then gathered up around the head, rather as a halo. Her hands hold an unopened red fan above her lap. As in the case of her mother, jewellery is sparse – a neck pendant and eardrops. She has pleasing, rounded features, but displays a wistful, almost sad demeanour.

The name of the artist raises a problem. The label records 'Langet', but no such artist can be traced. A clue appeared in the sale catalogue of 1922, where a portrait of Edward Dicey was stated to be by 'Lauget', but the latter name cannot be traced either. However, if either name resulted from transcribing unfamiliar handwriting, the original could have been 'Laugee', and there was a French history and portrait painter, Desiré Laugée (1823–96).

26 Godfrey Lewis Clark, G. T. Clark's son. Painting by Parker
Hagarty, 1919. *National Library of Wales.*

The sitter mentioned above must have been Edward James Stephen Dicey
(1832–1911), since his entry in *DNB* cites a portrait of him by Laugée.[15]
Dicey was the surname of G. T. Clark's mother's family, and that
connection will be discussed later.

In the National Library of Wales there is another portrait of Blanch, a
photographic vignette in profile, tinted and retouched with paint (a frequent
practice of the period). It is inscribed 'Blanche L. Clark age 18 London
May. Photographed by Dr Wallich, Trevor House, 2 Warwick Gardens,
Kensington W'. The date has to be 1869. The face looks a little younger than
that of the oil painting.

The Clarks also had one son, Godfrey Lewis Clark, born on 30 November
1855. In his portrait he appears as a person of consequence in public life. He is

standing and looking towards the left, dressed in a dark suit with check-patterned waistcoat, wing-collar and cravat. He sports a walrus moustache, but no side-whiskers. Godfrey Clark occupied various public positions in Glamorgan: he was high sheriff in 1897, a deputy lieutenant and a justice of the peace. He was also chairman of the Llantrisant and Llantwit Fardre Rural District Council and of the Pontypridd Board of Guardians. On the frame it is stated: 'This portrait was subscribed for by his friends as a mark of their appreciation of his character and public work in the county of Glamorgan.'

The painter was Parker Hagarty, who signed the picture and dated it '1919', that is, *after* the death of the sitter, which occurred on 11 February 1918. There is a further difficulty in the image itself, since Godfrey Clark looks only forty-five to fifty years of age, not sixty-two, his age at death. The picture must have been finished, if not wholly painted, posthumously, possibly from earlier photographs which showed his 'defining moment'. Such a practice is known elsewhere. A copy of this portrait hung in Glamorgan County Hall, Cardiff. The same image was reproduced in a photogravure print, signed 'Parker Hagarty, 1919'. Parker Hagarty was born in Canada in 1859, he went to study in Liverpool and Paris, and from 1885 lived in Cardiff, painting landscapes, portraits and figures. He was active in the South Wales Art Society, serving as its secretary for a period; his death was recorded in the minutes of the society in 1934.[16] He became an Associate of the Royal Cambrian Academy in north Wales. His sister, Mary S. Hagarty, was also a painter.

The portrait of Godfrey Clark's wife is the most striking of the whole collection. It makes an unmistakable statement about the social pretensions of the sitter and her family. In 1883 Godfrey married Alice Georgina Caroline Strong, daughter of Henry Linwood Strong, registrar of the Court of Probate, and his wife Fanny Louisa, who was daughter of the Hon. and Very Revd Henry David Erskine, dean of Ripon. There was already a Clark connection with the Erskine family: the dean's father, Lord Erskine, had nominated the young George Thomas Clark as 'gownboy' at Charterhouse in 1819. Alice is shown here wearing a long, flowing, grey-blue dress with cape and gossamer-like neck scarf. Her upswept auburn hair displays the high fashion of the 1890s. She is seated on a stone bench against a landscape garden background. On her lap she holds a wide-brimmed straw hat and a bunch of roses. Whether this was a studio set or a real scene from nature is immaterial: the message is the same.

The child sitting on a pillar to the right is her fourth son, Lionel, born in 1891. He wears a long white dress which to the modern eye looks more suitable for a girl, but in those days it was customary to dress little boys and girls alike. The pale faces and silvery garments of the two figures are bathed in

27 Alice Georgina Caroline, wife of Godfrey Lewis Clark, with their son, Lionel. Painting by Julian Russell Story, 1894. *National Library of Wales.*

28 Wyndham Damer Clark, in uniform of the Coldstream Guards.
Painting by Thomas Hasted Heath, 1905.
National Library of Wales.

light, contrasting with the darkness of the trees behind. Lionel has a turquoise band around his waist, tied at the back with a large bow. In his right hand he holds a stick, and from the other hand he trails an almost invisible ribbon or string, leading to a black labrador dog below. Meik, the dog, is stretched out at Mrs Clark's feet, its long black shape counterbalancing the dense foliage above. The tradition of painting family portraits *al fresco* in the company of favourite animals was well established as far back as the seventeenth century. The aim was to emphasize the status, landed wealth and leisure of the subject. An apt comparison is a portrait of 1776–8 by Thomas Gainsborough, now in Southampton Art Gallery, showing George Venables Vernon, 2nd Baron Vernon, of Briton Ferry House. The aristocrat stands in the sylvan setting of his own estate, while his favourite gun dog reaches up on two legs, its forepaws resting on its master's waistcoat.

The portrait of Mrs Godfrey Clark was painted in 1894 by Julian Russell Story (1857–1919), a fashionable portrait painter, born at Walton-on-Thames in England. After a period at Oxford University, Story studied in Florence and Paris. He eventually settled in Philadelphia, and is regarded as an American artist.[17] In 1882, while in Paris, he made a sketch of the distinguished botanist, Charles Coltman Rogers of Stanage Park, Radnorshire, as a preparation for an oil painting; there again he included a dog, Rogers's dachshund.[18]

The eldest son of Godfrey Lewis Clark and his wife was Wyndham Damer (1884–1961). The name Damer originated in his mother's family. His portrait shows him whole-length, advancing left, but turned full-face, in the uniform of an officer of the Coldstream Guards. There is a slight moustache on his upper lip, but no hint of his grandfather's side-whiskers. White gloves held in his left hand contrast with black shoes. He has a red sash around his waist and a red stripe down the side of his trousers; his sword hangs at his left side. This is a classic portrait of an army officer. It is surprising to find such a grand portrait of a young man so early in his career. A clue is found in the label at the foot of the frame, which states: 'Presented to / Wyndham Damer Clark / Coldstream Guards / on his 21st Birthday / By the members of the Pontypridd Board of Guardians / March 27th 1905.' His father, Godfrey, was chairman of the Pontypridd Board of Guardians, and this picture was no doubt intended as a tribute to the father.

Wyndham's portrait was painted by Thomas Hasted Heath, who exhibited between 1901 and 1905, and lived at various addresses in Cardiff.[19] His father and grandfather were also competent artists. One of the scanty facts known about his work is that he illustrated with line-drawings the melodramatic, but highly readable *Tales in Prose and Verse, and Dramas* (London, 1906), written by his grandfather, Thomas Edward Heath (1825–82), of Northlands, Cardiff. The book was edited and published by Hasted Heath's father.

29 Ann Mary (née Stephen), wife of Thomas Edward Dicey.
Painting, possibly by her son, Frank Dicey, date unknown.
National Library of Wales.

Wyndham Damer Clark presented to the National Library of Wales,
Aberystwyth, a great quantity of documents, archives and books relating to
G. T. Clark and the family, and he restored the principal family portraits to
Talygarn. He demonstrated his devotion to his grandfather's memory by
establishing and endowing the G. T. Clark Memorial Trust in collaboration
with the Cambrian Archaeological Association. The purpose of this Trust
was, and still is, to award prizes periodically for research work on the
archaeology of Wales and the Marches.[20] G. T. Clark joined that Association in 1850, soon after its foundation. He contributed over fifty articles to
its journal, *Archaeologia Cambrensis*, mainly on castles. The first awards of
Clark Memorial Trust were made in 1946, the centenary year of the

Association. The ninth distribution took place in 1997, actually at Talygarn, in a joint event with the Glamorgan History Society. Over the years, forty distinguished archaeologists have been honoured with these awards.

The last of the Talygarn pictures to be considered is that of Mrs Dicey, an aunt of G. T. Clark. This is a three-quarter-length portrait of a pensive, middle-aged lady with fine features and 'smiling' eyes. Her hair, parted in the middle, is draped in gossamer-like lace. She wears a white dress with lace sleeves, mostly concealed by a black cloak with red lining. Her left elbow rests on the arm of a chair, and the left hand is raised just to touch her face, revealing rings on the first and third fingers. A velvet purse is attached to her wrist. The picture is neither signed nor dated, but is labelled 'Mrs Dicey'.

The Diceys were a minor gentry family, descended from a seventeenth-century Thomas Dicey of Basingstoke. G. T. Clark's mother was Clara Dicey, daughter of Thomas Dicey of Claybrooke Hall, Leicestershire, and sister of Thomas Edward Dicey.[21] Clara had married the Revd George Clark, chaplain of the Royal Military Asylum, Chelsea, in 1806. Thomas Edward Dicey (1789–1858) merited an entry in F. Boase, *Modern English Biography* (1892). He was educated at both Oxford and Cambridge universities and became chairman of the Midland Counties Railway. He was a director of the North Staffordshire Railway from its foundation in 1846 until his death. He was also proprietor of the *Northampton Mercury*, the newspaper founded by his great-grandfather in 1720.

Thomas Edward Dicey's youngest son was Francis William (known professionally as 'Frank'), a first cousin of G. T. Clark.[22] He became a portrait and genre painter, having studied under Laugée and Bonnat in Paris. Between 1865 and his death in 1888 he exhibited in Liverpool, Manchester and Birmingham, as well as at the Royal Academy and other London venues. A watercolour of his figured in the Talygarn sale of 1922: 'A view of the Campagna di Roma'. Frank had three brothers: Henry Thomas Stephen Dicey, a barrister; Edward James Stephen Dicey, author, journalist and editor of the *Observer*; and Albert Venn Dicey, Vinerian Professor of Law at Oxford, who married Elinor Mary Bonham Carter. A. V. Dicey was author of the famous legal work, *A Digest of the Law of England with Reference to the Conflict of Laws* (1896).

The presence of only one Dicey portrait in the Talygarn collection is surprising. This circumstance is explained in part by the sale of 1922, which included at least nine portraits of family interest, four of them Diceys. First was G. T. Clark's mother, Mrs Clara Clark (née Dicey), painted by Frank Dicey, her nephew. The portrait listed as 'Mrs Dicey by Frank Dicey' probably referred to Ann Mary, sister-in-law of Mrs George Clark, in which case the artist would have been her son. The 'Mrs Dicey' in the Talygarn collection might have been a duplicate, also painted by Frank. Alternatively, there might only have been one portrait, which, failing to sell at the sale, remained with the Clarks. The dimensions of the two are almost identical, their widths differing by just over an inch, but such a discrepancy is not unusual when pictures are measured by different people. Ann Mary was daughter of James Stephen (1758–1852), master in Chancery and member of Parliament, who came of a distinguished family; she married Thomas Edward Dicey of Claybrooke Hall, and his portrait was also listed in the sale catalogue.

The 'Edward Dicey' by Lauget (identified as Laugée) was Edward James Stephen Dicey (1832–1911), second son of Thomas Edward Dicey, and a brother of Frank the artist. Also listed was a painting of an unidentified lady by 'C. Dicey', but no artist member of the family with this initial can be traced. The 'C' may be an auctioneer's error.

On the Clark side there was listed a 'group portrait' of Mr and Mrs Godfrey Clark by 'Phillips'; no further identification was given. A painting entitled 'Samuel Clark Esq. by Keelog, 1669' might have portrayed one of three learned clerical ancestors who bore this name (also spelled 'Clarke'), but the description is insufficient for identification. No artist named Keelog can be traced. Three 'clerical Clarks' were portrayed in various engravings. A particularly attractive and personable impression of the Revd George Clark appeared in an engraving by William Holl the elder, based on a drawing or painting by Joseph Slater; it bore the date 1816, when Clark would have been thirty-nine years old and already well established as chaplain of the Royal Military Asylum; he held this post with distinction for forty-four years in all. This engraved portrait was used as the frontispiece to *Sermons Preached in the Chapel of the Royal Military Asylum, Chelsea* by George Clark, posthumously published in 1872 by G. T. Clark, who wrote a sympathetic account of his father in the introduction.

To return to the sale catalogue, it contained also three Rudsdells, a family linked with the Clarks. The Revd George Clark was the surviving son of Joseph Clark and Sarah, only daughter of Jeremiah Rudsdell of Northampton, who came of a Yorkshire family of Puritan background. In the sale was a portrait of Ambrose Rudsdell, attributed to Gainsborough, which implied a sitter of consequence. Two portraits of 'J. Rudsdell', different sizes, artist not stated, may have shown Jeremiah Rudsdell, mentioned above, or alternatively a more famous J. Rudsdell: Sir Joseph Rudsdell, KCMG (1782/3–1871), an army officer who distinguished himself as chief secretary during the British occupation of the Ionian Islands. Local auction catalogues can be exasperating for their lack of precise detail!

The items mentioned above should be seen in the context of the whole picture collection offered for sale in 1922. There were 138 lots, mainly

30 Sitting room at 44 Berkeley Square, London, photographed probably in 1959, showing several of the Clark family portraits before their return to Talygarn.
English Heritage.

portraits, landscapes and still life. The portraits included Queen Elizabeth I of
England; Mary Tudor; Princess Elizabeth, daughter of James I of England,
later Queen of Bohemia; the King of Bohemia; Albert, Archduke of Austria,
and his wife; Charles I of England; and Catherine, Empress of Russia. With
nice impartiality, republican heads of state had been collected also: Oliver
Cromwell, George Washington and Benjamin Franklin. There were political
figures, such as Edmund Burke, Sir Robert Walpole and Lord Palmerston.
Clearly, these individuals were admired by the family. Among the artists cited
great names appear: Batoni, Beechey, Boucher, Gainsborough, Hogarth,
Hoppner, Janssens, Kneller, Lawrence, Lely, Reynolds, Rubens, Van Dyck,
Van Loo and Wilkie.

Landscapes and marine pictures numbered a couple of dozen, and included the inevitable Italian scenes, but, strangely, considering the apparent

quality of the portrait painters represented, there were no landscapes by Claude, Wilson or Sandby. One landscape had a Welsh subject: Kidwelly Castle, by 'H. Smythe', 1850. This artist's name may be misspelled and really represent the H. Smyth who made the drawings for eight of the views and plans of Kidwelly Castle which Clark used as illustrations for his admirable paper on that castle, published in *Archaeologia Cambrensis* in 1852.[23] There was a Kidwelly artist, Henry Smyth, who flourished *c.*1850, but little is known about him.[24] The engraver was John Henry Le Keux (1812–96), noted for architectural and antiquarian views; his father, John Le Keux, and his uncle, Henry Le Keux, also engraved similar subjects.

In the collection of oil paintings there were a few pictures on biblical themes – for example, 'Christ and the Woman of Samaria' – but listed under 'bedrooms' were numerous unidentified 'religious pictures', mainly prints. This point is interesting, because there was a strong religious tradition in the Clark family. The early diaries of G. T. Clark display both personal piety and a desire to make good, attitudes no doubt learned from his father.[25]

The forty-two lots of watercolour drawings and pastels made a miscellaneous assemblage, featuring a small number of obscure artists. There were many landscapes and topographical items, including two north Wales views by T. Sheraton (1865). The 111 lots of prints comprised portraits, landscapes and religious pictures, with an emphasis on historical and contemporary personalities. The Great and the Good of south Wales were well represented: Lord Tredegar, Dean Vaughan, the Marquess of Bute, Edward Pritchard, Christopher R. M. Talbot, Bishop Lewis of Llandaff and Lord Swansea. Famous female beauties had their place: Madame de Sévigné (coloured) and Mrs Siddons.

The accumulation of such a collection at Talygarn was partly a matter of convention, even of chance, but the choice of portraits in oils seemed to demonstrate artistic taste and discrimination; otherwise, interest was less defined. There were few specifically Welsh scenes. This huge quantity of pictures could more than fill the walls of Talygarn, and it should be remembered that much of the wall and ceiling space was already covered with 'built-in' decoration. Later generations of the family also had residences with their own picture collections, but no details are to hand.

The survey has so far accounted for Clark, Dicey and Rudsdell elements in the family collection, but an art historian might well ask why no Lewis portraits were acquired via G. T. Clark's wife. The Lewises of Greenmeadow were only a cadet branch of the Lewis family of the Van, and whatever portraits they held stayed at Greenmeadow. Even so, the full extent of that collection is not known because unfortunately most of it was destroyed in 1941 by fire due to enemy action. John Steegman, sometime keeper of art in the National Museum of Wales at Cardiff, recorded in *A Survey of Portraits in Welsh Houses*, only three Lewis portraits as 'formerly at Greenmeadow, Tongwynlais'.[26] The house itself has been demolished to make way for a housing estate. Those items are only of marginal interest to the present story: the earliest was of a young lady of the Lewis family of Llanishen, by an unknown artist, *c.*1740. Then came a father and son who both lived well into the twentieth century: Colonel Henry Lewis of Greenmeadow (1847–1925), painted by Oswald Birley in 1913,[27] and Captain Henry Lewis, formerly of Greenmeadow (1880–1956), painted by Louis William Desanges in 1900.[28] The former is shown as master of the Pentyrch Hounds, and the latter as an officer in the Royal Monmouthshire Engineers.

Portraits are a fragile asset in art and history. They are the first category of picture to be jettisoned when they cease to be of interest and relevance to their owners. They were often left unsigned and undated, their identities were easily lost – and often confused by later owners. Once parted from their original setting, they become flotsam on the art market, to be pur-chased cheaply as 'instant tradition' for country-house hotels. Among the Clark family portraits we rarely find the names of really famous portrait painters, but we do find an assemblage of paintings characteristic of many Welsh gentry houses, done by competent and respected artists. There is one difference: the Talygarn collection does not reach as far back in time as many others. Gentry portraits usually proclaimed their sitters' status and official *personae*; they were not intended to reveal an individual's innermost soul. The portrait of G. T. Clark by Henry Wyndham Phillips does show much of the humanity and personal character of the great man himself. His wife's image, on the other hand, is staid and enigmatic; the contrast between her modest pose and the elegant display of her daughter-in-law, Alice, could hardly be greater.

These images bring reality to the narrative of family history. The process of tracing the portraits has revealed a whole nexus of relatives, friends and business contacts linked with each individual portrayed, and has provided an insight into the social milieu in which the Clarks moved. Sadly, some interesting portraits which once belonged to the Clark family have dis-appeared untraced, but happily, the nucleus of the Talygarn collection has survived in good condition and is safely preserved in a place still accessible to the interested public.

APPENDIX: Catalogue of the Principal Portraits Discussed

Talygarn Collection

The painted portraits were recorded by Donald Moore in 1987 for the Welsh Portrait Archive of the National Library of Wales; the reference numbers apply to that archive.

The following abbreviations are used in the catalogue: H&S = head and shoulders; WL = whole length; TQL = three-quarter length; HL = half length; ns. = not signed; nd. = not dated; l. = left; r. = right; sgd. = signed; cm = centimetres; b. = born; d. = died; dau. = daughter; m. = married; s. = son; w. = wife; * = estimated measurement.

Oil paintings on canvas

1. GEORGE THOMAS CLARK, 1809–1898. *Henry Wyndham Phillips,* 1865/6. Date and artist confirmed by Clark's diary. 125.8 × 100.5 cm. TQL, seated, full-face with side-whiskers; wearing dark brown coat, blue waistcoat, grey trousers and cravat tied in bow; a letter in his l. hand. Two large books to l. NLW 0659

2. ANN PRICE (LEWIS), MRS CLARK, 1819–1885, w. of preceding. *Anon.,* nd, 120.2 × 86.5 cm. TQL, seated, full-face; wearing lace cap, black dress; a knitting needle in each hand and ball of wool on lap. NLW 0660

3. BLANCH LANCASTER (CLARK), later MRS FORESTIER-WALKER, 1851–1933, dau. of preceding. 110 × 84.4 cm. *Desiré Laugée* (mis-labelled 'Langet' on frame), *c.*1871. TQL, full-face; wearing light-blue dress trimmed with lace; holding closed fan. NLW 0661

4. GODFREY LEWIS CLARK, 1855–1918, brother of preceding. 135.6 × 90.2 cm, *Parker Hagarty,* 1919; sgd. & dated. TQL, standing, to l., walrus moustache; wearing suit, check waistcoat, wing-collar and cravat. NLW 0656

5. and 6. ALICE GEORGINA CAROLINE (STRONG), MRS CLARK, d. 1915, w. of preceding, and her fourth son, LIONEL CLARK, b. 1891. 196* × 130.6 cm. *Julian Russell Story,* [18]94 [label erroneously states 'Julian Strong']; sgd. & dated. She WL, seated in a park landscape, wearing long, light-blue dress, with hat and bunch of roses on lap. Child seated on pillar to r.; holding stick in his r. hand and ribbon or cord in l.; black labrador dog in foreground. NLW 0657

7. WYNDHAM DAMER CLARK, 1884–1961, son of preceding, aged 21. 200* × 104.4 cm. *Thomas Hasted Heath,* [1905]; sgd. WL, advancing to l., but full-face, with slight moustache; wearing officer's uniform of Coldstream Guards; sword at l. side. NLW 0658

8. Presumed ANN MARY (STEPHEN), MRS DICEY, 1796–1878, w. of Thomas Edward Dicey of Claybrooke Hall. 112* × 84.2 cm. Possibly by *Frank Dicey,* nd. TQL, seated, to r.; wearing black dress trimmed with lace, under red cloak; purse hanging from her r. wrist. NLW 0655

Sculptures

9. GEORGE THOMAS CLARK. Marble bust. 84 h. × 76 w. × 32 cm deep. *Joseph Edwards,* 1874. Date and sculptor's name incised on back. FSA after sitter's name. Head, with side-whiskers and moustache; 'toga' drapery. In entrance hall at Talygarn. NLW 0654

10. GEORGE THOMAS CLARK. Head, with moustache and side-whiskers, carved in high relief on square wooden panel, 23* × 23* cm, above fireplace in former billiard room at Talygarn. [*G. Biraghi*, installed 1895].

11. GEORGE THOMAS CLARK. Head, with moustache and side-whiskers, carved in low relief within medallion 14.5 cm diam. on wood panel, 31.5 × 30.5 cm, in corridor at Talygarn. [*G. Biraghi, c.*1885].

Cyfarthfa Castle Museum, Merthyr Tydfil

Sculpture

12. GEORGE THOMAS CLARK. Marble bust, 85 high × 65 wide × 37 cm deep. *Joseph Edwards.* Inscribed *verso* G. T. CLARK ESQRE F.S.A.&C./ commissioned / by the / Merthyr Tydvil / Board of Guardians./ Joseph Edwards, / Sculptor, / London, / 1872. Head, with side-whiskers and moustache; wearing 'toga' drapery.

Various sources

Photographs, drawings and prints

13. THE REVD SAMUEL CLARK (or CLARKE) (1599–1682), Minister of [St] Benet Fink and Vicar of Alcester. Three different but related portraits, all engraved prints:
(i) Frontis. to Samuel Clark's *The Marrow of Ecclesiastical Historie*, 1st edn., 1650. *Thomas Cross.* HL, seated at writing table, to r., short hair, moustache and pointed beard; wearing gown over open coat; broad collar; quill pen in his r. hand. Pillared arch above, with coat of arms in either spandrel and inscription *Aetatis suae 50 Octob: 10: 1649.* Verse below: 'All that thou sees't . . .' with *P. V. A. M. fecit.* Copies in BM, NPG, NLW.

(ii) Frontis. to *The Marrow*, 2nd edn., 1654. Same design and inscriptions, but sitter wearing skull cap; smaller moustache. Copies in BM, NPG, NLW.

(iii) Frontis. to *The Marrow*, 3rd edn., 1675. *John Dunstall*, nd. HL, not unlike two above, but face fuller, moustache and beard slighter. Wearing gown closely buttoned at front, smaller skull cap. No arch or pillars, but same two coats of arms on shaded background. Verse below: 'The skilfull Physiognomers . . .' with *J. C. A. M. fecit*. Copies in BM, NPG.

(iv) Other prints: *R. Gaywood*, HL, oval, and *R. White*, HL oval. Copies in BM, NPG.

See *Dictionary of British Portraiture*, i, 24; also for no. 14, below.

14. THE REVD SAMUEL CLARK (or CLARKE) (1626–1701), biblical commentator. Line engraving. *R. White*. HL oval. Copies in BM, NPG.

15. THE REVD GEORGE CLARK (1777–1848), Chaplain of the Royal Military Asylum, Chelsea. Frontis. to *Sermons Preached in the Chapel of the Royal Military Asylum*, ed. G. T. Clark (London, 1872). Vignette, 11 × 10 cm approx. H&S to r. clean-shaven, wearing gown and jabot. *William Holl, the elder* after *Joseph Slater*. 1816.

16. GEORGE THOMAS CLARK. Photographic print, 7 × 6 cm. *Arthur Pendarves Vivian*, 1854. HL, seated l., with side-whiskers; his r. hand on stomach; wearing coat, waistcoat and cravat tied in bow. NLW

17. GEORGE THOMAS CLARK. Lithograph in the *British Trade Journal*, 1 April 1877, with inscription below, 'INDUSTRIAL CELEBRITIES NO. 10', and sgd. 'Geo. T. Clark'. Vignette 13.5 × 12 cm. H&S, to r., with side-whiskers and moustache, wearing coat, waistcoat, shirt, high wing-collar and cravat tied in bow.

18. GEORGE THOMAS CLARK. Lithograph in drawn rectangle 35 × 28.8 cm, on card 56.5 × 47 cm. Sgd. 'G. T. Clark', bottom r., but no details of artist or publisher. Inscribed below: GEORGE THOMAS CLARK, TALYGARN, GLAMORGAN, with coat of arms in centre. H&S, full-face, with side-whiskers and moustache; hair parted on his l. Wearing coat, waistcoat, shirt, wing-collar and cravat tied in bow. GRO D/D Xee 2/1A

Same image, reduced, as frontispiece to Clark, *Cartae* (1910 edn.), in vignette, 14 × 12 cm.

19. GEORGE THOMAS CLARK as officer in Glamorgan Rifle Volunteers. Photograph. WL, full-face, with side-whiskers; in uniform, seated; sword across knees, plumed shako on sideboard to l. CCM

20. GEORGE THOMAS CLARK AND HIS MILITARY STAFF. Photograph. Clark seated at table, centre, with ten members of his unit grouped around, all in uniform; outside portico of Dowlais House, Merthyr Tydfil. GRO D/D G Ph 4/1

21. MRS GEORGE T. CLARK. Drawing in charcoal touched with white chalk in oval, 35.2 × 29.2 cm., on irregularly trimmed card. H&S, full-face, similar to painted portrait; wearing lace cap and collar. *Helen Shaw*; sgd. nd. GRO D/D Xee 2/1A

22. BLANCHE [*sic*] LANCASTER CLARK, age 18. Photograph, vignette on white ground, 9.2 × 5.6 cm, tinted, partly overpainted. *Dr Wallich*, 2 Warwick Gardens, Kensington, W., May 1869. H&S, to r. in profile, with jewelled ear-drop, collar buttoned up. NLW

23. GODFREY LEWIS CLARK. Photogravure print, 30.5 × 20.3 cm (image), sgd. *Parker Hagarty*, 1919; published by W.H. Beynon & Co., Cheltenham. TQL, standing l.; with moustache; wearing coat, check waistcoat and trousers. NLW

Talygarn sale catalogue, 1922

(Details as given by auctioneers, Gottwaltz & Perry, 11 High Street, Cardiff; all oil on canvas; lot numbers on right.)

24. MRS CLARA CLARK, *née* DICEY, 44″ × 31″, by Frank Dicey. 2034
25. MR and MRS GODFREY CLARK (a group), 45″ × 41″, by Phillips. 2040
26. SAMUEL CLARK, ESQ., 30″ × 25″, by Keelog [*sic*], 1669. 2032
27. EDWARD DICEY, ESQ., C.B., 15″ × 18½″, by Lauget [= Laugée]. 2038
28. MRS DICEY, 43″ × 32″, by Frank Dicey. 2035
29. THOMAS EDWARD DICEY, ESQ., of Claybrooke Hall, 23½″ × 19″. 1989 [A portrait of the above, 'After Raeburn', is owned by a descendant of G. T. Clark.]
30. AMBROSE RUDSDELL (HL), 30″ × 25″. *Gainsborough.* 2016
31. J. RUDSDELL, ESQ., 30″ × 24½″. 2036
32. J. RUDSDELL, ESQ., 11½″ × 9½″. 2037

Greenmeadow, Tongwynlais (portraits formerly at)

See John Steegman, *A Survey of Portraits in Welsh Houses*, ii (Cardiff, NMW, 1962), 103.

Acknowledgements

The author desires to express his thanks to all the other members of the G. T. Clark Centenary Commemoration Committee, especially the editor, Brian James, for their readiness to share information in a project which has called for great common effort. Thanks are also due to the Department of Pictures and Maps and the Department of Manuscripts and Records of the National Library of Wales, and to the Glamorgan Record Office for facilities afforded in the course of this research; to Dr T. F. Holley of Merthyr Tydfil for newspaper references.

Notes

[1] Personal communication from Derrick Kingham.

[2] Rupert Gunnis, *Dictionary of British Sculptors 1660–1851* (London, Abbey Library, 1968).

[3] Diary, 1872: NLW MS 15,006B; also the *Western Mail*, 2 September 1872.

[4] 1 April 1877, 198–9.

[5] Diary: NLW MS 15,005B.

[6] I am indebted to David Griffiths, portrait painter, of Cardiff, for comments on method.

[7] Diary: NLW MS 15,003B.

[8] U. Thieme and F. Becker (eds.), *Allgemeines Lexikon der bildenden Künstler*, xxvi (Leipzig, 1932).

[9] Diary: NLW MS 15,004B.

[10] 14 April 1877.

[11] George Clark, *Sermons Preached in the Chapel of the Royal Military Asylum, Chelsea* (London, 1872), introduction by G. T. Clark.

[12] Corresp. Glamorgan Rifle Volunteers, 1862–3. NLW MS 15,010E.

[13] Letter to Lord-Lieut. of Glamorgan, 10 October 1859. NLW ibid.

[14] Eira M. Smith, 'Mrs Clark of Dowlais', *Merthyr Historian*, 8 (1996), 213–18.

[15] E. Bénézit, *Dictionnaire des peintres, sculpteurs etc.* (Paris, Librairie Gründ, 1976), vi; Bryan's *Dictionary of Painters and Engravers* (London, Bell & Sons, 1930), iii. Laugée also painted a portrait of A. V. Dicey (1873), now at Trinity College, Oxford. Richard Ormond and Malcolm Rogers (eds.), *Dictionary of British Portraiture* (London, Batsford, 1979–81), iii, 55.

[16] Thieme and Becker (eds.), *Allgemeines Lexikon der bildenden Künstler*, xv (1922).

[17] J. Johnson and A. Grentzner, *Dictionary of British Artists 1880–1940* (Woodbridge, Antique Collectors Club, 1980).

[18] John Steegman, *A Survey of Portraits in Welsh Houses*, ii (Cardiff, National Museum of Wales, 1962), 224: Stanage Park.

[19] Johnson and Grentzner, *Dictionary*.

[20] *Arch. Camb.*, 94 (1939), 242–3: 'G. T. Clark Trust'.

[21] Burke's *Landed Gentry* (1871), 349.

[22] Thieme and Becker (eds.), *Allgemeines Lexikon der bildenden Künstler*, ix (1913).

[23] *Arch. Camb.*, NS 3 (1852), 1–20: 'Kidwelly Castle'.

[24] Hunt & Co., *Directory and Topography of the Towns of South Wales and Bristol* (London, 1850), 55, cited in Paul Joyner, *Artists in Wales c.1740–c.1851* (Aberystwyth, NLW, 1997).

[25] Diary, 26 September 1830, NLW MS 15,003B.

[26] Steegman, *A Survey of Portraits*, ii, 103: Greenmeadow.

[27] Christopher Wood, *Dictionary of British Artists*, iv (Woodbridge, Antique Collectors Club, 1995); also Bénézit, *Dictionnaire*, iii.

[28] G. Meissner (ed.), *Allgemeines KünstlerLexikon*, xi (Munich, K. G. Sauer, 1995). .

CHAPTER 9

Clark of Talygarn

DERRICK C. KINGHAM

Talygarn is famous throughout the south Wales valleys as a convalescent home and rehabilitation centre where, since 1923, many thousands of miners have been restored to fitness and health following accident and injury at work. But the 'dominant figure at Talygarn'[1] is George Thomas Clark who, in the latter part of the nineteenth century, created there a great house and garden which remain of outstanding interest and beauty.

On Tuesday, 4 July 1922 at the Park Hotel, Cardiff, 'the TAL-Y-GARN ESTATE – comprising Tal-y-garn Mansion and the Freehold Estate approaching in extent 1,200 acres' – was offered for sale by auction by Messrs Gottwaltz and Perry of 11 High Street, Cardiff. To quote from the catalogue:

TAL-Y-GARN MANSION is situate about a mile from Llantrisant Station on the London and South Wales Branch of the Great Western System, the estate being contiguous to and for the most part south of Pont-y-clun, a part of the historical parish of Llantrisant, within and near to which are the many richly mineralised areas for which Glamorgan is famous, its situation being in direct touch with the well-known Ely Coal Valley just now in the early stages of development.

IT has been the County Seat of the Vendor's family since the beginning of the latter half of the Nineteenth Century, their predecessor in occupation being the late Dr Lyle. Very extensive and costly additions were effected by the late Mr George Thomas Clark, and ever since, the comfort of the Mansion and the beauty of its surroundings have been more than maintained.

IT REPOSES on an elevated position in the midst of exceedingly choice specimens of Ornamental Timber in association with delightfully pictur-esque Pleasure Grounds and Gardens containing beautiful examples of Flowering Shrubs, all giving in their season a perfect wealth of bloom, the

31 Talygarn: the south front, seen from near the lake. The tall building left of centre is the water tower. Photograph, *c.1922*. *Glamorgan Record Office.*

Lake below, nearly Eight Acres in extent, bordered with Rhododendrons, affording from the South Front an enchanting view.

George Thomas Clark had acquired the 'Mansion' from Dr Lisle's daughter, Miss Frances Lisle – the catalogue spelling of the name is incorrect – in 1865, and until his death in 1898 had been enlarging and decorating the house, improving the gardens and enlarging the estate. His son, Godfrey Lewis Clark, maintained the house and added to the estate but his grandson, Wyndham Damer Clark, who inherited when Godfrey died in 1918, decided to sell.

Before Clark there had been Dr Lisle, and before him a succession of owners of both lordship and house reaching back to the fourteenth century and possibly earlier. It is clear that the descent of the lordship and the house were quite separate; in other words, Talygarn Fawr was not the manor house. Talygarn is listed with other lordships in the Statute of 27 Henry VIII (1535/6) creating the shire of Glamorgan. It belonged to the lords of Afan in 1340 and possibly earlier. The ultimate heiress of the lordship whom we can identify in the Welsh pedigrees was Elizabeth, daughter of William Mathew

32 Talygarn: the north front. Photograph, *c.*1922. *Glamorgan Record Office.*

of Llantrithyd, probably as part of her marriage settlement. By 1595 the lordship had been sold, and sometime before 1705 came into the possession of the Jenkinses of Hensol, from whom it descended to the Talbots. It was finally bought by G. T. Clark in the late nineteenth century, and he became the first resident lord of Talygarn.

The medieval family owning the house, Talygarn Fawr, were cousins of Llywelyn ap Cynwrig, lord of Radyr, the great Welsh magnate of Meisgyn. The family continued at Talygarn for 300 years, ending in the heiress Ann David, who married John Price Meyrick who died in 1617. Her son, David Price Meyrick, still owned Talygarn in 1653. It then passed through various hands – in George Clark's words, it 'fell into the hands of farmers' – until in 1817 or 1818 Thomas Popkin sold it to Dr Lisle.[2]

The Revd Dr William Berkin Meackham Lisle was an interesting but difficult man, often at odds with his bishop. He became rector of St Fagans in 1792, a benefice he held until his death at the age of 90 in 1856, having been the longest serving rector in the history of the parish. Soon after 1792 he became also the vicar of Llanishen, a living he soon exchanged for the more lucrative one of Llantilio Pertholey in Monmouthshire, which he again held until his death. He was a prebendary of Llandaff Cathedral. Over the years he appears to have performed few duties in any of these parishes. He

33 Talygarn: part of the south front, showing the conservatory or winter garden. Photograph, *c*.1922. *Glamorgan Record Office.*

was, it seems, employing curates at a pittance to undertake his duties while he lived in comfortable circumstances at Talygarn, the cause of some of his difficulties with the bishop.

He had bought Talygarn as a summer residence but was soon living there more or less permanently and farming on a large scale. He was a man of large private means who, when he first went to Talygarn, found the roads in the district 'unfit for a gentleman's carriage' and had them widened and signposts erected. He improved the house at Talygarn including the building of a single-storey extension on the west end. He was eccentric and was said to have kept his room temperature always at 90°F; local tradition has it that he was a poisons expert who kept a snakepit at Talygarn to house his deadly reptiles.[3] Sometime before his death he returned to the rectory which he had built at St Fagans when he first went there. He died at St Fagans in 1856 and is buried in the churchyard there. After the death of Mrs Lisle at Talygarn in 1861 their only surviving child, Frances Ann, went to live in Bristol and the house remained empty and neglected.

This, then, was the Talygarn first seen by George Thomas Clark in 1865. He was in his fifty-seventh year, had already had more than one successful career and was then living in Dowlais House as the resident trustee of the

Dowlais Iron Company. He had been seeking a country estate for some years, and friends had kept him informed of what properties were available – Miskin in 1858, St Donats in 1861, Sant-y-Nyll in 1864, Cottrell and Talygarn in 1865. There was, it seems, a dispute between Clark and his friend John Bruce-Pryce who both wanted Talygarn – Bruce-Pryce for his son, the Revd William Bruce of Bath. Bruce-Pryce advised Clark to buy Cottrell, 'the most desirable estate in Glamorganshire', but Clark it was who acquired Talygarn.[4]

Towards the end of his life Clark set down a detailed and probably chronological account of how he came to purchase Talygarn and the alterations which he had made to both house and gardens. This is quoted extensively in an unpublished document, a copy of which is in the South Wales Miners' Library at the University of Wales Swansea. On it is a note that it was written by 'Ronald F. – finished end Sept. 1959'. This was Ronald Frankenberg, the social anthropologist, who was at that date Education Officer for the South Wales Area of the National Union of Mineworkers. Clearly the G. T. Clark notes were available to him, and I have used his version of them extensively.[5]

When I purchased Talygarn, seen for the first time 6th May and purchased July 1st 1865, for, I think, £7,600, I found myself in possession of a queer, rambling sort of house, and about 300 acres, more or less, of land about it. The house had been the manor house of the ancient lordship of Talygarn mentioned in the Act of 26 or 28 Henry VIII, constituting the county, and after many changes of hands, had fallen into the hands of farmers, and finally had been purchased and patched up by Dr Lisle, who had added to its West end a block about 54ft. square of a ground floor only, containing four rooms of equal size, divided by a passage, and now represented by a dining room and pantry on one side and the two libraries on the other side, divided as before by a passage somewhat widened.

The house was in poor condition.

The kitchen and offices occupied a sort of East Wing, on the ground, above which, in the roof were many very poor attics. The only water supply was from an open and rather dangerous well, 100 ft deep in the limestone rock, placed just outside the backdoor. In it were the broken remains of a hand forcing pump, superseded by a winch with a rope and bucket. There was an imperfect attempt at a water-closet, and the kitchen and offices were of a wretched description, and the whole place permeated by damp, rising from the foundations and leaking through the roof, partly thatched.

This is Clark's own description. It is not the sort of place one would have expected this man to live in, but he knew what he was doing, and he must have appreciated the potential of the site.

> I mended and patched up the place and made it water-tight, if not damp proof and furnished it from a shop in Saint Augustine's Back, Bristol at a cost of about £1,500 2nd July, 1865. Any further outlay for some years was upon the land. I built somewhat expensive farm buildings, and drained several fields all of which I might have spared for all the good it did.
> I also planted rather largely about the house, chiefly foreign conifers and with great success, for they grew wonderfully. Slept there for the first time 11th October, 1865.

He visited the place every twelve or fourteen days; now and then his wife went with him. Sometimes he slept there 'but we kept no establishment; only a gardener and his wife, who lived in the house'. At last their visits became more frequent, and

> we decided to build, though slowly and by degrees. The walls were mostly thick, but not much above six to eight feet high; but seemed strong enough to bear any reasonable weight. I began with the old clock tower, taking off the roof and raising the walls to about forty feet high. In the top storey was placed an iron water tank, at a level to supply the future house. I also fixed a small steam pumping engine near the brook, and laid a main to the water tower, the lift being about 140 feet. This was completed in 1870, and in the following year the interior of the tower was fitted up in floors and a staircase laid.

Clark, at this point, was looking ahead to the building or rebuilding of Talygarn, but there is some suggestion that he was not quite ready to begin. Some years passed before any major alterations took place, and there may indeed be some correlation between the profitable years of the Dowlais works and the intensive periods of development at Talygarn.[6] It was not until the 1880s that he made it his permanent home. As late as 1877 he still regarded Dowlais as his main residence. On 6 January of that year, the *Merthyr Express*, reporting an inquiry into the incorporation of Merthyr Tydfil, quotes him as saying:

> I do reside at Dowlais. I am not here every day of my life it is true. I have a house down in this county . . . but I don't suppose I have slept in it 50 times. I have a house in London too, and may for the last few years have occupied it for three weeks in the year. I am a regular attendant of the

34 Talygarn: part of the south front.
Photograph, 1922, published in the sale catalogue.

Board of Guardians, and whatever business I may have in London or elsewhere I generally manage to be down on Friday for the School Board, and for the Guardians on Saturday. Dowlais is my home, and I always consider it so. I am sure I am perfectly right in saying that I live at Dowlais House, and nowhere else.

Was he exaggerating? He may have been, to make his point, but clearly Talygarn was not yet his main home.

Meanwhile, at Talygarn, work continued.

It was not, till October 1877, that I removed the old Vinery and began the further limb of the new conservatory. The square pavilion at the angle was completed in about six months. In December was laid the foundation of the new kitchen, and the well was closed, the dome resting upon the limestone rock. And as the roof of the four living rooms let in water, and I proposed being much on the spot while building, I reslated the roof temporarily.

In July, 1878, finding the bricks of the water tower spongy and damp I painted the two exposed on the North and West fronts, though without much advantage. In February 1879, I laid out the flower garden anew in the two levels divided by a dwarf wall with two flights of steps. Also the billiard room was begun and six months later the window frames fixed in that and Blanch's room above. May 6th 1879 opened the new entrance from the high road, and planted a band on each side of it. In this year also began the hall, boudoir, drawing room and staircase, all on new ground. The old front door stood where now is the small store room. Also was begun the new front door, and the entrance lobby and gallery.

This year, 1879, was the beginning of the great period of activity which entirely transformed the house. Clark was seventy years old but there was no lack of energy and enthusiasm. He had owned Talygarn for fourteen years, during which he must have been planning the direction in which he wanted ultimately to go.

'In April, 1880, the timber ribs of the hall roof were fixed, and in June the slates were on, and the boards laid for the slating of the great bedroom, dressing and bath rooms, and the staircase.' There are stories locally that the staircase and the suite of rooms above were built for a proposed visit by the Prince of Wales, later Edward VII, that never actually took place. Clark himself never mentions this and there is no confirmation elsewhere, but the great bedroom was always a very grand room: there is an old photograph showing a very large four-poster bed with fine tapestries on the walls. Intriguingly, the staircase, now usually called the 'grand' staircase, was also known as the 'royal' staircase and a generation later Viviane, wife of Wyndham Damer Clark, calls it the 'state' staircase. But by this time the great bedroom had, according to Viviane Clark, become the *spare* bedroom!

We know that the timber ribs of the hall roof were made at Merthyr Tydfil, so Clark was obviously making use of carpenters and other craftsmen at the Dowlais works. This is confirmed by the finding in recent years of a timber support to one of the built-in bookcases in the former drawing room bearing the pencil inscription 'Wm Lewis, Alma Street, Dowlais, June 27, 1883'.

Clark brought John Jones, the foreman of the joinery shop at the Dowlais works, to Talygarn to superintend his building work. Jones, who as a young man had come from Carmarthenshire in 1852, had been there to greet Mr and Mrs Clark when they moved into Dowlais House in 1856. His work was commemorated later by Godfrey L. Clark in a small window in the hall at Talygarn. The *Merthyr Express* of 7 September 1918, reporting his recent death 'at the advanced age of 91 years', also recalls that 'the building of Talygarn Church was completed under the superintendence of the deceased who was thought so highly of by Mr [G. T.] Clark that he had his name in conjunction with his own placed on the corner stone of the building'.[7]

In 1880 also

the old kitchens and offices were unroofed and part of the wall preserved in a new servants hall lobby at the base of the small tower, housekeepers room, larder and small dairy. The hall was floored and glazed and the large fireplace built. The woodwork was by Howard of Berners St., the upper stage copied from a drawing of a tomb at Assisi supplied by me. The parquet, also by Howard, was laid in the drawing room bay and in some other places, and two mosaic slabs were laid as sills before the two door windows of the drawing room. The three Verona marble chimney pieces are by Terrazzi of Verona, and the drawing room doors by Cortelazzo of Vicenza.

In 1882 the entrance lobby and gallery were floored and glazed, the front door made here, fixed, and the old stables removed, and the space walled in as part of the kitchen-garden. A little later the laundry was built, and still later the dairy, a large tank underlying the floor, and a similar tank of iron placed in the roof. Between the dairy and the house are two underground tanks, part of the old house.

In this year too the two towers were completed, the back staircase laid, and the old clock furbished up was fixed in the great tower.

This clock is interesting, made by a Cornish clockmaker in the previous century and obviously at Talygarn before Clark. A brass plate bearing the maker's name and date was fixed to the clock when I first saw it, but it has now gone as a result of some petty vandalism. It is presumably the clock from the former clock tower which Clark transformed into the water tower to supply his new house. No one can be sure who built the original clock tower, but it is shown on the 1841 tithe map for the parish of Llantrisant.

The clock is still in the tower and the present writer had it working once, and the bell on top of the tower, which I believe is still there, wired up. Unfortunately, the two distinguished amateur clock repairers, who went round restoring interesting old clocks in their spare time, moved away before the work was finished. Interestingly, commenting on the installation of the clock and the bell striking mechanism, they said that this was not clockmaker's but very definitely engineer's work.

The interior decorations were completed very leisurely. The carved wood generally was from Venice, and the balusters were copied from those in the old house at Margam, of which Mr Talbot lent me one. The veneered panels are mostly my own work, as are a great number of small tables here and in London. The drawing room chimney-piece in white marble is from Sinclair in Wardour Street, that in the entrance gallery in carved wood is

35 Talygarn: part of the south front. A postcard, date unknown.
Madame Alys Cattoir-Clark.

Italian, and that in my library old English, both purchased in London. The tiles in the entrance lobby and conservatory and the two battle-pieces are from Giustiniani of Naples, bought when I was there with Talbot.

The three painted ceilings in the drawing-room, boudoir and lobby were done at Venice, the fixing and gilding by Newton of London, and the frames cast in plaster from those in my small sitting room in London. Two badly veneered doors came from Dowlais House, and the four, if not six square pieces of needlework and the coverlet for the best bedroom are all by a lady of Milan. The two drawing-room doors and doorcases are by Cortelazzo of Vicenza – those of the boudoir and hall were made and veneered on the premises, and the others were from Gloucester . . . The woodwork of the drawing room and the carved panelling throughout was by Biraghi, as was the staircase. The actual panelling was done at Gloucester – the plain panels at home. The bookcases were made at Merthyr and Gloucester.

Previous owners may have had gardens at Talygarn – Dr Lisle certainly did – but of these there is now no trace. Dr Lisle was a known tree enthusiast and although he may have planted some specimen trees his contribution was mostly 'plantation planting' to protect his crops and vines from the easterly winds. Clark planted trees early on. In 1877 he removed Dr Lisle's old vinery and built a conservatory. When in May 1879 he made the new drive from the high road he planted bands of trees on either side. It has been said

166

36 Talygarn: the terraces, the south front in the background, the water tower on the extreme right. A postcard, date unknown. *Madame Alys Cattoir-Clark.*

that if his tree-planting had been properly maintained in later years Talygarn could have rivalled the arboretum at Westonbirt.

It may be noted here that G. T. Clark was well known in horticultural circles. At Dowlais House he grew pineapples in his glasshouses. A letter from Lady Aberdare, dated 25 June 1874, thanked him for two splendid pines – 'they look as only South Wales pines can look!' She was keeping them for a party the following night. At Talygarn, Clark grew vines and bananas. His garden and farm account books were meticulously kept and every detail recorded. Clark received bulbs from friends on their travels, for instance Sir Bartle Frere sent bulbs from the Cape, and Clark in turn forwarded some of this consignment to the Royal Horticultural Society for their collection.

Clark was elected to the Council of the RHS on 10 February 1876, and on 1 March of the same year became one of its vice-presidents, a position which he held for ten years until 9 February 1886. He attended the fortnightly Council meetings regularly and was in the chair on a number of occasions, but does not seem to have had an input into any particular aspect of horticulture. The principal reason for his election appears to have been to take advantage of his financial abilities.[8]

'It was in 1882', Clark continues, 'that the new rockwork was begun, and, I think, soon after the lodge built (by 1888), and the gate piers and gates completed – and Poplars Cottage was almost entirely rebuilt, and finally Hirst was put into it.' Matthew Hirst (1825–99) was headmaster of the

37 Aerial photograph of Talygarn, 1974. *East Glamorgan NHS Trust.*

schools at Dowlais founded by the Guests and supported by Clark; he mentions Hirst again later. 'Also the Cot was rebuilt and the garden then laid out, and Mr and Mrs Sheppeard lodged there. Also a double and rather expensive cottage was built below the stable yard, and the coachman lodged there.' That double cottage has now become two very desirable semi-detached residences with a fine coat of arms above one of the front doors!

A road was then made down to and across the dam – the ground beyond the water had been long planted and was doing well. Somewhere about this time the small field North of the house was excavated as a lower lawn, and laid out to grass with a fountain in the centre, and banks of earth on the North and West sides – thickly planted with flowering shrubs and herbaceous plants.

In 1893 the rose garden was made at the base of the water tower. This involved much earthwork, excavating below and filling above, and masonry for relaying wall and cut stone for the belt for the balustrade. Also a platform was made for tea drinking, and the iron gratings made especially at Venice and two doors were fitted into the spaces of the verandah of the water tower. Also I had designed and cast a large leaden tank, the idea from one of St. Fagan's – in the middle of the rose garden. While this was being done we began upon the lake, for which see the water supply.

38 Talygarn: the drawing room. Photograph, 1922, published in the sale catalogue.

The 'tea platform' can still be identified on the south lawn, near the site of the water tower. The late Sir Cennydd Traherne remembered as a child coming to Talygarn – in a pony and trap – to visit the Clark children and having tea, brought out to the tea platform by the butler, on a silver tray. The water tower was demolished after the 1939–45 war, but is clearly seen in old photographs. Some of the iron gratings may now be in use as gates. The leaden tank is probably the one which appears on later photographs on the north front of the house and which was also removed after the war.

> The white and gold furniture in the drawing-room came from Dijon, the mirror frames from there and from Lausanne (when I was there with Wimborne and his daughter). The bookcases came from Merthyr, the ornamental cupboards for china from Venice. The foundations of the square pavilion in which the conservatory ends were laid, and a large underground tank, from about 1884, and the superstructure added about 1890 – the workshop also was an addition.

The magnificent conservatory was another casualty of the post-war period. It had by that time deteriorated badly and was pulled down to be

39 Talygarn: the boudoir. Photograph, 1922, published in the sale catalogue.

rebuilt and used as a gymnasium for the miners' rehabilitation centre. It was later known as the Winter Garden and is still called that. Old photographs show the exterior in the later Clarks' time and some from the early and mid-1920s show, with its iron columns, the interior apparently little changed.

The North Lawn was originally too narrow; it was widened about 1875, and soon after the stone balustrade fixed – then many years later about 1879 the field beyond which had been enclosed in a belt of trees, was excavated to an equal depth of about six feet, and laid out as a square lawn with a central basin, and afterwards the semi-circular seats added in Ham Hill Stone. The brick wall was finally completed about 1880, and the slope forming the two sides of the lawn were planted with shrubs. A walk had already been laid out enclosing the field at the top . . . and in 1882, north of this a road was laid out, by which carts could carry plants and soil to the slopes and to the north walk.

After Clark's wife Ann died, on 6 April 1885, his son Godfrey and his family came to live with him. Clark notes this by saying: 'Soon after my wife's death when Godfrey and his family came to reside with me, the attics

40 Talygarn: the gallery. Photograph, *c.*1922. *Glamorgan Record Office.*

41 Talygarn: the tapestry bedroom. Photograph, *c*.1922. *Glamorgan Record Office.*

in the roof were fitted up as bedrooms and very many alterations made so as to give separate rooms to Mrs Godfrey and the children, both sitting and sleeping.'

Work continued downstairs and in the grounds. Clark was using two rooms on the north side of the Lisle extension as libraries to house his vast collection of books and 'in 1892–93 the two libraries were doubled in area by throwing forward the wall into the north lawn, also the entrance lodge was built, and the pair of wrought iron gates from Venice were hung, and two stone piers built copied from a house in Somersetshire'. It is unlikely that the present gates are the original Venetian ones. The stone piers are new, recently rebuilt after being demolished by a large lorry, but to the same design and in the same kind of stone.

He mentions again the large double cottage which was built below the stables,

with bow windows and the walls of the upper floor covered with red tiles. Also, before this a large house had been built for the gardener and Poplar cottage was repaired and re-roofed, for Mr Hirst and his wife. Hirst was schoolmaster at Dowlais, now retired with a pension. We gave him the house and garden free, and he gave an hour or two in the morning to Wyndham in arithmetic and reading and English.

The new church has been built and called St. Ann's in memory of my wife, the churchyard doubled in area. The old church or chapel is preserved and used as a Sunday School.

In 1894 I built a new and large billiard room below the conservatory. It is about 40 × 24ft with a large bay window and two other windows connected with it is a smaller window[9] in which Alice intends to receive her school children.

Clark's notes, as far as they survive, end with his last addition: 'November 1895, billiard room and adjacent room nearly finished and two-thirds of the woodwork came from Venice' – again the work of G. Biraghi who had done so much wonderful work throughout the house.

'Talygarn', according to John Newman, 'is unique in the county. So too was its owner, for Clark, industrialist and architectural historian, was also Glamorgan's only Victorian amateur architect.' Clark had created a house 'on an astonishing scale and its internal decoration takes the breath away'.[10] The gardens were also very fine. Old photographs show how magnificent they were, with lawns sweeping down to the lake and pathways lined with fine shrubs. Game abounded on the estate – partridge, pheasant, hare, woodcock, snipe and wild duck. Only one thing was missing. On 1 January 1881 Clark's brother wrote from Pembroke wondering if he would like to have some peafowl to give the place a 'baronial aspect', but there is no evidence that the offer was ever taken up.

How then did Clark and his Talygarn home appear to others at that time? On 23 April 1887, David Jones of Wallington called on Clark. He had arrived at Llantrisant Station – which was actually in Pontyclun – and walked the mile or so to Talygarn. Leaving his small portmanteau at the Lodge, he walked along the old private road to the house which, he said, had 'been much enlarged and is a huge nondescript place, having that irregularity about it purposely designed to give the idea of being a sort of ancient castle adapted somehow to modern requirements'. He was admitted through 'a series of irregular corridors' to what he supposed to be Mr Clark's private room. Clark shortly came in and Jones describes him as 'a man approaching 80 showing his age but he is still active and with a mind possessing great energy. His head is large and massive – plenty of grey hair, a shaggy beard and immense projecting eyebrows nearly white but with a few intensive black hairs amongst them.'

David Jones stated directly the object of his visit whereupon, he says, Clark 'fired up'.

Indeed, there was a perfect explosion of temper when he knew that I had a genealogical question to put. Was he a herald that people should pester him in that way? Shoals of letters came down upon him, and that was bad enough. But to call upon him, that was an *impertinence* . . . beyond all endurance.

Clark in his old age had become rather deaf and David Jones found it difficult to enter upon his exculpation but at last managed to make him understand that before venturing to call upon him he had consulted a mutual acquaintance and on hearing this Clark became interested in what Jones had to say. After discussing the subject of the interview, the Morgan family, George Clark said that his own late wife was a Morgan heiress – the heiress of Morgan of Rhiwbina. He showed Jones the Lewis shield, of which family she was a member, in which the Morgan arms were quartered. The interview then terminated and Clark showed David Jones to the door, they shook hands and he departed.[11]

David Jones had visited Llantwit Major to stay with the Nicholls some eighteen months earlier, in 1885, and had been told about Clark by his hosts.

By some means or other he has accumulated a large fortune – he is quite a millionaire they say . . . This new house [Talygarn] is of his own designing, nondescript as to its style, very large, very costly and very extraordinary. While at Dowlais he used to travel on the continent a good deal every summer and was always on the look out for rare and costly old carvings and sculptured masonry suitable for the fittings of a house or even a palace, and before he began building had accumulated a large store of this sort of material. Two of the principal rooms are decorated in this way so sumptuously that an architect of repute who went over the house lately estimated the cost of decorating the two rooms at £20,000 . . .

The effect on the whole was said to be bizarre rather than pleasing, while the arrangements were anything but convenient. But,

as long as Mr Clark is pleased, he having to pay the piper, no one else need find fault and he it seems is not only satisfied with his house and skill in designing but is actually proud of it. Every one knows that among archaeologists he stands in the front rank as an authority on castramentation; it is to be suspected that his skill in 'reconstructing' medieval buildings has carried him away from nineteenth century conveniences and requirements and developed a fondness for designing 'passages that lead to nowhere' which appears to be one of the characteristics of his new house.[12]

St Ann's church must be mentioned here; it is part of the history of 'Clark of Talygarn'. His wife, Ann Price Clark, had died in London in 1885 and her body was brought to Talygarn and buried in the churchyard of the old chapel on the other side of the road from Pontyclun to Cowbridge. David Jones of Wallington said that Clark had intended to 'beautify the chapel or perhaps rebuild it'[13] in her memory. Instead he built a completely new church. There had been a chapel of ease on the site since medieval times. Sir Leoline Jenkins, said to have been born nearby at Tŷ Ffald, had, according to the inscription above the outer vestry door, restored the chapel in 1687. In addition, Dr Lisle had rebuilt the south wall which had collapsed when he was at Talygarn.

Although it was Ann's death which made Clark decide to build the church when he did, he must have had it in mind as soon as he came to Talygarn, because on 8 May 1868 the *Bridgend Chronicle* had reported that Talygarn church had been repaired, the clergyman, the Revd R. H. Jones, provided with a new surplice and that 'Mr G. T. Clark intends soon building a new church at Talygarn'. The church was designed by Clark himself in 1887, but John Newman is not impressed – 'the overall effect, it must be admitted, is inartistic'.[14] An 'engineer's building', perhaps.

Clark's activities often figured in newspaper reports. On 22 April 1887, the *Glamorgan Gazette* reported that 'Mr G. T. Clark left Talygarn for his London seat, which he purchased of a nobleman a few years ago. He has taken his horses and carriage and 15 servants and will stay there for three months returning home in the first week of August.' The fact that he took so many servants probably indicates that he intended to do a lot of entertaining. This was the year of Queen Victoria's Golden Jubilee and London would have been full of foreign royalty and other important visitors and Clark, one supposes, was not one to miss an opportunity to further his business interests.

Later that year (on 11 November 1887) the same newspaper reported that

Mr G. T. Clark has returned to Talygarn after a stay at his London house. He will superintend some improvements and the formation of two carriage drives which will give employment to workmen for some time to come. A handsome pair of carriage horses has been purchased by Thomas Phillips, the Talygarn coachman. They were bought in London and cost 300 guineas. They are very much admired.[15]

Clark apparently remained well and active and improving his garden. On 8 March 1890, in his eighty-first year, he wrote to Lord Aberdare: 'I am enjoying the *soft* rain, which is pouring life into my fresh-planted evergreens, and water into my new tank. A touch of April is that, but the wind is high and quite worthy of March.'[16] In September of the same year, his old friend Lady Charlotte Schreiber accepted his invitation and spent a few days with him in Talygarn.[17] Five years later Lord Aberdare came to stay at Talygarn. In a letter to his son-in-law, he gave a rare picture of the aging Clark. 'Here I am with one of the oldest and most intimate of my living friends, reviving the fast-fading past of our joint lives. At eighty-five, though deaf and infirm of foot, his intellect is as clear, his memory as fresh, his sense of humour and power of language as keen as they were forty years since.'[18]

George Thomas Clark died at Talygarn on 31 January 1898 in his eighty-ninth year. He had apparently been unwell for a few days but had been working in his library earlier in the day. He was buried in St Ann's (now St Anne's) churchyard with his wife. The cast-iron plaque, presumably added later and entirely appropriate for an engineer and ironmaster, records simply: 'Here lies all that is mortal of George Thomas Clark and his wife Ann Price Clark'. The memorial tablet inside the church is presumably how the family saw him at the time:

> In memory of George Thomas Clark of Talygarn. High Sheriff for Glamorgan in 1867. For many years Resident Trustee of the Dowlais Iron Works, which attained under his direction to a high degree of prosperity. He took a leading part in establishing the Volunteer Forces in Wales, and was Colonel of the 2nd Battalion of the Glamorgan Rifles. He was an eminent Antiquarian and a high authority on Archaeological subjects. Born 26th May 1809. Died 31st January 1898.

He was survived by his daughter, Blanch Lancaster Clark, who had married Clarence Forestier-Walker of Castleton in Monmouthshire, and by his son, Godfrey Lewis Clark, who inherited the estate. Godfrey had his own career, not in his father's field of iron and steel but as chairman of the Rhymney Railway Company and in local government, in Llantrisant and Pontypridd, where he was chairman of the Rural District Council and the Board of Guardians. His wife, Alice, daughter of Henry Linwood Strong, died in 1915; Godfrey survived her by three years, dying on 8 February 1918.

Talygarn then passed to Godfrey's eldest son, Wyndham Damer Clark, who, faced with the problem of increased taxation and death duties, decided to live in London. In 1921 he moved his wife and young family to the beautiful William Kent house at 44 Berkeley Square which had been acquired on a long lease by G. T. Clark some half a century earlier. The sale of 440 outlying acres in Llanishen and Lisvane, mostly inherited from the Lewises,[19] followed very quickly after G. L. Clark's death, and in 1922

Talygarn itself, with its contents and 1,200 acres of land, was put up for auction. The mansion and estate that G. T. Clark had so keenly built up thus passed out of the ownership of his family after only two generations.

The contents of the house were disposed of at a massive sale in 1922 – it was scheduled for ten days and went on for twelve. The catalogue of the sale lists the collections of paintings, silver, porcelain, armour, fine furniture and thousands of books put together mainly by George Clark. It can also be read as something of a social document. After the finest furniture and works of art had been sold, the remaining contents were listed and sold room by room, from the fine, sumptuously furnished principal rooms to the attic servants' quarters where, in the maids' rooms, there were often just a bed and a chair and, perhaps, a small cupboard or chest of drawers.

Later in the same year the entire Talygarn estate was put up for auction. Many of the farms and estate houses were sold but the house and gardens did not find a buyer until 1923 when they were acquired by the South Wales Miners' Welfare Committee at a cost of £20,000; Talygarn would achieve further distinction as the miners' convalescent home and later as a rehabilitation centre for mineworkers. That the miners of the time appreciated the magnificence and beauty of the property they had acquired is shown by articles in the *Colliery Workers' Magazine* by the Right Hon. Thomas Richards and Oliver Harris. Tom Richards, general secretary of the South Wales Miners' Federation, said: 'surrounding the building are 140 acres of woodland, lawns, gardens, lakes, conservatories and shaded walks, while to look in any direction is to see a prospect that is pleasing, beautiful and restful'.[20] Harris describes the

> beautifully carved wainscotting around the walls of some of the rooms and the halls, and the finely carved mantelpieces . . . the exquisite Venetian candelabra, and the painted ceilings . . . Some of the tapestry on the walls is pure silk, and that in the room known as the Tapestry Room on the first floor is a revelation, both in texture and design, of the art of the weaver; the whole must have cost an immense sum of money, but the general effect produced is certainly something that is seldom seen in private houses.[21]

Later generations of the Clarks

This chapter has been primarily an account of G. T. Clark and Talygarn. He is buried with his wife across the way in St Anne's churchyard. Godfrey Clark and Alice are buried nearby in the family vault. Blanch, who lived until 1933, is also buried there. Nearby is the small grave of Godfrey's second son, Jocelyn, who died in 1889 aged three and a half years. The present family members are now scattered and none of them lives in Wales, although they retain an interest in property in Cardiff. They are very much aware of their distinguished ancestor, and it was pleasant to see so many of them at the commemoration service in Talygarn church and the garden party at Talygarn House on 23 May 1998.

Godfrey Lewis Clark had four sons, Wyndham Damer, Jocelyn George Erskine (who died in infancy), Godfrey Henry Jocelyn and Lionel Clement Erskine. Wyndham Damer Clark, the last of the family at Talygarn, married in 1912 Viviane Margaret Nellie Bourke and they had four children: Everid Viviane, born in 1913; Delia Alys, 1915; George Hubert Wyndham, 1917; and Juliet Ann Gertrude, 1919. Viviane's book, *Early Memories*, privately printed by W. D. Clark in 1960, is a fascinating look at her early life before she married Wyndham and came to Talygarn. It is dedicated 'To Everid, Delia, George and Juliet from Their Mother. I have started this book to tell you a little of what times were like when I was young. It may amuse you, or it may bore. Then throw away this book. V.C.'

Everid married, in 1940, Joseph John Gurney of Northrepps Hall in Norfolk, then a captain in the Welsh Guards. In recent years, a chance meeting with the writer, Verily Anderson, brought me into contact with her cousin Joe Gurney and his brother Anthony who, after Everid's early and tragic death in 1956, had kept in close contact with her brother George. This in turn led me to George's son, Guy, who lives in Scotland and has been very interested in and supportive of the G. T. Clark Centenary Project. Through Guy I was able to meet Juliet Coyne, the youngest and only surviving child of Wyndham. She was born at Talygarn in 1919 and has been most helpful to the present writer. She and her daughter Penny visited Talygarn in June 1995. My first contact with the family had been with Jocelyn Clark and his Canadian wife Hope, following a letter which I wrote to *The Times* about the Torcello mosaic from St Anne's church, which is referred to elsewhere in this volume.[22] He was a great help initially, but sadly he died in 1997 during the writing of this chapter.

The future of Talygarn

Ironically, in G. T. Clark's centenary year, the future of Talygarn is uncertain. As a miners' rehabilitation centre it became part of the National Health Service in 1951 and the house and the surviving estate were conveyed to the then Minister of Health in 1955. It is now in the ownership of the Secretary of State for Wales. With the decline of the coal industry and the introduction of safer working conditions there was less need for a specific *miners'* rehabilitation centre and from the 1970s onwards Talygarn accepted patients from other industries and is now open to all who need its specialist facilities. In recent years, the house has become a listed building, Grade II*; the gardens are on the Cadw/ICOMOS Register of Landscapes, Parks and Gardens of Special Historic Interest in Wales, also Grade II*; and the whole is a Conservation Area based on the surviving Clark landscape.

In 1996 the Bro Taf Health Authority announced that, in 1999, the Centre would be closed and the facilities transferred to a new district general hospital presently under construction near Llantrisant. The Authority will then be required to dispose of the property on the open market to the highest bidder, irrespective of the proposed future use. As a result, a group known as the Talygarn Forum was formed to campaign against closure. The Forum believes that Talygarn is a centre of excellence and that much-needed facilities could not satisfactorily be reprovided at the new hospital. It is also concerned about the future of the beautiful house and gardens and believes that, whatever happens, their integrity should be maintained and that some way should be found to ensure their future use as a cultural, educational and sporting asset for the local community. At the time of writing, the outcome remains unresolved, but let us hope that Talygarn will find a future of which G. T. Clark would have approved.

Notes

[1] John Newman, *The Buildings of Wales: Glamorgan* (London, Penguin Books; Cardiff, University of Wales Press, 1995), 625.

[2] I owe these facts on the early history of Talygarn to Mr J. Barry Davies.

[3] D. J. Francis, *The Border Vale of Glamorgan* (Barry, Stewart Williams, 1976), 140–1.

[4] Susan Muir, 'Pigs and Pineapples' (a submission to the Architectural Association School of Architecture towards the AA Graduate Diploma in the Conservation of Historic Landscapes, Parks and Gardens, 1988).

[5] I have been unable to establish the present whereabouts of the original notes or, indeed, whether they have survived.

[6] Edgar Jones, *A History of GKN*, i, *Innovation and Enterprise, 1759–1918* (London, Macmillan Press, 1987), 303.

[7] This information regarding John Jones, including the *Merthyr Express* report, was recently sent to me in a letter from his great-grandson, D. Keith Jones of Cowbridge.

[8] Muir, 'Pigs and Pineapples'.

[9] He presumably means a smaller *room*.

[10] Newman, *Glamorgan*, 103, 626.

[11] T. J. Hopkins, 'David Jones of Wallington', in Stewart Williams (ed.), *Glamorgan Historian*, iv (Cowbridge, D. Brown and Sons, 1967), 87–8.

[12] Ibid., 89.

[13] Ibid. It is now known as St Anne's church.

[14] Newman, *Glamorgan*, 626.

[15] I am grateful to Mr David Francis for these references to the *Bridgend Chronicle*.

[16] *Letters of the Rt. Hon. Henry Austin Bruce, G.C.B., Lord Aberdare of Duffryn* (Oxford, privately printed, 1902), ii, 271.

[17] *Lady Charlotte Schreiber: Extracts from her Journal, 1853–1891* (London, John Murray, 1952), 205.

[18] *Letters of Henry Austin Bruce*, ii, 334.

[19] Philip Riden and Keith Edwards, *Families and Farms in Lisvane 1850–1950* (Cardiff, Merton Priory Press, 1993), 21.

[20] Thomas Richards, ' "Talygarn", Miners' Convalescent Home', *Colliery Workers' Magazine*, 1, 6 (June 1923), 138–9.

[21] Oliver Harris, 'Talygarn, G. T. Clark and the Dowlais Workmen', *Colliery Workers' Magazine*, 1, 6 (June 1923), 140–4. The tapestries are no longer present, alas, as they were deemed 'unhygienic' in a hospital and were disposed of.

[22] See Chapter 11.

CHAPTER 10

Clark's London House: 44 Berkeley Square

RICHARD HEWLINGS

The London house (figure 42) which G. T. Clark occupied from 1877 until his death (and which his heirs retained until the late 1950s) is one of the most lavish private houses of Georgian London.[1] So distinctive is its architecture, particularly its stair, that it was chosen by Soane to illustrate his Royal Academy lectures in 1815,[2] and it is one of only three still surviving London domestic interiors to be illustrated in the canonical architectural history of the period: Sir John Summerson's *Architecture in Britain 1530–1830*, written in 1953.[3]

It was designed in 1744 by William Kent (1685–1748), then regarded as the most fashionable architect available, and now as the most creative of that time.[4] Kent's first career was as a painter, and in pursuit of that he had spent the years 1709–19 in Italy.[5] He returned in the company of the third Earl of Burlington, himself an architect, and he enjoyed Lord Burlington's patronage for the rest of his life, initially his employee, later the holder of official posts which Burlington had helped him to obtain, living for much of his life in Burlington's own house, and at the end buried in Burlington's own vault at Chiswick.[6] It was doubtless through Lord Burlington's social influence that Kent obtained the most attractive private commissions of his day, working for Queen Caroline, the Prince of Wales, four dukes, two prime ministers and other leading politicians.[7] Kent's letters to Burlington reveal that he was a close and trusted friend of the family.[8] The latter included Lady Cecilia Isabella Finch, Lady Burlington's half-aunt, and, from the quantity alone of the correspondence between them, evidently also Lady Burlington's closest intimate. In the Burlington family she was known as Lady Bel,[9] and it was for her that Kent designed 44 Berkeley Square.

Burlington's architectural ambition was to build in the style of the ancient Romans,[10] and to a large extent that intention was imparted to or shared by his numerous protégés. Doubtless he envisaged Romanization as a means of

181

42 East elevation of 44 Berkeley Square. *English Heritage.*

both ornamenting and civilizing the relatively rude and ignorant culture of his native country, whose commercial expansion had in his lifetime first shown its apparently unstoppable global power and energy. Ancient architecture adhered to a system, of which its ornament especially was a component, and ancient ornament had meanings which could be assembled like signals from a code book. Meaningful architecture could impart messages, including moral or political messages, and contemporary opinion was clear that moral guidance was exactly what was needed.

However, sources of information on ancient Roman ornament were limited, and eighteenth-century British architects were obliged to assume that Italian Renaissance ornament was an equivalent thesaurus on which they could draw more easily. Chief among the Renaissance architects whose published work transmitted to them the architecture of the ancients was Andrea Palladio, and the British architects who acknowledged their debt to

43 Ceiling of the saloon at 44 Berkeley Square. *English Heritage.*

183

44 Upper part of staircase at 44 Berkeley Square. *English Heritage.*

him are therefore called Palladians. William Kent's ten years in Italy, however, had acquainted him with a wider range of sixteenth-century architecture. Thus ceilings ornamented by dense patterns of broad ribs with enriched soffits, as in the five principal rooms of Lady Bel Finch's house, are also common to most of the leading Italian architects of the sixteenth century. The pattern which Kent used in the saloon (figure 43) is that of the side niches in the loggia of the Villa Madama, Rome, the most celebrated architectural work of Raphael,[11] which Kent had evidently seen.[12] But he could also have seen other versions of it, for instance in Vincenzo Seregni's S. Vittore al Corpo, Milan, of 1560.[13] The pattern in the barrel vault over the stair (figure 44) is a design which Kent often used, abstracted from that

45 Second-floor stair landing at 44 Berkeley Square. *English Heritage.*

of the main arcade vault in St Peter's Basilica, by Bramante.[14] Again he could equally well have seen it in Alessio Tramello's Madonna di Campagna, Piacenza, of 1522.[15] The tripartite windows of semi-parabolic shape at the top of the stair (figures 44 and 45) are taken from a similar internal window in Vignola's S. Andrea in Via Flaminia, Rome, of 1551–3.[16] Kent was to use this same (and unusual) window type on the main elevation of Wakefield Lodge, Northants, designed just before his death in 1748 and built a few years later.[17] Palladio, specifically, may not have aided Kent, but sixteenth-century Italy, generally, did.

In 1877, however, few British people can have considered the civilization of ancient Rome as one superior to their own. Victorian Britain was manifestly more advanced materially, morally and politically, and Clark himself had been a major contributor to the engineering triumphs which were the most conspicuous advertisement of that superiority. Roman civilization was of interest as a historical phenomenon, one of many, only more useful as the direct ancestor of modern success. To few can the relativism of the ancient Roman legacy have been more apparent than to the archaeologist, and Clark's direct experience of this body of knowledge would also

185

46   South-east ground-floor room at 44 Berkeley Square.
English Heritage.

have conditioned his response to the Roman world. Such Romanisms as he
may have detected in the architecture of Lady Bel Finch's house are unlikely
to have impressed him.

Its Italianisms, on the other hand, were presumably more influential.
Clark's Italophilia is quite clear from his choice of decoration at Talygarn,
in particular the copy of a painting by Veronese installed on the drawing-
room ceiling, and from his use of Italian tradesmen (especially Cortelazzo of
Vicenza and the carver Biraghi). Furthermore, the paintings on the drawing-
room ceiling are set in a frame of plaster beams which is a version of a
similar pattern in the front ground-floor room of his London house (figure
46), and the ornament on these beams was directly cast from presses of the
beams in London. Clark evidently believed Kent's designs to be a suitable
complement to his Italian paintings, conceivably even to be stylistically

186

47 Front door at 44 Berkeley Square. *English Heritage.*

indistinguishable from them. For G. T. Clark, therefore, his house was as close an equivalent as London could offer to an Italian palace of the *cinquecento*.

He could, of course, have built a new house. London offered architects who were profoundly familiar with *cinquecento* architecture, a branch of architectural education which first manifested itself in the later work of Sir John Soane,[18] and became conspicuous in the work of Sir Charles Barry, especially his Pall Mall clubs of 1830–2 and 1838–41.[19] The rich surface treatment of buildings in Barry's style was widely deemed suitable for banks and bankers, and, slightly later, for the buildings of the newly portentous and triumphalist state.[20] In the third quarter of the nineteenth century 'Italianate' was thus identified with plutocracy and officialdom.

48 Lower part of staircase, looking south: 44 Berkeley Square.
English Heritage.

There was, however, another constituency for Italian visual culture, which responded to it more sensuously and intuitively. The approbation given to what were styled 'Primitives' by critics and painters from the later 1840s was an early example of this response, which valued Italian paintings and buildings for different qualities from those which appealed to bankers and public men. The best-known manifestation of this sensibility in the visual arts is the Pre-Raphaelite Brotherhood, and in literature the Brownings, Walter Pater and John Addington Symonds. But there was also an architectural response. William Burges designed some powerful interiors

49 North-west first-floor room, looking east: 44 Berkeley Square. *English Heritage.*

at Gayhurst House, Buckinghamshire, between 1858 and 1872, in a style which is a 'primitive' version of the Italian Renaissance, comparable to his better known 'early' Gothic.[21] At Worcester College, Oxford, between 1864 and 1879 he transformed the anaemic classicism of James Wyatt's chapel and hall into a vigorous interpretation of the *quattrocento*.[22] In church architecture one of the best examples of this taste is J. D. Sedding's Church of the Holy Redeemer, Clerkenwell, of 1887–1906.[23] G. T. Clark's taste for Renaissance Italy may best be seen as part of this sensibility, itself one of the expressions of the Aesthetic Movement.

In addition Clark may have been attracted to Lady Bel Finch's house for a more specific reason. It closely resembled another house designed by Kent: 22 Arlington Street. No. 22 had a similar façade[24] (though without Lady Bel Finch's assertive door surround) (figure 47), a stair with identical balustrade and cantilevers (figure 48),[25] and a Great Room whose ceiling was painted with grisailles on blue or red grounds, as in Lady Bel's saloon, framed by beams whose pattern is another version of that on Lady Bel's ceiling.[26] The similarity, which is intense, cannot have been overlooked. Nor can Clark have failed to see it, for in 1871 22 Arlington Street was bought by the first Lord Wimborne, owner of the Dowlais ironworks and Clark's friend.[27] It is difficult to avoid concluding that Clark was drawn to Lady Bel Finch's house because of its close affinity with Lord Wimborne's house, much larger though that was.

Lady Bel Finch's house stands on the west side of Berkeley Square, which until the 1730s had been a field called Brick Close, part of a small estate on the north side of Piccadilly which belonged to the Lords Berkeley of Stratton, whose principal estate was at Bruton in Somerset.[28] In 1664 the first Lord Berkeley built a palatial house behind a forecourt on the Piccadilly edge of this estate.[29] In 1696 the third Lord sold this house to the first Duke of Devonshire and, although reconstructed (also to Kent's design) after a fire in 1733, Devonshire House, as it became, survived until 1924–5.[30] The land east and west of it was laid out as Berkeley Street and Stratton Street in 1683.[31] Projected northward into Brick Close, the alignments of these streets form the east and west sides of Berkeley Square. In 1736 the site of the east side of the Square was leased from the fourth Lord Berkeley by two carpenters, Edward Cock and Francis Hilliard, who laid it out in building plots.[32] On Lord Berkeley's death in 1741 Cock and Hilliard obtained a second lease which enabled them to lay out the west side of the Square.[33] Lady Bel Finch obtained a sub-lease of her plot, which became No. 44, from Cock and Hilliard on 9 September 1742.[34]

Lady Bel's account book tells us that building began in the same month.[35] The bill for digging the foundations was settled on 30 April 1743; that for slating the roof on 2 September 1744. Kent's responsibility is attested by the tradesmen's receipts, all annotated 'Recd. of the Rt. Honble. the Lady Isabella Finch from the Hands of Wm Kent Esqr.' Stephen Wright, Kent's assistant who later designed Cambridge University Library and Clumber Park for the Duke of Newcastle,[36] witnessed all the agreements with tradesmen and was subsequently paid for 'measuring Abstracting & making up the Several Artificiers Bills for the carcase of Main House & Kitchen Offices Subteranes etc in 1742–3 & part in 1744'.

A number of these 'artificiers' were connected with Kent. William Barlow, the carver, had worked for Kent at 22 Arlington Street;[37] he was an artist with some reputation, publishing a book of ornamental designs called *Friezes with Foliages, Festoons, Shells and Flowers*;[38] he contracted to make chimney-pieces for the Mansion House in 1751, having been admitted to the freedom of the London Masons' Company for the purpose.[39] John Marsden, the joiner, had made a model of a hunting lodge proposed by Kent for Richmond Park in 1735;[40] he worked for Kent at 22 Arlington Street[41] and at Wakefield Lodge,[42] and he was to be a witness to Kent's will.[43] William Almond, the gilder, was also to work at Wakefield Lodge in 1751.[44] Ralph Crutcher, the bricklayer, worked at the Horse Guards between 1750 and 1759;[45] Kent was its architect, although it was only begun after his death.[46] Edward Mist, the paviour, was presumably a relation of John Mist, who had worked under Kent on the Treasury building in 1733;[47] John Mist was Master Paviour to the Board of Ordnance,[48] and worked with Gibbs[49] and Roger Morris.[50] He died in 1737,[51] and the Mist who worked under Flitcroft at Wimpole, Cambridgeshire, in 1744 may well have been Edward.[52] John Devall, the plumber, was the leading plumber of the day, appointed Sergeant Plumber in the Office of Works in May 1742;[53] but he had worked to Kent's designs at Holkham Hall in 1732, 1736 and 1742,[54] and was to do so again at the Law Courts in 1749,[55] the Horse Guards in 1750–9,[56] and Wakefield Lodge in 1749–51.[57] The mason, Joseph Pickford, had worked at Holkham in 1739–40[58] and at 22 Arlington Street in 1741,[59] and was to work at the Horse Guards in 1750–3.[60]

Pickford also worked under Stephen Wright at Claremont in 1750,[61] at Cambridge University Library in 1754–6,[62] at Oatlands, Surrey, in 1756[63] and at Ashburnham Place, Sussex, in 1759–63.[64] Stephen Wright was his executor.[65] Benjamin Holmes, the smith, also worked at Cambridge University Library under Wright.[66] Two of the tradesmen must have known Kent through Lord Burlington. These were Evan Thomas, the slater, and Edward Wethersby, the painter, both of whom had worked at Chiswick House in 1726–8.[67] The glazier, Richard Cobbett, is not known from earlier work, but he may be the glazier of that name who was to work at Hovingham Hall, Yorkshire, among a number of other Londoners, in the 1760s,[68] and at Somerset House between 1776 and 1793.[69] Two tradesmen seem to be unknown from anywhere else, the ironmonger Francis Bedwell and, most surprisingly, the plasterer Robert Dawson, whose work gives the house so much of its character.

By the time of Clark's occupancy surprisingly little had been altered. The two first-floor rooms at the rear have chimney-pieces and wainscot (above the dado only) of a 1790s character (figure 49), which have been attributed to Henry Holland,[70] as the then owner, the Earl of Clermont, was a friend of Holland's greatest patron, the Prince of Wales.[71] Even so, these rooms still retain ceilings, doors, architraves, skirtings and dados of 1740s type. And examination of the tiny upper service stair reveals that its top flight is of mid-nineteenth-century character, indicating that an extra storey of service accommodation was added then, before Clark's arrival. The records of the parish of St George, Hanover Square, and of the City of Westminster do not include any applications for alterations between 1877 and 1962; so Clark, surprisingly, may have made no changes. By 1962 his descendants had sold it to the Clermont Club. The subsequent alterations, by Philip Jebb, were the most considerable to be made since 1744.[72] These were, however, designed with skill and discretion, and the house would still be recognizable to Clark and his family today.

Notes

[1] London, Westminster Archive Centre, Parish of St George, Hanover Square, Ratebooks, C707, 28 March 1877 (the last to show Sir Percy Burrell, the previous owner), and C709, 28 March 1878 (the first to show G. T. Clark). Sir Percy Burrell, Bt., MP, had died at 44 Berkeley Square on 19 July 1876. F. Boase, *Modern English Biography* (London, Frank Cass, 1965), i, 491. Clark noted in his diary on 10 April 1877: 'Rent ½ year for 44 Berkeley Square, £49.7.6'. NLW MS 15,007B.

[2] David Watkin, *Sir John Soane* (Cambridge, Cambridge University Press, 1996), 289, 369, 377, 570, 608, 630.

[3] John Summerson, *Architecture in Britain 1530–1830*, 6th edn. (Harmondsworth, Penguin, 1977), pl. 287. The others are Home House (pl. 348) and 1 Bedford Square (pl. 373).

[4] Mark Girouard, '44 Berkeley Square, London', *Country Life*, 132 (27 December 1962), 1648–51.

[5] Cinzia Sicca, 'On William Kent's Roman sources', *Architectural History*, 29 (1986), 134–47.

[6] Howard Colvin, *A Biographical Dictionary of British Architects 1600–1840*, 3rd edn. (New Haven and London, Yale University Press, 1995), 580–2.

[7] Richard Hewlings, *Chiswick House and Gardens*, 2nd edn. (London, English Heritage, 1991), 51.

[8] Chatsworth, Devonshire MSS, folder of Kent's letters.

[9] Ibid., Letters 219.0–20.

[10] Richard Hewlings, 'Chiswick House and Gardens: Appearance and meaning', in Toby Barnard and Jane Clark (eds.), *Lord Burlington: Architecture, Art and Life* (London and Rio Grande, Hambledon Press, 1995), 4, 128, 131–3.

[11] Christoph Luitpold Frommel *et al.*, *Raffaelo architetto* (Milan, Elemond, 1984), 352.

[12] Sicca, 'Roman sources', 139.

[13] Wolfgang Lotz (rev. Deborah Howard), *Architecture in Italy 1500–1600* (New Haven and London, Yale University Press, 1995), pl. 221.

[14] Frommel *et al.*, *Raffaelo architetto*, 304, 306, 307.

[15] Lotz, *Architecture in Italy*, pl. 89.

[16] Ibid., pl. 184.

[17] Richard Hewlings, 'Wakefield Lodge and other houses of the second Duke of Grafton', *Georgian Group Journal* (1993), 47; Marcus Binney, 'Wakefield Lodge, Northamptonshire', *Country Life*, 154 (2 August 1973), 298. Neither of these articles, however, identifies the source of this motif.

[18] Dorothy Stroud, *Sir John Soane, Architect* (London, Faber, 1984), 110–11.

[19] Henry Russell Hitchcock, *Early Victorian Architecture in Britain* (New Haven, Yale University Press, 1954), i, 162–84.

20 Michael Port, *Imperial London* (New Haven and London, Yale University Press, 1995), 233.
21 J. Mordaunt Crook, *William Burges* (London, John Murray, 1981), 142–6.
22 Ibid., 146–52.
23 Gavin Stamp and Colin Amery, *Victorian Buildings of London 1837–1887* (London, Architectural Press, 1980), 153–4; Roger Dixon and Stefan Muthesius, *Victorian Architecture* (London, Thames and Hudson, 1978), 227.
24 Peter Campbell (ed.), *A House in Town* (London, Batsford, 1984), 109.
25 Ibid., opposite p. 160.
26 Ibid., opposite p. 112.
27 Ibid., 140.
28 B. H. Johnson, *Berkeley Square to Bond Street* (London, John Murray, 1952), 58.
29 Ibid., 51–7.
30 Ibid., 161–8.
31 Ibid., 69–70.
32 Ibid., 174–7.
33 Ibid., 177–8.
34 London, London Metropolitan Archives, Middlesex Land Registry, 1742/2/432.
35 London, Sir John Soane's Museum, shelf AL 39B.
36 Colvin, *Biographical Dictionary*, 1099–1100.
37 Geoffrey Beard, *Craftsmen and Interior Decoration in England 1660–1830* (Edinburgh, Bartholomew, 1981), 245.
38 Idem.
39 Sally Jeffery, *The Mansion House* (Chichester, Phillimore, 1993), 126–7, 299.
40 H. M. Colvin (ed.), *The History of the King's Works*, v (London, HMSO, 1976), 221.
41 Campbell, *House in Town*, 112–13.
42 Hewlings, 'Wakefield Lodge', 49.
43 Campbell, *House in Town*, 113.
44 Hewlings, 'Wakefield Lodge', 55.
45 Colvin, *The King's Works*, v, 438.
46 Ibid., 436–7.
47 Ibid., 432.
48 O. F. G. Hogg, *The Royal Arsenal* (London, Oxford University Press, 1963), i, 267–8.
49 Terry Friedman, *James Gibbs* (New Haven and London, Yale University Press, 1984), 306–7.
50 Colvin, *The King's Works*, v, 232.
51 Francis Sheppard (ed.), *Survey of London*, xxxi (London, London County Council, 1963), 286.
52 London, British Library, Add. MS 36,228.
53 Colvin, *The King's Works*, v, 473.
54 I am indebted to Prof. Dr Leo Schmidt for this information.
55 Colvin, *The King's Works*, v, 388.
56 Ibid., 438.
57 Hewlings, 'Wakefield Lodge', 49.
58 I am indebted to Prof. Dr Leo Schmidt for this information.
59 Campbell, *House in Town*, 112–13.
60 Colvin, *The King's Works*, v, 438.
61 Michael Symes, 'The garden designs of Stephen Wright', *Garden History*, 20 (Spring 1992), 13–14.
62 Cambridge, Cambridge University Library, UAc.2(3).
63 Symes, 'Garden designs', 15, 18.
64 Christopher Hussey, 'Ashburnham Place, Sussex – II', *Country Life*, 113 (23 April 1953), 1249.

[65] Edward Saunders, 'An 18th century provincial architect', *Country Life*, 152 (9 November 1972), 1206.
[66] Cambridge, Cambridge University Library, UAc.2(3).
[67] R. T. Spence, 'Chiswick House and its gardens, 1726–1732', *Burlington Magazine*, 135 (August 1993), 525–31.
[68] Giles Worsley, 'Hovingham Hall, Yorkshire – III', *Country Life*, 188 (22 September 1994), 58.
[69] Colvin, *The King's Works*, v, 465.
[70] Arthur Oswald, 'Georgian London: No. 44 Berkeley Square, the residence of Wyndham Damer Clark, Esq.', *Country Life*, 86 (8 July 1939), 17.
[71] *CP*, iii, 276–7; Girouard, '44 Berkeley Square, London', 1651.
[72] London, Westminster Archive Centre, Westminster Drainage Plans, Box 227/8806.

CHAPTER 11

George Clark and the Arts

PETER LEECH

This essay studies Clark as collector, patron and literary practitioner. It is not possible to separate entirely a polymath's activities into tidy compartments such as Arts, Science, Recreations, etc., but the following tentative pages will, it is hoped, help to elucidate more of this extraordinary man, the revelation of whose energy and curiosity and competence in so many fields is the paramount purpose of this celebratory volume.

I

The first, brief section of the essay is a quick introduction to some of the multifarious concerns that George Clark had, as represented in the auction catalogue of the sale at Talygarn House in 1922. We start by rapidly considering his enormous library, selecting a comparatively few titles to represent the main categories.[1]

There was a comprehensive span of English literature from Chaucer to Trollope. Of periodicals and journals there was a collection ranging from the *Gentleman's Magazine* and the *Edinburgh Review* to full sets of publications by the British Archaeological Association, the Royal Archaeological Institute, the Somerset Archaeological Society, the Huguenot Society, the Royal Agricultural Society of England, the Journals of the House of Lords, *Archaeologia*, *Archaeologia Cambrensis*, the *Antiquary*, the Bristol and Gloucestershire Archaeological Society's papers, and so on.

There was not just Burke's *Peerage* and *County Families of the United Kingdom* but also other peerages (by Lodge, by Collins), *The Plantagenet Roll of the Blood Royal* and many genealogies, heraldic manuscripts and books of arms revealing an intense interest, far beyond personal pride in descent and connection, in matters of genealogy. There were printed records, charters and rolls, with a copious supply of legal volumes: the

50 Talygarn: the hall. Photograph, *c*.1922.
Glamorgan Record Office.

Parliament Rolls, Rymer's *Acts*, the *Judges of England*, the poll books of
Northampton – major and minor works touching the original documented
history of the kingdom, a long list which, with his own extensive publications, denote a very profound concern with the past in the form of its
original written sources.

   There was a large religious section in Clark's library: Luther, Lancelot
Andrewes, Jeremy Taylor, Richard Baxter, Wesley, Keble, Pusey and
Newman and, of course, included in the broad sweep of theological opinion
a special place for the very considerable literature written by his Clark
ancestors. Some of the Clarks were in the forefront of controversy and the
publishing of sermons and the compilation of holy precepts in the sixteenth,
seventeenth and eighteenth centuries. The works of Charles Darwin were
also among Clark's books.

   His own immediate background included strict Protestant influences from
both his mother's and his father's side. The Diceys, as well as the Clarks,
gave the young George his personal knowledge of Christian reformers such

51 Talygarn: one of the two interconnecting library rooms. Photograph, *c.*1922.
Glamorgan Record Office.

as Hannah More and William Wilberforce, whose published works were certainly on his shelves. Clark's father, the Revd George Clark, was chaplain, moral tutor and headmaster of the Royal Military Asylum. He was a well-known evangelical clergyman. George Clark jun. collected and published some of his father's sermons. He also republished earlier forebears' pastoral exhortations that had only just gone out of print.

Much then, on Clark's library shelves, of the Church Militant. Much also of more mundane military matters, in quite detailed accounts and treatises: not only were there some of the few works that dealt with fortification before he himself had started to study castles 'in a scientific manner' but also there were volumes on contemporary wars, the full *Campaigns of Napoleon*, the huge set of Wellington's *Dispatches* (which concerned battles fought in Clark's childhood) and (of the wars fought in Clark's maturity) *The Tactical Problems* and *Speeches* of von Moltke, Bismarck's military right hand. The Iron Duke and the Prussian practitioners of 'Blood and Iron' were part of Clark's thinking, for we must remember that he took a serious interest in the military effectiveness of castles, not a quiet antiquarian's. He was not playing at soldiers as Lieutenant-Colonel of the Dowlais Volunteers, however picturesque he looks in the photographs of him in that capacity. In his earliest days he was surrounded by a military as well as a religious atmosphere.

Studying then sometimes holy works, sometimes the theory and practice of war, he also had at hand books that show something of a leaning towards the theatrical. Quite apart from Shakespeare, Massinger, etc., Clark's library included a stock of plays for *acting* – Lacy's *Acting Plays* (42 volumes), Inchbald's *British Theatre* and Planché's *Extravaganzas* (betraying, the last, perhaps a bias towards pantomime?).

Clark had a hoard of dictionaries: Latin, French, Greek, Italian, Dutch, Anglo-Saxon, the *Etymological Dictionary of the Scotch Language*, Cornish-Cambrian, and Hindoostani. He read his Roman classics in the original Latin: Virgil, Ovid, Horace, Caesar, Cicero, Livy, Martial, Pliny, Suetonius, Tacitus and (also in Latin) the Greek comedies of Aristophanes. There were works in French in abundance: Montaigne, Bossuet, Dumas (20 volumes), Beaumarchais, George Sand, *Annuaire de la noblesse* (48 volumes), with numerous *mémoires* and *histoires*, e.g. of Richelieu, Marie Antoinette, Marshal Ney, Lucien Bonaparte, and twenty volumes of 'Eminent French Authors'.

Clark's fine art folios and books encompassed Raphael, Dürer, Parmigianino, Reynolds, Vasari's *Lives*, Redgrave's *Century of British Painters, Les Peintures de Charles Le Brun et d'Eustache Le Sueur* and the contemporary critical-historical works, in translation, of Morelli and Kugler.

There are more titles of Scottish history and topography than of Welsh, but the following titles do occur: *Lives of the Cambro-British Saints*, Pennant's *Tours*, Meyrick's *Cardiganshire*, Coxe's *Monmouthshire*, Jones's *Brecknockshire*, Fenton's *Pembrokeshire, Royal Tribes of Wales, Annals of the County Families of Wales*.

There were horticultural volumes such as *Arboretum et Fruticetum Britannicum* and Loudon's *Shrubs and Formal Gardens*; and there *were* manuals of technical and scientific procedures as one would expect on an industrialist's shelf, but this brief library list ought to impress anyone of George Thomas Clark's huge interest in so many matters outside the works office at Dowlais. It is a small fraction of the full list at the sale in 1922, and many parcels of books were unlabelled, but it is enough to establish the prodigious scholarly background of Clark of Talygarn.

The library was dispersed in 1922 and so were the other collections, the paintings and engravings that included works, according to the auctioneer, by Gainsborough, Rembrandt, Janssens, Zucchero, Van Dyck, Longhi and

Batoni. Neither the National Gallery nor the National Museum of Wales has record of buying any of them. The framed works at Talygarn would seem to be not out of the ordinary for a man of Clark's means and the engravings included portraits of Clark relatives and friends and contemporary personalities that would be expected for a man so aware of his past and in touch with so many living notables.

There was, though, a very Clarkian selection of military artefacts. Again they are simply given a bare lot number and remain undescribed in the catalogue but they included a fierce array of warriors' accoutrements: helmets, shields, bucklers, pieces of body armour, damascened swords, battle-axes, maces, knives, scimitars, together with three 14″ bronze mortar cannon and three 16″ bronze mortar cannon, and *twenty-three* suits of armour (some full-size, some boys', some miniature). Talygarn House presumably bristled with warlike devices: ferocious metal standing perhaps near bookcases containing potent, if not actually thundering, divines.

More delicately, there was porcelain, but this was Mrs Clark's province. A small portion of her collection found its way into the National Museum of Wales at Cardiff. There was much silver, chiefly Georgian, some small bronzes and medallions featuring the Iron Duke, Cromwell, Schiller, Molière and Dante. There was fine table glass, much of it Venetian.

According to photographs of the principal rooms taken in the 1920s, the furniture looks very expensive but there is not much authentic detail in the vague (yet hopeful) auctioneer's list. The great 'Louis XV' console table, opulently gilded with cupids, incorporates Clark's cipher and coat of arms and so one doubts the dating of the piece. The Clark heraldry, and even more so the Clark cipher, was found everywhere at Talygarn, in all shapes and sizes, in stone, marble, wood, on canvas, ironwork, tapestry, endlessly, subtly sometimes, sometimes inescapable. We shall return to it.

Before ending this account of what was dispersed from the mansion, note might be made of the billiard room with its forty-two cues and the massive table 'fitted with patent pockets and ball-returning railway'. In the hall was a full Steinway grand piano, one of three at the house, another being an upright grand in the drawing room. And, to cap all, the working equipment of *this* ironmaster included two lecturer's magic lanterns in portable cases, plus four boxes of slides.

II

The second section of this essay touches upon Clark as patron. We do not examine the decoration and permanent artwork that remains at Talygarn

199

without soon encountering the name 'Layard'.[2] Austen Henry Layard was a cousin of Lady Charlotte Guest (and later her son-in-law by marriage to her daughter Enid). He had long been a friend of Clark's and both of them as young men had frequently been welcome visitors to the Guests at Dowlais House. In the 1840s the young Layard had become famous as 'Layard of Nineveh', sending back from Mesopotamia massive archaeological specimens such as the huge winged bulls and lions that became the foundation of the Assyrian Department of the British Museum. He wrote of his adventures well, and profitably, and became a household name, went into politics, was a Cabinet minister and ended as envoy to Spain and, as ambassador to the Sultan, Disraeli's adviser during the Turko-Russian crisis of 1878.

He and his wife Enid retired to Venice, where they became the centre of British social activity. They entertained British and German royalty and also encouraged and supported Venetian firms and individual craftsmen.[3] Layard was supremely interested in Italian art and had been since his childhood in Florence. His collection of Renaissance paintings was bequeathed to the National Gallery of which he was a trustee and adviser on purchasing.[4] Ceaselessly energetic, he was a patron on a great scale. He had, before permanently settling in Venice, re-established the Venice Murano Glass Factory, with Dr Salviati. Salviati's glass mosaics are found throughout Britain because of Layard's advice and encouragement to patrons ecclesiastical and secular.

Another protégé of Layard was Antonio Cortelazzo of Vicenza. Layard had discovered Cortelazzo as a brilliant faker and persuaded him that he could make more profit by turning from his clever life of forgery to a legitimate career as an outstanding craftsman in his own right. To accomplish this transformation Layard had to provide a market for the unknown Cortelazzo and this he did in the 1870s. The Layards, together, introduced the reformed Cortelazzo to a number of English friends – Enid's brother Sir Ivor Guest (later the first Lord Wimborne) and Sir William Drake, chairman of the Burlington Fine Arts Club, and George Thomas Clark.

A third name associated with Layard is the wood-carver Biraghi of Venice. Biraghi, in 1885, redecorated the stairway at Canford, the Guests' seat in Dorset. In the 1840s Lady Charlotte and Sir John Guest engaged the architect of the Houses of Parliament, Sir Charles Barry, to build a sumptuous Gothic edifice at Canford. When, much later, part of the structure was burnt down, Layard recommended the wood-carver Biraghi as decorator.

The work of all three Veneto craftsmen, Salviati, Cortelazzo and Biraghi, was introduced by George Clark into different stages of the beautifying of his own house, and the church he built, at Talygarn. Clark bought Talygarn in 1865, 'a queer old rambling house' with 300 acres.[5] Gradually he improved the property but it is not till the 1880s that Talygarn House, as we know it, came into being. The first craftsman from Italy that Clark employed was Cortelazzo. Clark states that the Cortelazzo doors of the drawing room at Talygarn were made considerably before the room itself was finally decorated. In 1871 Cortelazzo designed a very fine belt in beautifully worked steel for Lady Layard. What is more interesting for us is the exhibit now in the Victoria and Albert Museum of a similar Cortelazzo belt given by George Clark to his wife, and later donated to the V. & A. by his grandson, Wyndham Damer Clark.[6] The belt consists of twelve segments delicately engraved with gold on steel and further ornamented with the unmistakable Clark cipher and the enamelled, but not quite accurately tinted, heraldry used by Clark, and his wife's family's lion rampant in miniature. There are also two mosaic flower panels and two cameos. The central panel is a Medusa's head, a symbol of Athene.

Cortelazzo's chief work for Clark was the decorating of the doors and mantelpiece of the drawing room at Talygarn. All is exuberantly covered with arabesques and satyrs writhing gracefully in prolific grandeur. Amongst this activity, rather subtly, the Clark cipher and his principal heraldic charge, the fleur-de-lis, are worked into the elaborate overall design.

Biraghi is responsible for the carved panelling in the drawing room, the hall, the cedar-wood corridor, the two main stairways and, later (1895), the extensive marquetry-lined walls of the billiard room. At Canford in 1885 Biraghi fills the huge stairway with bas-relief Renaissance decoration – vases, cupids, trophies of war. The impression is perhaps overpowering. Canford is on a scale that dwarfs Talygarn and the Dorset display of carved magnificence leads up to a very large Gothic-style window that armorially celebrates the ascending Guests' achieving a viscountcy and marrying on a ducal level. At the bottom of the Canford stairs, and almost hidden, two small carved portraits are introduced into the general magnificence. They are quite easily missed: they are labelled on swags decorously held by putti. On one side of the stairway is Layard and on the other side Biraghi is supported in the background by the gouges and chisels of his craft. He is labelled 'G. Biraghi. Venezia. 1885'.

At Talygarn Biraghi's work is on a lighter scale, in dimension more domestic and the stock cornucopias and putti are interspersed with specific Venetian themes – the winged lion of St Mark, the Doge's cap, and from time to time, and subdued, the Clark cipher and heraldry. Again, as at Canford, Biraghi carves his own head and his patron's. Not once, but twice. In the corridor he is profiled, with a coat of arms beneath his head which is, as at Canford, framed with the tools of his trade. In the billiard room at

52 Talygarn: painted ceiling of the drawing room, the 'copy' of Veronese's *Musica* in the centre. Photograph, *c*.1922. *Glamorgan Record Office.*

Talygarn, for which he supplied the marquetry panels, he appears again – a small head, a few inches across, above the mantelpiece facing a similar small head of George Clark over the mantelpiece at the other end of the very long room: patron and craftsman unequivocally linked, as at Canford.

Biraghi features twice then, in miniature, as does Clark, but there are two other small heads in the corridor at Talygarn. One is not surprised that the third head is of Layard. A more complete declaration of Clark's enthusiasm for Veneto craftsmanship and their great supporter, Layard, is hard to imagine. There is, though, a fourth labelled head in the corridor, which is enigmatic. It is of a Renaissance Venetian 'Nicolaus Barbadicus' (Nicolò Barbarigo) who in some way is connected with the Sultan Murad III[7] and, presumably, also with a theme that connects Layard, Biraghi and Clark. The inclusion of Barbarigo in a context of patrons and craftsmen is so far unexplained. It may have something to do with the fact that the Barbarigo family had one of their *palazzi* on the site of what became the Salviati mosaic factory: or there *may* be an etymological link between 'Biraghi' and 'Barbarigi'. Research proceeds.

The largest painting at Talygarn is in the ceiling of the drawing room, part of an elaborate scheme set in gilded plaster based on designs from Clark's Berkeley Square house (by William Kent). A superficial glance at this painting, on canvas, made for Clark by Santi, a copyist in Venice, suggests that it is not unlike the copy of *Musica* by Veronese which Layard had in his *palazzo* on the Grand Canal. The original *Musica*, in the Marciana Library in Venice, is famous for having won the young Veronese a special prize, a gold chain, bestowed on the advice of Titian and Sansovino, the architect of Venice's prestigious Library. In Veronese's original and in Layard's copy, there is an intricate arrangement of two young ladies and a young gentleman singing and playing delicately, while in the background of leafy shadows an incomplete sculpture of the god Pan glowers down on the small and vulnerable figure of Syrinx who, nude back to us, gazes at the broken reed pipe that is tied to a branch above her. Clark has the copyist alter the picture. In place of the small Syrinx figure is a full-scale, third young woman who sings serenely from a page of music. This arrangement, removing Syrinx, leaves us a painting of no more than a delightful singing party with a garden ornament in a shady background. Why does Clark have the painting altered? Bowdlerization? An attempt to fit an originally circular canvas into an oval framework? A removal of disharmony?

Puzzling as may be some of Clark the patron's requirements, a different sort of mystery surrounds the 'Torcello' mosaic.

Layard's Salviati Company supplied Clark with several mosaic pieces, including a sizeable reredos that Clark donated to his old school, Charterhouse, when it moved from Smithfield in London to Godalming in Surrey in the 1870s. It took the form of a *Last Supper*. It was later removed from Charterhouse when superseded by Sir Giles Gilbert Scott's War Memorial reredos in the 1930s and is now to be found in the church at Clayton in Yorkshire.[8]

An extremely large Salviati mosaic was fixed to the east wall of the hall at Talygarn. It was a copy of an eighteenth-century painting depicting Venice honouring her last great warrior doge, Francisco Morosini, for conquering the Turks in the Peloponnese in the seventeenth century. The mosaic appears in a photograph (*c*.1920) and may be glimpsed momentarily in Jill Craigie's film, *Blue Scar*, made in 1946. A matron later deemed that the mosaic was becoming detached from the wall and had become a danger to patients, and it is now safely in storage.

Smaller mosaic decorations remain in both Talygarn House and St Anne's church, but what is no longer present is the *ancient* mosaic, not a creation of the nineteenth century but from the cathedral on the remote island of Torcello (north-east of Venice) which had been for very many centuries the seat of the Patriarch. So far nothing has come to light in Clark's papers, but this eleventh-century piece of glittering tesserae was attached to the wall of what was then Clark's family pew in the church – 'this chapel of St Ann'[9] – he had just built in memory of his wife in 1887. In 1986, a new incumbent, the Revd Martin Reynolds, while making a photographic record of the church, 'rediscovered' the treasure. The mosaic was authoritatively examined and pronounced a very small part of the great *Last Judgement* mosaic which fills the entire west wall of the basilica at Torcello and is one of the greatest examples of Venetian-Byzantine art.[10] In 1987 the mosaic was sold at Sotheby's for £240,000 and passed into a private collection in the United States. A replica is fixed to the north wall of the nave of St Anne's.

Why Clark chose the mosaic for his very own special part of the church is conjectural. The head is of an apostle. In 1986 it was thought it might be of St Philip or St Thomas. Maybe Clark thought it was the apostle Thomas and found it appropriate to place his namesake in the church dedicated to the namesake of his wife Ann. The area where the mosaic 'presided' is now the vestry and it is still decorated with small shields of Clark's armorials and cipher. Nearby is a carved 'poppyhead' decorated with Clark heraldry and his wife's family's rampant lion.

Clark was in Venice with his daughter Blanch soon after his wife's death in 1885 and it is assumed that Layard, who certainly accompanied them to Torcello one afternoon, arranged for the purchase of the mosaic. The head, with one or two other fragments, had been removed from the west wall at Torcello by the restorer Moro some years earlier when he was replacing damaged mosaic from the row of apostles' heads. It appears that his contract permitted him to keep any original mosaics for himself after making and fixing 'better' versions. It is not clear whether Clark bought the head as a comparatively impromptu purchase or whether he had in mind some long-planned acquisition, perhaps of an artefact that alluded to his own second name. There is a story, recorded earlier this century, that the clergy at Torcello had dealings with an English 'milord' at the time of the transaction, but no transaction is mentioned specifically in any papers that have yet come to light. There is no suggestion that the mosaic was come by illegally.

It is certainly a striking piece of work when viewed at close quarters and, although only a minute part of the huge mosaic wall of apocalyptic grandeur, it has its own air of solemn majesty. It was made by the craftsmen who were also at work in St Mark's, Venice, roughly at the time of the Battle of Hastings. If the head is of Thomas the Apostle, or if George Thomas Clark thought it was, this would be a final confirmation of a pattern that emerges from Clark's patronage of the much later Venetian craftsmen. The work from Venice is concerned primarily with his desire to make Talygarn a specially dynastic home.

The church of St Anne has no blatant family advertisement and indeed at Talygarn House itself the ciphers and heraldry are for the most part quietly introduced into the decoration. At Canford the initials of Josiah John Guest and Charlotte Elizabeth Guest are sometimes found unmistakably announcing the one-time owners' presence. With Clark things are more subtle, more blended. The family ciphers, the intertwined Cs, are often difficult to find, are wrought or painted or carved in a great variety of ways, not all of them immediately obvious. 'George' never dominates; little is made of 'G. T. C.', the initials he modestly uses at the end of so many of his written articles: it is the House of the Clarks that matters, and both indoors and in the grounds that is what is indicated, lightly introduced into the ambience. If the cipher is emphasized, as in the light blue and gold device near the window of the drawing room, then it is done exquisitely. His grave in the churchyard is in no way ostentatious: a slim Celtic cross marks his resting place with Ann.

Another point about the interior decoration of the house: there are in some rooms allusions to childhood. Clark does not refer to them in his account of the growth of Talygarn, but children's figures delicately animate some ceilings and are found in smaller pieces of decorated glass in some of the windows. One ceiling, it is true, in one of the smaller rooms, is covered with supposedly Clark and Lewis devices, almost as if giving a history lesson in pedigree, but in the 'Governess Room', for example, children are depicted in pursuits proper to the four seasons, and elsewhere one finds playful and elegantly frolicking small human beings and one group of very happy little cupids, magnificently framed in gold plaster, who have dispensed with their arrows and quivers and are celebrating harmoniously in a ring-dance.

Most unchildlike, in contrast, the hall in Clark's time would have appeared much more Gothic than now. Photographic evidence shows three miniature suits of armour in niches on the replica thirteenth-century Assisi fireplace, and halberds alongside the large Morosoni mosaic which displays the warrior doge in full armour. The large window which remains is copied from Claybrooke church, in Leicestershire, and its imitation late fourteenth-century tracery is fenestrated with heraldic glass representing ancient families with Glamorgan connections.[11] Today the hall, full of family portraits and billiard tables, has a grand *domestic* atmosphere rather than the more medieval effect that G. T. Clark intended.

Another theme, to be found in the drawing room, includes references to the gods at peace, and the Muses. Around the 'Veronese' group in their melodious serenity are the gods (in grisaille) at ease, and in the ceiling of the window alcove the Muses are depicted very elegantly in quiet colouring. Clark does not elaborate on the craftsmen or copiers involved: it is presumed that Santi had some hand in the work, especially the slightly stiff, grey divinities.[12] In Clark's time the large tondo (School of Botticelli) of the *Virgin and Child,* to be seen in a 1922 photograph, would have added to the tranquility of the drawing room. (Incidentally this tondo is not the one displayed in the National Museum of Wales, as has been suggested.)

The gods calm, the Muses quietly being themselves, the children in playful abandon; it may be that Clark was trying to fuse, at times, his sense of the past, the heraldry, the Gothic and Renaissance allusions, with his hope for future generations and their fruitful, peaceful expectations. The Biraghi work is omnipresent, binding all, whatever may be the theme of any particular room. Nobody thinks that Clark was other than a rather heavy-handed architect[13] but he seems to be altogether a more accomplished co-ordinator of interior design and, with Layard's friendly Venetians, Clark appears to have been a true patron, not a mere collector but one who inspires, fathers even, the design, and is deeply part of the creating process.

III

There is a third aspect to consider: Clark the writer, the practitioner in the craft of words: a creative artist himself. For sixty-five years he wrote. He wrote official reports as public health superintending inspector, engineering reports in India, and the Great Western Railway guidebooks. There were the great works of archaeology and history for which he is already known. There are also the articles, 'for the general reader', at the beginning and end and throughout his long working life. Let us briefly review his total *œuvre* and see what Clark tells us, obliquely, about himself through his themes and style, which may reveal a little of someone who probably never gave a second thought to autobiography. There is usually something especially innovatory in what he is writing and it will be for the most part extremely lucidly put.

The 1839 Great Western Railway guidebook[14] is both the first guidebook to Brunel's railway and also the first guidebook to offer such a comprehensive encyclopaedic array of information. The book was dedicated to Brunel and was published anonymously. It is quite small, very handy, but packed with crystal-clear help for the railway traveller. One of its chief purposes must have been to enthuse and encourage travel by rail. The wildest terrors were circulating in those early years when a horse-drawn population was not at all sure of this fiery contraption that had already claimed Mr Huskisson, a former Cabinet minister. Clark's easeful introduction to the railroad allays suspicion of the dragon and hints at the positive advantage to be found in this means of locomotion. Nothing could be more encouraging than to be set at rest by the evident simplicity of boarding, settling down and enjoying the ride as Clark describes it *and,* in so doing, profiting intellectually by it.

In the preface Clark makes it clear, quite modestly, that there had never been a guidebook like this:

An attempt is here made to introduce into the pages of a guide book subjects of a nature not hitherto found there. From the manner in which railways are constructed, and for the facilities which they afford for visiting even very remote parts of the kingdom, it seems probable that the study of various natural sciences, and more particularly of Geology, together with the subject of Archaeology, will be more generally followed. Hence some of such subjects have here been entered upon . . .[15]

In the guidebook proper the passenger who approaches the Paddington terminus is put at ease by a most accommodating overture:

The company's servants have strict orders to behave with civility, and to refuse money; and any known breach of these regulations is followed by instant dismissal.

All private carriages to go by the Railway, should be brought through the archway, at the least quarter of an hour before train time.

A bell rings at five minutes before the hour, as a signal to secure seats and deliver up tickets; and a second bell at the hour, when the offices are closed and the carriage doors shut and locked.

The passenger should therefore enter at the proper booking office, at the doors of which the porters will take charge of the heavier luggage. Having procured a ticket, passed into the departure shed, seen the luggage stowed away, taken a seat in a carriage, and given up his ticket to an attendant, the starting bell will ring, and upon the two minutes allowed for making up the way bill having elapsed, the train will move off across the depôt.

Upon quitting the shed, immediately upon the right is the coach-house; beyond which, the multiangular building, is the engine-house, with the forges and fitters' workshops.[16]

Passing under the Westbourne Road Bridge, a skew of seven arches . . . are the Company's temporary shops on the left; and on the right, the embankment of the Harrow Road, and a public house lately constructed by the Company . . .

Beyond the Black Lion Lane Bridge upon the left is the retaining wall of Westbourne Park, lately occupied by Lord Hill, but now, with the remainder of Mr Cockerel's estate, in the possession of the Railway Company. The cottage on the right, near the turnpike, is part of the same estate, and was formerly occupied by Mrs Siddons.[17]

Clark now proceeds more diagrammatically. A column down the middle of the page gives precise details of the permanent way and, on each side of this technical column, landmarks and 'the subjects of a nature not hitherto found in a guidebook' are digressed upon briefly, as the traveller makes his effortless way through a landscape that is still, for the most part, Regency.

We are told the details, in the central column, of each section of the track, the bridges we pass under, the radius, in chains, of every curve of the line, and a careful announcement is made of every gradient: and we are afforded a generous compilation of all that is to be seen on both sides of the line: the house of a Mr Whippy; the home of one who was provost of Eton (his coat of arms given in full); the site of Richard Baxter's house, just after Acton – 'famous 70 years ago for its mineral springs'; Wharncliffe Viaduct; 'Harrow on the Hill, and the country between, are seen to great advantage'; Middlesex Lunatic Asylum; 'North Hyde Barracks, now disused'; 'Eight ovens for the preparation of coke for the locomotive engines'; the 'celebrated "Mons" of Eton may be seen from the Railway. The mount itself appears to be the centre of a camp or earthwork, probably of Celtic or Danish construction.' Brunel's hardly used rails are taking Clark's traveller deep into the green heart of the Thames Valley and 2,000 years of history.

And before our reading traveller finishes, he is further treated to more portions of archaeology, architecture, philology, geology, together with an abundance of thoughtful advice on the possibilities of continuing westwards by steamship to New York. If he ventures not so far he is informed of the exact fare of Hackney carriages, and the surplus cost of dogs 'conveyed separately'. Such is the packed cornucopia of George Clark's guide to the GWR. It is clear, it is attractive, it is reassuring, it is eminently readable, it is manna to the historian of railways, and still engaging to all who may come upon it.

When, ten years later, Clark (turning forty) writes his dozens of Board of Health reports the same precision is evident. However Clark and his fellow inspectors write to something of a formula suggested by Chadwick, the public health promoter. Clark's *Newport* report is not unlike Rammell's *Cardiff* in clarity.[18] Again, of course, Clark is involved in a collective, pioneering enterprise.

We now turn to Clark's writing unconnected with his professional callings, what might be thought of as his 'hobby' writing. There can be no doubt that *Mediaeval Military Architecture* was innovatory. He makes it quite clear that his first description of Caerphilly Castle (in 1834, at twenty-five) was original and pioneering: 'It was, I believe, the first attempt to treat, in a scientific and accurate manner, the plans and details of a great mediaeval fortress.'[19] Fifty years later, at the suggestion of Professor E. A. Freeman, he publishes a very full collection of his lifetime's research, 'generally accurate accounts of most of the principal castles of England'.[20] The double volume of over a thousand pages deals with ninety-three castles.

In dedicating the work to Freeman Clark eulogizes the great historian and claims little for himself:

> [Freeman] a topographer and master of mediaeval architecture . . . Materials which in their original form are dry and uninstructive give, in his hands, weight and substance to some of his most brilliant sketches. As a collector of some of these materials, I have often felt surprise and delight at the use to which they have been applied; and, although my work has been rather that of a quarryman or brickmaker, I am sometimes led almost to regard myself as sharing in the glory of the architect.[21]

Whatever scholars think of his overall conclusions on medieval military architecture, and nobody accepted them in their entirety, his place is assured as a pioneer in the field and on a vast scale and unlike his 'professional' writing Clark expands his style sometimes when speaking of castles. It is basically clear but, now and again, it becomes richer idiosyncratically.[22] He quotes several times some lines by Mason:

> Time
> Has moulder'd into beauty many a tower,
> Which, when it frown'd with all its battlements,
> Was only terrible.

Romanticism interweaves occasionally with customary precision. The first sentence of the first castle described, Alnwick, includes a surveyor's accuracy and a hint in the last three words of a Border balladeer: 'The castle of Alnwick stands upon a moderate eminence on the south bank of, and 150 yards distant from, the river Alne, which was thus its immediate defence against the Scot.'[23]

There is a pleasant stateliness sometimes. At Caernarfon the custodians (the 'men from the Ministry' in Clark's day) are noted – 'Mr Salvin, than whom no man could more skilfully restore an ancient castle, was consulted upon its necessary repairs, and Mr Turner, as deputy-constable, watches over the fabric with no common care'.[24] Pure lyricism occasionally occurs but there is sometimes, quite unexpectedly, a comic twist at the end: Clun is set in

> this rich and smiling land, amidst hamlets, churches, manor-places, farm-houses, and cottages, with frequent orchards and gardens, green pastures of root crops, and waving corn-fields, the river Clun pursues its sinuous course, giving life and fertility to the scene, which, indeed, is throughout imbued with an aspect of peace and – perhaps rather indolent – prosperity.[25]

The lyrical Clark waxes incisively humorous for a moment but follows with scholarly details, dimensions, minute calculations and several full pages of genealogy and lordship: seriousness reigns for the rest of the description.

Clark offers a human touch in other ways. Harlech's last constable 'was the late W. W. E. Wynne, Esq., of Peniarth, as good a man as he was an eminent antiquary'.[26] Familiar, epigrammatic, homely, our author also interweaves local patriotism and native fervour into the narrative as at York where Clark prefaces his great tour of the gates and walls with: 'The men of York cannot but feel for their birthplace something of the love of children for a parent . . . of that secret charm by which every man, worthy of the name, is attracted to his native land.'[27]

But at his grandest Clark calls for all available trumpets, as it were. After seventy pages of detailed exposition of the architecture and history of the Tower of London he terminates with a hugely magnificent fanfare and a peroration *allegro reale*.

> It is the work of the great Norman conqueror of England, founded by the founder of her monarchy. It is the citadel of the metropolis of Britain, and was long the most secure residence of her greatest race of kings. Here they deposited the treasure of the empire and the jewels and regalia of their crown. Here they secured the persons of their prisoners, and minted and stored up their coin. Here the courts of law and of exchequer were not unfrequently held; here the most valuable records were preserved; and here were fabricated and preserved long-bow and cross-bow, sword, lance, and pike, armour of proof, balistae, scorpions, and catapults, then the artillery and munitions of feudal war. Here, too, as these older machines were laid aside, was first manufactured that 'subtle grain', that 'pulvis ad faciendum le crak', and these 'gonnys and bombards of war' which were to revolutionise the military art, until they themselves should be superseded by later inventions, of which the ancient keep is still the grand storehouse and armoury of the country . . .

53 The meeting of the Royal Archaeological Institute at Caerphilly Castle, 27 July 1871. Photograph, 1871. *Cadw: Welsh Historic Monuments. Crown Copyright.*

Here, too, captive within these walls, and through these gates led to death, were More and Fisher, martyrs for the ancient, and Anne Askew for the purer, faith . . .

No other fortress, no bastile in France, no bargello in Italy, no prison-castle in Spain or Germany, is so deeply associated with the history of its nation, or with the progress of civil and religious liberty.[28]

Before we leave *Mediaeval Military Architecture* there are one or two points to make about Clark's treatment of the castle he dealt with from the very beginning of his studies and on which he restated his opinions on various occasions, Caerphilly. The 1834 description is in four parts: history of lordship; topography; the physical explanation of the castle with map and diagram; the account of the castle as he found it in ruin, plus an account of Edward I as strategist – a straight exhaustive account.[29]

In 1871 on the famous excursion of the Royal Archaeological Institute to Caerphilly Clark indulges in a grand public lecture for 500 visitors to the castle who lunched, sumptuously catered for by the young Marquess of Bute. Clark revels in the occasion. His account of the provisions collected

211

for the great siege is gargantuan.[30] He peoples the ruined walls with an animated scene of bannered and trumpeted medieval soldiery, makes an aside on the art of modern warfare, gives a crisp description of the castle itself, with the aid of a huge map, pays a particularly fulsome vote of thanks to the present Lord of Glamorgan (i.e. the Marquess himself), gallantly salutes all the ladies and is obviously enjoying the event immensely. He had a reputation for bringing old ruins to life and on this occasion outdid himself. Incidentally it is thought that the photograph of the event, with crinolined and top-hatted crowds gazing at the photographer, *may* show Clark himself in the foreground. Certainly it is a great day at Caerphilly Castle and the band of the Volunteers is playing in the picture, that stout company whom Lt.-Colonel Clark led on manœuvres against the castle on at least one occasion.

In the final account of Caerphilly in *Mediaeval Military Architecture* (1884) there is none of this spirit of *en fête* but at the very end of the description there are a few lines added to the allusion to the manor-house on the hill. It remains something of an 'in-joke'. Clark slyly ends his scholarly account of Caerphilly with a reference to the dovecote and manor-house of the Van, the Lewis edifice built partly from the stones of the ruined castle, 'the spoils of Caerphilly'. Clark finishes with: 'In appropriating the stones of Caerphilly to the erection of their manor-house, the Lewis family, from whom the ground was originally wrested, may have committed a breach of taste, but none had a better moral right to help themselves from that source.'[31] Not many of his readers would realize that this was a very droll remark indeed coming from one who had married into the Lewis family.

There is humour to be found even in the opening of *The Land of Morgan*. In his introductory survey of the county of Glamorgan Clark laments that vines no longer flourish as they did in medieval times. 'Its wines are, alas! no more; not even the patriotic efforts of Lord Bute, in his vineyard at Castell Coch, have as yet been able to raise a murmur from the local temperance societies'[32] – a way of putting it that might not have endeared Clark to some of his moderately Puritan ancestors. There are other lapses in seriousness – the surrealist cartography with which he delineates the shape of the county as a diving porpoise,[33] and more gallantry offered to the fair wives of the county. Most of the book of course is a full scholarly argument of what actually happened in the Norman settlement of Glamorgan and overturns the legends that passed for history with rigorous criticism.

We shall end with some specimens of his earliest and latest essays, drawing out more clearly his main themes and something, perhaps almost conclusive, of this man of intense energy and production, and reserve.

Perhaps we have already glimpsed a little more of the man behind the forge, the man behind the battlements. When the young doctor Clark practised in Bristol he joined a group that wished to elevate the intellectual standards of Bristolians. Based on the Bristol Institution, Library, Laboratory and Lecture Theatre, this little band were of some distinction. They included the physician father of John Addington Symonds, the brother of John Henry Newman and the Revd W. D. Conybeare, rector of Sully near Cardiff and later dean of Llandaff, and already a geologist of great fame. Not only was Clark (at twenty-seven) of their company: he edited their new journal, *The West of England Journal of Science and Literature*. It lasted but a few numbers, for which he apologizes that it is mainly his fault as he himself wrote a great many of the articles, the promises of some would-be contributors having not been fulfilled.

In his first, editorial, piece he states very clearly the polymath intention of combining science and literature and especially in relation to the large surrounding area, which included Bristol, Bath, Cornwall and south Wales. It would be a channel of information and discussion covering geology, zoology, natural history, philosophy, philology and archaeology, and literature – but only *classical* (i.e. no new 'original') poetry: 'It will be by no means our ambition to open a foundling hospital for weak and unprovided offspring of this description.'[34] Ethnography, the study of mythology, antiquities, would be welcomed but not the mere chronicling 'of old vessels or brass farthings. Actual Statistics, no less than Antiquarian researches, will demand our notice.'[35]

George Clark never made a more succinct statement of the multifarious pursuits that engrossed him throughout his life and he was keen to add that although 'disclaiming *controversial* Theology, we shall ever be anxious that every line we pen may be found throughout marked by a general Christian spirit and Christian tendency'.[36] The venture lasted about a year and Clark apologizes in his closing remarks for 'the dryness of the articles . . . [which] of necessity proceeded from one, and that an inexperienced pen: so that some of the papers are crude and ill-arranged'.[37] But one of his pieces alone will give the lie to his apology.

His article on a 'Visit to Antwerp at the capitulation of 1833' had been written at the age of twenty-three, but he reads like a mature and seasoned war correspondent of the first rank.[38] His use of military nomenclature is masterly. He speaks of lunes, lunettes, hornworks, *chevaux de frise*, gabions, petards, *troups de loups*, casemates, ravelins,[39] bastions, as he takes us through the ruined city. Fascines, counterscarp, revetments fall into his narrative of the siege (the countryside ruined, the mud of flooded dykes, the shattered market gardens are redolent of much later wars long after his

213

time). He details precisely the artefacts of war, 'le gros mortier de Liège', a 22″ calibre mortar around which the sightseers stand open-mouthed. He defines the effect of shells landing and the skill of the battery experts and the mangling of cannon by superior artillery. Clark knew the reality of military devastation in his own lifetime probably before he adopted Caerphilly as his first study of ancient warfare. And he does not flinch from poignancy and horror. He notes children playing at marbles with grape and shot. He recalls at length the poor, half-decapitated fellow whose 'comrades had buried him as best they could, and a shell had rendered their pious offices useless . . . An Englishman, standing by, detached a loose mass of the rampart with his foot, and a second time sepulchred the remains.'[40] (It would be interesting to know who 'an Englishman, standing by' really was.) Clark knew war, its glory and panoply, and consequence, and he hopes it will not haunt his own land. 'Those who live in . . . England value but little the blessings of peace, for they are happily ignorant of the miseries of war.'[41]

Over sixty years later, what is probably his finest late piece harks back not to battles and siege-engineering but to the long essay of railway memories and his earliest days, his recollection of the time, not long after Antwerp, of pioneering with Brunel. It does not sound like a promising work from its title, 'The birth and growth of the broad gauge',[42] but it is a piece of railway history that becomes a consummation of so much that George Clark valued. It is occasioned by G. A. Sekon's newly published history of the GWR (1895) which Clark finds 'wanting in those qualities that give life to a narrative'.

Clark begins with something of the wonder aroused by Stephenson's *Rocket* and its undreamed of speed, incredibly outdoing its expected 10 m.p.h. There is a splendid account of the early railway promoters – 'most of whom were politically reformers and ecclesiastically Dissenters'![43] – and the intricate chicanery that accompanied the long passage of the GWR Bill through Parliament. Brunel emerges, of course, as the hero of the piece. First, as the very young apprentice to his father, from whose comprehensive methods Isambard Kingdom learns so much of every trade that he could possibly want to use as a supreme civil engineer. The younger Brunel, educated at the Lycée Henri Quatre, also has an exceptional draughtsman's hand, a great love of the beauty to be incorporated into design and a brilliant command of figures – 'a readiness in calculations not common with Englishmen, and which gave him an enormous advantage when defending his estimates before a parliamentary committee'.[44] Brunel's masterly forty days dominating the opposition in committee is detailed with great verve and Clark, of course, revels in a full description of the choice of route from Paddington west.

Brunel's methods and use of assistants, the fact that in overall design he had kinship with Wren, his supreme conquering of the problems of Maidenhead Bridge,[45] the cheerful support of his workmen and assistants who 'obeyed his orders as troops obey a victorious general',[46] Clark cannot but eulogize. Brunel was above all a master of engines, every minute detail being scrutinized and yet the North Country locomotive builders were never dominated by him. Clark may well have learnt not to override his tried subordinates from his erstwhile superior, Brunel, when he was laying down the track of the GWR, and may also have noted with admiration the conciliatory skills he employed in negotiating the railway's entry into London.

After technical and legal battles the great day of the opening of the line as far as Taplow arrives. Now Clark turns from the engineering and parliamentary agent's niceties to human situations that are remarkably effective in bringing the world of iron and steam into a highly personal context. Following feverish activity by Brunel to make safe the track because of intense rain, the opening took place. The day was dominated by the *North Star*,

> a magnificent engine designed and built by Messrs. Stephenson . . . With the engine had been sent up from Newcastle its driver, Appleby, who shared in its popularity, and was indeed a fine specimen of the north countryman – tall and broad in stature, shrewd in the expression of his features, skilful in the management of his engine, and not a little pleased by the crowds who came to see her arrival and departure.[47]

A few days later the directors of the company make their own trial trip. Clark is present (he is the engineer accompanying Stephenson the Elder) and records:

> George and Robert Stephenson were invited to accompany them. Robert took his place on the footboard of the engine, beside the driver; George came late, and occupied himself with visiting the works of the terminus, until the return of the train. When its approach was signalled, as the engineer who accompanied him relates, he became much excited, and when, true to its time, the train ran into the station with Robert upon the footboard, his eyes sparkled with pride and affection, and he rushed forwards to greet him. The affection of the old man for his son, and his confidence in him were well known, and formed a bright feature in both their characters, for they were reciprocal.[48]

We are immediately informed that the train made 57 m.p.h. and are back to technicalities but Clark, among others, had been moved by this touching incident of footplate piety.

Just before these very human moments in this 'Broad Gauge' narrative Clark uses a word that is helpful in summing up what the present essay has tried to illuminate. In describing the end of the broad gauge railway Clark speaks of the 'general inosculation that now exists between the most distant groups of railways'.[49] 'Inosculation'[50] is a term that encapsulates so much of Clark's activities, the intertwining, the interweaving of so many tracks and lines of interest and research.

It would be agreeable to have a simple picture of Clark's life, something like a clear Underground Map that one could read at a glance, but no polymath can be unravelled so easily and it is part of the problem of investigating a life so multifaceted as Clark's that an overall portrait is extremely difficult, if not impossible, to achieve. We can deduce from his library and the decorative surroundings that he co-ordinated at Talygarn and in his writings something of the man – his self-confidence in marshalling so much historical detail into enthralling narratives, his eye for the humorous, his delight in grandiloquence, his love of sciences and the arts, his deep regard for ancestry and the binding of the generations, his steady gaze at the misery of war and urban squalor – but we still have to tease out so much of the inner character: so often the extrovert George Clark paradoxically remains private, rarely expressing his heart, or the faith of his fathers. A later student of south Wales geology quotes Seneca: 'Let us not be surprised that what is buried so deeply should be unearthed so slowly.'[51]

The present writer hopes to pursue the study of Clark's patronage and his writings (and those of his forebears) and perhaps even to present a selection of his written work which has been given an accolade from a surprising quarter, from the historical novelist, the lately deceased Alexander Cordell, who fulminating against the Guests at Dowlais (in *The Fire People*), nevertheless writes of 'Lady Charlotte Guest who translated the *Mabinogion*; she whose agent was the magnificent writer G. T. Clark.'[52] This is an interesting quotation to end with. Its author very unexpectedly trumpets Clark's literary powers while thinking of him merely as an agent, praising one aspect alone, unaware of George Thomas Clark's parallel excellence in other spheres: the scholar ironmaster so richly accomplished among the arts of Vulcan *and* Athene.

Notes

[1] The sale, by Gottwaltz & Perry of Cardiff, took place at Talygarn 5–20 July 1922. Some of the books were, however, presented to the NLW, together with G. T. Clark's personal papers.

[2] See *Austen Henry Layard: Symposium Internazionale* (University of Venice, 1987), especially Dr Judy Rudoe on Cortelazzo, in her essay 'The jewellery of Lady Layard', 213–17.

[3] For great help with the Venetian aspects of this essay the author is bound in gratitude, and over a long period, to Lady Clarke and John Millerchip in Venice; also to Peter Philp, the National Museum of Wales Art Department (Oliver Fairclough and Dr Mark Evans), the National Gallery (Nicholas Penny), the Victoria and Albert Museum, the Courtauld Institute. Robin Protheroe-Jones (Welsh Industrial and Maritime Museum) helped with some early enquries about Clark as engineer. Staff of Canford School, Dorset, have also, over the years, been most kind (especially Robin Whicker, now retired).

[4] Layard was a great friend of Morelli who had much influence on art criticism and patronage in the late nineteenth century. Layard also edited a version of Kugler's *Handbook of Painting* for John Murray.

[5] Clark's own information on Talygarn is set out in a few typed pages that are accepted generally, but have no provenance. See Chapter 9.

[6] Victoria & Albert Museum, Jewellery Gallery, Case 20 Board J.

[7] 'NICOLAUS.BARBADICUS.OBAT.AMUBTHEM.III.TURC.IMP.' which, allowing for Venetian orthography, links Barbarigo with the Sultan Murad III (reigned 1574–95).

[8] Information kindly supplied by the archivist of Charterhouse School. Mention might also be made here of two other examples of ecclesiastical patronage: Clark's gift of the elaborate central lancet window in the west front of Llandaff Cathedral in memory of his friend Dean Conybeare; it was destroyed in the blitz of 1941 (see Nevil James, *The Stained Glass of Llandaff Cathedral* (Llandaff, Llandaff Cathedral Shop Committee, 1997), 26); and Clark's influence on the building and furnishing of the Welsh church (St Mary's) in Dowlais, now demolished, which is still being investigated.

[9] This is from the inscription on the date-stone. The spelling now in use is 'St Anne'.

[10] Sotheby's Catalogue, 9 July 1987.

[11] The author is indebted to the Revd Jennie Bradshaw, rector of Claybrooke, Diocese of Leicester, for her kind assistance.

[12] Clark's typescript mentions e.g. 'Paolindi' but he is not specific. Barbetti, probably from Siena, is said to be the sculptor on whose work the small sphinxes in the drawing room are based.

[13] John Newman, in *The Buildings of Wales: Glamorgan* (London, Penguin Books, 1995), and others do not find that Clark was at his best as an architect, but it is agreed that his co-ordinating touch indoors was of a much higher order than his skill at designing buildings.

[14] *A Guide Book to the Great Western Railway* (London, 1839).

[15] Ibid., Preface.

[16] Ibid., 25.

[17] Ibid., 26.

[18] For a list of the public health reports, see the bibliography of G. T. Clark under years 1849, 1850 and 1851; for a discussion of these see Chapter 2.

[19] *Mediaeval Military Architecture in England* (London, 1884), i, Preface. Discussed in Chapter 5.

[20] Ibid., i, Dedication.

[21] Ibid., i, Preface.

[22] Most of *MMA* gives solid facts, copious measurement and very comprehensive military engineering details. The extracts that are presented here exhibit stylistic devices that adorn his consistent lucidity, rather like a little icing on a very rich but digestible cake.

[23] Ibid., i, 175.

[24] Ibid., i, 309.

[25] Ibid., i, 402.

[26] Ibid., ii, 81.

[27] Ibid., ii, 595.

[28] Ibid., ii, 272.

[29] *West of England Journal of Science and Literature*, i (1835–6), 62, 101, 135, 185.

[30] *Arch. J*, 28 (1871), 325–9.

[31] *MMA*, i, 335.

[32] *The Land of Morgan* (London, 1883), 13.

[33] Ibid., 14.

[34] *West of England Journal*, first editorial.

[35] Ibid.

[36] Ibid.

[37] Ibid., last editorial.

[38] Ibid., i, 228. The article had been first printed in the *Gent. Mag.*, in 1833.

[39] Ibid., i, 230. cf Major-General Stanley in *The Pirates of Penzance*.

[40] Ibid., i, 234.

[41] Ibid., i, 237.

[42] *Gent. Mag.*, 279 (1895), 489–506.

[43] Ibid., 492.

[44] Ibid., 493.

[45] Ibid., 497. Cf. Turner's ethereal evocation of Maidenhead Bridge, in *Rain, Steam, and Speed – the Great Western Railway* (1844), with Clark's brick-by-brick description of its construction five years earlier.

[46] Ibid., 498.

[47] Ibid., 502.

[48] Ibid., 502.

[49] Ibid., 501.

[50] Inosculation (a medical term): anastomosis, hence applied generally of the passing of one thing into another. A rare word today perhaps among GPs, but current among surgeons in the nineteenth century. *OED*.

[51] Quoted on the last page of F. J. North, *The Stones of Llandaff Cathedral* (Cardiff, University of Wales Press, 1957), 117.

[52] Alexander Cordell, *The Fire People* (London, Hodder and Stoughton, 1987), 247.

A Bibliography of G. T. Clark's Writings

(*omitting newspaper articles and short reviews*)

Compiled by BRIAN LL. JAMES

1833

'On the inscriptions found on the Babylonian bricks', *Gent. Mag.*, 103 part i: 3–4.

'Visit to Antwerp, at the capitulation', *Gent. Mag.*, 103 part i: 409–14, 492–6.

Review of four Saint-Simonian pamphlets, *Gent. Mag.*, 103 part ii: 250–3.

1835

'Notices of Dethick and Ashover, co. Derby, and the families of Dethick and Babington', *Coll. Top. & Gen.*, 2: 94–101.

'Castles of Gwent and Dyfed. No. I. Castle of Ogmore', *Gent. Mag.*, NS 3: 243–6.

'Castles of Gwent and Dyfed. No. II. Newcastle', *Gent. Mag.*, NS 3: 489–90.

'Essay on Caerphilly Castle', *West of England Journal of Science and Literature, Part II – Literature*, 1 (1835–6), 62–71, 101–4, 135–43, 185–99.

The West of England Journal of Science and Literature, 1, Nos. 1–5 (January 1835–January 1836), ed. G. T. Clark. Clark was the author or possible author of several articles published in this journal. 'Essay on Caerphilly Castle' is signed, and 'Visit to Antwerp' had already appeared in *Gent. Mag.* over his initials. He is the possible author of the following unsigned articles in *Part I – Science*: 'Observations upon the polders of Flanders', 1: 64–8; 'On the anatomy and physiology of the organs of the senses', 210–17; 'A geological description of the parish of Portishead', 261–72; 'Short notes upon the diluvial and alluvial deposits of the Taffe Valley', 272–87; 'A sketch of the present state of our knowledge of the laws of chemical combination', 310–20; 'Some account of the mer-de-glace', 320–3. In *Part II – Literature*: 'Essay introductory to the archaeology of the West of England', 95–101, 130–4, 199–217; 'Observations on English castles', 217–28; 'Remarks on the history of inventions', 241–8.

1836

'Visit to Antwerp at the capitulation of 1833', *West of England Journal of*

Science and Literature, Part II – Literature, 1 (1835–6), 228–41. A slightly revised version of the article in *Gent. Mag.* (1833).

1838

'Topographical prosings: Hints for antiquarian tourists', *Gent. Mag.*, NS 10: 375–8.

1839

A Guide Book to the Great Western Railway, containing some Account of the Construction of the Line, with Notices of the Objects best worth Attention upon the Course. 72, 19–22 pp.
'Topographical prosings, no. II. Local guides', *Gent. Mag.*, NS 11: 385–7.

1843

'Church notes at Kingston upon Soar, co. Notts.', *Coll. Top. & Gen.*, 8: 264–73.
'The pedigree of the family of Babington of Dethick and Kingston', *Coll. Top. & Gen.*, 8: 313–60.
[A note on the Rastall family], *Gent. Mag.*, NS 19: 338.
'Topographical and historical notes upon the castle of Tamworth', *Gent. Mag.*, NS 19: 592–3.
'Description of Berkhampstead Castle', *Gent. Mag.*, NS 20: 36–8.
'The church of Cogan, Glamorgan', *Gent. Mag.*, NS 20: 129–30.
Review of *Chronica Jocelini de Brakelonda*, edited by J. G. Rokewode, *British and Foreign Review*, 15: 54–79.
Review of Froissart's *Chronicles*, *MR*, 1: 1–28.
'Wars in France. Edward the Third'. Review, *MR*, 1: 213–49.
'Welsh fiction'. Review of *The Mabinogion*, translated by Lady Charlotte Guest, and *The Eastern Origin of the Celtic Nations*, by J. C. Prichard, *MR*, 1: 431–68.
Review of *A General Armory*, by J. and J. B. Burke, *MR*, 2: 16–34.

1845

'Military architecture', *Arch. J.*, 1: 93–107.

1846

The History and Description of the Great Western Railway. Text by G. T. Clark, lithographs by J. C. Bourne. iv, 76 pp.

1847

Report . . . on the Engineering Features of the Concan and the Great Western Ghauts. 8 pp.
'On the neighbourhood of Bombay, and certain beds containing fossil frogs', *Quarterly Journal of the Geological Society of London*, 3: 221–4.

1848

'Rev. George Clark, A.M.', *Gent. Mag.*, NS 29: 311–13.
'Iron manufacture in south Wales', *Westminster Review*, 50: 76–108 (attributed in *Wellesley Index* to W. B. Adams).

1849

'Sanitary reform', *BQR*, 9: 41–70. A review article on four publications (not attributed in *Wellesley Index*).
'Cotton-growing – American and Indian', *BQR*, 9: 354–85. A review article on four publications (not attributed in *Wellesley Index*).
William Wells, *A Sermon Preached in the Chapel of the Royal Military Asylum, Chelsea, on the 30th January, 1848, upon the Occasion of the Death of the Rev. George Clark, A.M. . . . Together with three Sermons Preached by the Deceased.* 59 pp. Includes 'Notice' and 'Biographical sketch' by G. T. Clark.
Reports to the General Board of Health on the sanitary state of the following places: Bangor, Brecon, Bulkington, Carmarthen, Durham, Harrow, Kendal, Nuneaton, Penzance, Preston, Rugby, St Thomas (Exeter), Stratford on Avon, Swansea, Taunton, Totnes, Warwick, Watford, Wigan, Worcester.

1850

'Castell Coch', *Arch. Camb.*, NS 1: 241–50.
'Caerphilly Castle', *Arch. Camb.*, NS 1: 251–304.
Reports to the General Board of Health on the sanitary state of the following places: Bangor, Beverley, Bodmin, Bridgend, Bristol, Brynmawr, Bulkington, Calne, Coity Lower, Harrow, Launceston (two), Leamington, Llandilo Fawr, Llanelly, Melcombe Regis, Newmarket, Newport (Mon.), Newton Abbot, Nuneaton and Chilvers Coton (two), Padstow, Sawtry, Sherborne (two), Swansea, Tenby, Towyn, Watford, Welshpool, Wrexham.

1851

Reports to the General Board of Health on the sanitary state of the following places: Brynmawr, Calne, Carmarthen, Corsham, Leamington Priors, Llangadock, Long Itchington, Newmarket, Padstow, Swindon, Welshpool, Wrexham.

1852

A Description and History of the Castles of Kidwelly and Caerphilly, and of Castell Coch. 82 pp.
'Kidwelly Castle', *Arch. Camb.*, NS 3: 1–20.

1857

The Schools of the Dowlais Iron Company: Annual Report for 1856–7. Includes Clark's address at prize giving, 8 October 1857, pp. 10–18.

1858

Some Account of Morlais Castle. 18 pp.

1859

'The earls, earldom and castle of Pembroke', *Arch. Camb.*, 3rd ser. 5: 1–13, 81–91, 188–202, 241–5.

'Some account of Morlais Castle', *Arch. Camb.*, 3rd ser. 5: 97–114.

1860

'The earls, earldom and castle of Pembroke' (cont.), *Arch. Camb.*, 3rd ser. 6: 1–11, 81–97, 189–95, 253–72.

'On the military architecture of Wales', *Arch. Camb.*, 3rd ser. 6: 285–99, 355.

1861

'Some account of the parish of Penmark', *Arch. Camb.*, 3rd ser. 7: 1–22. By G. T. Clark and R. O. Jones.

'Earls and earldom of Pembroke' (cont.), *Arch. Camb.*, 3rd ser. 7: 185–204.

1862

'Some account of the parishes of St. Nicholas and St. Lythan, co. Glamorgan', *Arch. Camb.*, 3rd ser. 8: 92–116, 177–201. By G. T. Clark and R. O. Jones.

'Some account of Cardiff Castle', *Arch. Camb.*, 3rd ser. 8: 249–71.

'An outline of the topography of Glamorgan', *Gent. Mag.*, NS 12: 15–22.

Report of talk at Restormel Castle, *Arch. Camb.*, 3rd ser. 8: 310–12.

Report of paper on the military architecture of Wales, *Arch. Camb.*, 3rd ser. 8: 324–5.

1863

On the Proposed Welsh University. 3 pp. A letter to Hugh Owen dated in 1863, but perhaps not published until 1870.

1864

'Glamorganshire documents', *Arch. Camb.*, 3rd ser. 10: 247–50.

'Mansell evidences', *Arch. Camb.*, 3rd ser. 10: 281–91.

1865

'The cross of St. Donat's', *Arch. Camb.*, 3rd ser. 11: 33–48.

'Benton Castle, Pembrokeshire', *Arch. Camb.*, 3rd ser. 11: 82–4.

'Some account of the parish of Llancarvan', *Arch. Camb.*, 3rd ser. 11: 261–76, 343–60.

'Corfe Castle', *Arch. J.*, 22: 200–40.

1866

'Some account of the parish of Llancarvan' (cont.), *Arch. Camb.*, 3rd ser. 12: 1–29.

'The castle and family of Penrice', *Arch. Camb.*, 3rd ser. 12: 276–95.
'Contribution towards a history of the parish of Llantrithyd', *Arch. Camb.*, 3rd ser. 12: 389–97. By G. T. Clark and R. O. Jones.
'Some remarks upon Bronllys Tower', *Arch. Camb.*, 3rd ser. 12: 441–5.
'Scarborough Castle', *B*, 24: 921–2.
Report of talk on the Tower of London, *Arch. J.*, 23, 324–6.

1867

'The military architecture of the Tower of London', in *Old London*, pp. 13–139.
'The lords of Avan, of the blood of Jestyn', *Arch. Camb.*, 3rd ser. 13: 1–44.
'Contribution towards a history of the parish of Llantrithyd' (cont.), *Arch. Camb.*, 3rd ser. 13: 205–33. By G. T. Clark and R. O. Jones.
'Contribution towards a cartulary of Margam', *Arch. Camb.*, 3rd ser. 13: 311–34.
'The family of Nerber of Castleton', *Arch. Camb.*, 3rd ser. 13: 375–80.
'Mediaeval military architecture in England', *Arch. J.*, 24: 92–109, 319–39.
'Tutbury Castle', *B*, 25: 185.
'Grosmont Castle', *B*, 25: 274.
'Tamworth Castle', *B*, 25: 405–6.
'Leicester Castle', *B*, 25: 487–8.
'The castle of Arques', *B*, 25: 548–9, 565–8.
'Château-Gaillard', *B*, 25: 643–4.
'The castle of Bôves', *B*, 25: 848.

1868

'Contribution towards a cartulary of Margam' (cont.), *Arch. Camb.*, 3rd ser. 14: 24–59, 182–96, 345–84.
'The castle of Coucy', *B*, 26: 191–2, 206–7.
'Berkhampstead Castle', *B*, 26: 529.
'Bedford Castle', *B*, 26: 689–90.
Evidence to the Royal Commission on Trades Unions. *PP* 1867–8 [3980–I] xxxix: 88–99.

1869

'East Orchard Manor House', *Arch. Camb.*, 3rd ser. 15: 63–78.
'Admiral Sir Thomas Button', *Arch. Camb.*, 3rd ser. 15: 246–57.
'The rise and race of Hastings', *Arch. J.*, 26: 12–19, 121–36, 236–57.
'Penard Castle', *B*, 27: 689–90.
'Alnwick Castle: Its military architecture', *B*, 27: 782–6.
'Remarks upon the basalt dykes of the mainland of India', *Quarterly Journal of the Geological Society of London*, 25: 163–8.
Review of *The History and Description of Leeds Castle, Kent*, by Charles Wykeham Martin, *Arch. J.*, 26: 411–18.

1870

'An outline of the topography of Glamorgan', *Arch. Camb.*, 4th ser. 1: 1–22.
'Letter of Sir Hugh Luttrell of Dunster', *Arch. J.*, 27: 53–7.
'Hawarden Castle', *Arch. J.*, 27: 239–54.
Isambard Brunel, *The Life of Isambard Kingdom Brunel, Civil Engineer*. Contains reminiscences of Brunel by G. T. Clark, pp. 94–8.

1871

Thirteen Views of the Castle of St. Donat's. 33 pp., 12 plates. Text by G. T. Clark, drawings by Frances Stackhouse Acton.
An Address on the Delivery of the Annual Prizes to the Students of the Cardiff Schools of Science and Art, Nov. 30, 1870. 28 pp.
'The Kenfig charters', *Arch. Camb.*, 4th ser. 2: 172–90, 243–56, 313–19.
'An extent or survey by inquisition of the county of Glamorgan', *Arch. J.*, 28: 60–5.
'Herbert charters, probably relating to Herefordshire', *Arch. J.*, 28: 159–60.
'Extentae de Kairdiff . . . Glamorgan', *Arch. J.*, 28: 309–14.
'Clifford Castle', *B*, 29: 984–5.
'Penrith Castle', *B*, 29: 1021.
Report on the South Wales Coalfield (Eastern Division) for the Royal Commission on Coal in the United Kingdom. *PP* 1871 [C.435] xviii: 31–7.

1872

'Glamorgan charters', *Arch. Camb.*, 4th ser. 3: 33–6.
'Piracy under Penarth', *Arch. Camb.*, 4th ser. 3: 47–50.
'The tower of Llanquian', *Arch. Camb.*, 4th ser. 3: 144–6.
'Glamorgan adventurers in Ireland', *Arch. Camb.*, 4th ser. 3: 210–11.
'Admiral Sir Thomas Button' (cont.), *Arch. Camb.*, 4th ser. 3: 223–34.
'Heraldry of Wales', *Arch. Camb.*, 4th ser. 3: 315–29.
'Some account of Guildford Castle', *Arch.J.*, 29: 1–25.
'The late Earl of Dunraven', *Arch. J.*, 29: 78–82.
'Gloucestershire charters', *Arch. J.*, 29: 268–72.
'Odiham Castle, Hants.', *Arch. J.*, 29: 331–41.
'Llantrissaint borough charter', *Arch. J.*, 29: 351–9.
'Urquhart Castle, in the county of Inverness', *B*, 30: 124–5.
'The keep of Middleham Castle', *B*, 30: 284–5.
'The ancient defences of Southampton', *B*, 30: 1023–5.
'Taunton Castle', *Somerset Arch. Proc.*, 18: 60–76.
George Clark, *Sermons Preached in the Chapel of the Royal Military Asylum, Chelsea, between 1840 and 1847*, by the late Revd George Clark. Edited by his son.

1873

'Charter by Richard III', *Arch. Camb.*, 4th ser. 4: 78–9.

'Kilpeck Castle', *Arch. Camb.*, 4th ser. 4: 50–8.
'Sir Robert Mansell', *Arch. Camb.*, 4th ser. 4: 31–45, 217–35.
'Richard's Castle', *Arch. J.*, 30: 143–52.
'Earthworks in Brecknockshire', *Arch. J.*, 30: 264–6.
'Pickering Castle', *Arch. J.*, 30: 349–57.
'Contemporaneous copy of the convention for the surrender of Rennes . . . 1357', *Arch. J.*, 30: 399–402.
'Mr. Albert Way', *Arch. J.*, 30: 389–94.
'The castle of Pontefract', *B*, 31: 162–4, 209–10.
'The castle of Barnard Castle', *B*, 31: 482–4.
'The castle of Ewias Harold', *B*, 31: 763–4.
'The keep of Clitheroe', *B*, 31: 1023–4.
Report of field visit to Berkhamsted Castle conducted by Clark, *Arch. J.*, 30: 407–11.

1874

'The castle of Builth', *Arch. Camb.*, 4th ser. 5: 1–8.
'Wigmore', *Arch. Camb.*, 4th ser. 5: 97–109.
'Bridgenorth, Oldbury and Quatford', *Arch. Camb.*, 4th ser. 5: 263–7.
'Bodiham Castle', *Arch. Cant.*, 9: cv–cxvi.
'Remarks upon the worthies of Devon', *Arch. J.*, 31: 127–51.
'Defences of York', *Arch. J.*, 31: 221–61.
'Charters of the Berties', *Arch. J.*, 31: 284–8.
'Carlisle Castle', *B*, 32: 169–71.
'Helmsley Castle', *B*, 32: 67–9.
'Tickhill Castle', *B*, 32: 126–7.
'Mitford Castle', *B*, 32: 191.
'The castles of Eaton-Socon and Huntingdon', *B*, 32: 431–2.
'Earth-works of the English period', *B*, 32: 585–7, 624–6.
'Cockermouth Castle', *B*, 32: 944–7.
'Sherborne Castle', *Somerset Arch. Proc.*, 20: 20–34.

1875

'Harlech Castle', *Arch.Camb.*, 4th ser. 6: 101–15.
'Moated mounds', *Arch.Camb.*, 4th ser. 6: 63–9.
'The castle of Kenilworth', *Arch. J.*, 32: 55–85.
'Rochester Castle', *Arch. J.*, 32: 205–28.
'The earthworks of the Wiltshire Avon', *Arch. J.*, 32: 290–309.
'Dover Castle', *Arch. J.*, 32: 436–61.
'Moated mounds: Cambridge, Towcester, Tempsford, Toternhoe and Caerleon', *B*, 33: 232–4.
'The defences of York', *Yorks. Arch. J.*, 4 (1875–6), 1–42.

1876

The Remarks of the Lord Lieutenant of Glamorgan Remarked upon. 13 pp.

British Iron Trade Association. Inaugural Address of the President, Mr G. T. Clark. 32 pp. Reprinted in *Eclectic Engineering Magazine*, 14, and in the *Merthyr Express*, 4 and 11 March 1876.

'Tretower, Blaen Llynfi, and Crickhowel', *Arch. Camb.*, 4th ser. 7: 276–84.

'Charter of Adam, abbot of St. James's, Northampton', *Arch. J.*, 33: 83.

'Lincoln Castle', *Arch. J.*, 33: 212–28. Also printed in *Reports and Papers Read at the Meetings of the Architectural Societies*, 13 (1875–6), 176–89.

'Norham Castle', *Arch. J.*, 33: 307–24.

'Berkeley Castle. (Original royal letters preserved at Berkeley Castle.)', *Bristol & Glos. Trans.*, 1: 115–37.

'Arundel Castle', *B*, 34: 161–2.

'Castle Rising', *B*, 34: 341–4.

'The castle of Bramber', *B*, 34: 555–7.

'The castles of Brougham and Brough', *B*, 34: 683–6, 691.

Review of *Notes on Irish Architecture*, by the Earl of Dunraven, *Arch. J.*, 33: 437–47.

1877

'Coyty castle and lordship', *Arch. Camb.*, 4th ser. 8: 1–22.

'The castle of Ewias Harold', *Arch. Camb.*, 4th ser. 8: 116–24.

'Ludlow Castle', *Arch. Camb.*, 4th ser. 8: 165–92. Reprinted in *Trans. of the Shropshire Archaeological and Natural History Society*, 6 (1883), 271–98.

'The manorial particulars of the county of Glamorgan', *Arch. Camb.*, 4th ser. 8: 249–69.

'Coychurch, co. Glamorgan', *Arch. Camb.*, 4th ser. 8: 294–8.

'The land of Morgan', *Arch. J.*, 34: 11–39.

'Muckross and Inisfallen', *Arch. J.*, 34: 149–63.

'Charter of confirmation by Richard Earl of Cornwall . . . 1256', *Arch. J.*, 34: 180–6.

'Borthwick Tower', *B*, 35: 394–6.

'The castle of Christchurch', *B*, 35: 652–4.

'Porchester Castle', *B*, 35: 756–60.

'The castle and barony of Clun: Hopton Castle', *B*, 35: 1047–50.

'The castle of Montgomery', *Mont. Coll.*, 10: 313–26.

'The castle of Dolforwyn', *Mont. Coll.*, 10: 326–8.

'The moated mounds of the Upper Severn', *Mont. Coll.*, 10: 329–48.

1878

'Manorial particulars of the county of Glamorgan' (cont.), *Arch. Camb.*, 4th ser. 9: 1–21, 114–34.

'A plea in curia regis', *Arch. Camb.*, 4th ser. 9: 51–9.

'Oswestry and Whittington', *Arch. Camb.*, 4th ser. 9: 179–94.

'The appeal of Richard Siward', *Arch. Camb.*, 4th ser. 9: 241–63.
'The land of Morgan' (cont.), *Arch. J.*, 35: 1–18, 313–38.
'The earthworks of Brinklow, Lilbourne, and Earl's Barton', *Arch. J.*, 35: 112–19.
'Rockingham', *Arch. J.*, 35: 209–41.

1879

'The land of Morgan' (cont.), *Arch. J.*, 36: 117–44.
'The Babingtons, knights of St. John', *Arch. J.*, 36: 219–30.
'Dunster Castle', *Arch. J.*, 36: 309–20.
'Knaresborough Castle', *Yorks. Arch. J.*, 6 (1879–80), 98–108.
'Observations on some moated mounds in Yorkshire', *Yorks. Arch. J.*, 6 (1879–80), 109–12.

1880

The Earls, Earldom, and Castle of Pembroke. 132 pp.
Merthyr Tydfil School Board. Memorandum by the Chairman, March 1880. 14 pp.
'Heraldry', in *Encyclopaedia Britannica*, 9th edn., xi, 683–712.
'The castle of Montgomery', *Arch. Camb.*, 4th ser. 11: 114–28.
'The moated mounds of the Upper Severn', *Arch. Camb.*, 4th ser. 11: 200–12.
'The land of Morgan' (cont.), *Arch. J.*, 37: 30–54, 117–28.
'Some remarks upon earthworks', *Arch. J.*, 37: 217–26.
'Roman defensive work', *Arch. J.*, 37: 378–85.
'Notes on earthworks', *B*, 38: 249–52.
'St. Leonard's Tower, West Malling', *B*, 39: 640–2.
'On volcanic foci of eruption in the Konkan', *Records, the Geological Survey of India*, 13 part 1: 69–73.

1881

Letter to the Merthyr Board of Guardians Resigning the Chairmanship of the Board. 13 pp.
'Of the castles of England at the Conquest', *Arch. Camb.*, 4th ser. 12: 1–16.
'Of the political value of castles under the successors of the Conqueror', *Arch. Camb.*, 4th ser. 12: 109–25.
'The political influence of castles in the reign of Henry II', *Arch. Camb.*, 4th ser. 12: 177–86.
'Earthworks of the post-Roman and English period', *Arch. J.*, 38: 21–41.
'The castles of England and Wales at the latter part of the twelfth century', *Arch. J.*, 38: 258–76, 336–51.
'The castle and keep of Durham', *Arch. J.*, 38: 418–21.
'Chepstow Castle', *Bristol & Glos. Trans.*, 6 (1881–2), 51–74.
'The rectangular keep of a Norman castle', *B*, 40: 283–6.
'Norman castles: Of the shell keep', *B*, 40: 397–8.

'A Norman castle. The castle garth', *B*, 40: 581–3.
'Castles of the Early English period', *B*, 41: 386–7.
'The castles of Skenfrith and White Castle, otherwise Llantilio', *B*, 41: 814–6.
'The castles of Brougham and Brough', *Cumb. Antiq. Soc. Trans.*, 6 (1881–2), 15–37.
'On the mediaeval defences of the English border', *Cumb. Antiq. Soc. Trans.*, 6 (1881–2), 38–49.
'Bowes Castle', *Yorks. Arch. J.*, 7 (1881–2), 80–5.
'West Riding poll-tax and lay subsidy rolls, 2d Richard II', *Yorks. Arch. J.*, 7 (1881–2), 187–93.
Samuel Clark (1599–1682), *The Saint's Nosegay*. Reprinted with a memoir of the author, by his descendant, G. T. C. xlvii, 173 pp.
Evidence to the [Aberdare] Committee Appointed to Inquire into the Condition of Intermediate and Higher Education in Wales and Monmouthshire. *PP* 1881 [C.3047-I] xxxiii, 630–3, 881–2.

1882

'The custumary of . . . Rothley, co. Leicester', *Archaeologia*, 47: 89–130.
'The castles of England and Wales at the latter part of the twelfth century' (cont.), *Arch. J.*, 39: 154–76.
'Some account of the keep of Colchester Castle', *Arch. J.*, 39: 239–56.
'The moated mound of Sekington', *Arch. J.*, 39: 372–5.
'On some East Anglian earthworks', *B*, 43: 176, 185–7.
'Fortified churches on the Northumbrian border', *B*, 43: 363–4.
'Pevensey Castle', *B*, 43: 424–6.
'Hastings Castle', *B*, 43: 533–5.
'Richmond Castle, Yorks.', *B*, 43: 643–4, 676–7.
'Hertford Castle', *B*, 43: 819–20.
'Dunster Castle: A descriptive sketch', in Sir H. C. Maxwell Lyte, *Dunster and its Lords, 1066–1881*, pp. ix–xv.
Samuel Clark (1599–1682), *The Duty of Every One that Intends to be Saved*. Reprinted with a preface [by G. T. Clark]. xiv, 253 pp.

1883

The Land of Morgan. 166 pp.
Some Account of Sir Robert Mansel . . . and of Admiral Sir Thomas Button. 110 pp.
'The Dane-John mound', *Arch. Cant.*, 15: 343–7.
'Fillongley', *B*, 44: 241.
'Croxall Mound', *B*, 44: 241–2.
'Ludlow Castle', *Trans. of the Shropshire Archaeological and Natural History Society*, 6: 271–98.
'Conisborough Castle', *Yorks. Arch. J.*, 8 (1883–4), 125–57.
'Scarborough Castle', *Yorks. Arch. J.*, 8 (1883–4), 179–97.

1884

Mediaeval Military Architecture in England. 2 vols.

1885

Cartae et alia Munimenta quae ad Dominium de Glamorgan Pertinent, i, *1102–1350*. ix, 310, 42 pp.

'Richmond Castle', *Yorks. Arch. J.*, 9 (1885–6), 33–54.

1886

Limbus Patrum Morganiae et Glamorganiae. Being the Genealogies of the Older Families of the Lordships of Morgan and Glamorgan. 620 pp.

'[Memorandum concerning orthodoxy and loyalty of Basil, Earl of Denbigh]', *Arch. J.*, 43: 177–8.

'The castle of Lewes', *Sussex Arch. Coll.*, 34: 57–68.

1888

Pedigree of the Babingtons. Single sheet, 6′7″ × 6′.

1889

'The parish of St. Hilary, in Glamorganshire, and its lords', *Arch. Camb.*, 5th ser. 6: 214–23.

'Bamburgh Castle', *Arch. J.*, 46: 93–113.

'Contribution towards a complete list of moated mounds or burhs', *Arch. J.*, 46: 197–217.

'Castle Acre', *Arch. J.*, 46: 282–5.

'Bute Docks and the trade of Cardiff', *Shipping Gazette and Lloyds List*, 30 January 1889.

1890

Cartae, ii, *1348–1721*. xx, 421, 59 pp.

'Cardiff Castle', *Arch. Camb.*, 5th ser. 7: 283–92.

'The tenth Earl of Northumberland', *Yorks. Arch. J.*, 11 (1890–1), 462–85.

Review of *Annals of the House of Percy*, by E. B. de Fonblanque, *Yorks. Arch. J.*, 11 (1890–1), 1–16.

1891

Cartae, iii, *441–1300*. xl, 595, 60 pp.

'Schedule of a parcel of the lands of Henry, Duke of Suffolk, within the manor of Lutterworth', *Arch. J.*, 48: 190–2.

'The house of Percy, entitled Barons Lucy of Cockermouth', *Cumb. Antiq. Soc. Trans.*, 11: 399–432.

'The archaeology of the land of Morgan', in *Handbook for Cardiff and District Prepared for the Use of the British Association*, ed. Ivor James, pp. 1–58.

Review of *Rockingham Castle and the Watsons*, by Charles Wise, *Arch. J.*, 48: 472–6.
Letter to the editor on 'Scottish heraldry and genealogy', *Arch. J.*, 48: 426–33.

1892
'Professor Edward A. Freeman', *Arch. J.*, 49: 86–8.
Review of *A Treatise on Heraldry*, by John Woodward, *Arch. J.*, 49: 92–4.
Review of *The Douglas Book*, by William Fraser, *Arch. J.*, 49: 303–14.

1893
Cartae, iv, *1215–1689*. xxxvi, 660, 44 pp.
'The signory of Gower', *Arch. Camb.*, 5th ser. 10: 1–16, 292–308.
Review of *The Old Manorial Halls of Westmorland and Cumberland*, by M. W. Taylor, *Arch. J.*, 50: 107–9.
Review of *Napoléon et Alexandre Ire*, by Albert Vandal, *QR*, 177: 416–42.

1894
'The signory of Gower' (cont), *Arch. Camb.*, 5th ser. 11: 122–30.
'The campaign of Waterloo'. Review of *The Campaign of Waterloo*, by J. C. Ropes, *Gent. Mag.*, 276: 251–68.
'Napoleon'. Review of *Napoléon et Alexandre Ire*, by Albert Vandal, *Gent. Mag.*, 277: 228–49.

1895
'The birth and growth of the broad gauge'. Review of *A History of the Great Western Railway*, by G. A. Sekon, *Gent. Mag.*, 279: 489–506.
John Martineau, *The Life and Correspondence of Sir Bartle Frere*. Contains reminiscences of Frere contributed by G. T. Clark, i, 44–6.
Samuel Clark (1684–1750), *A Collection of the Promises of Scripture*. A new edition, by G. T. Clark. lxxxiii, 272 pp.

Index

Subscribers

The following have kindly associated themselves with the publication of this volume through subscription:

Michel Cattoir, Brussels
Alys Cattoir Clark, Brussels
Andrew Clark
Charles G. L. W. Clark
Guy W. N. H. Clark, Inverkip, Renfrewshire
Mrs Jocelyn G. Clark, Cobham
Jonathan Clark
Lucinda Clark
Nicola F. V. Clark
Philippa Clark, London
Thomas H. M. W. Clark
J. Coyne, Stanford in the Vale
J. J. Gurney, Northrepps Hall, Norfolk
Cynthia Hogg
Angela Mackenzie
Diana Mackenzie, London
Elizabeth Anne Mackenzie, London
Delia Thorley

David and Ann Allen, Pontyclun
Clive A. Andrewartha, Penpedairheol
The late Major H. E. Bailey, Aberthin
Arthur Melville Banbury, Talygarn
Jill Bartlett, Caerphilly
Mario Basini, Cardiff
Gerald Beaudette, Barry
S. G. Beckley, Swansea

Glenda M. Bell, Trerhingyll
L. M. Beresford, Bedfordale, Western Australia
E. R. Beynon, Bedlinog
F. E. Bird, St Mellons
J. D. M. Blayney, Llanblethian
John R. E. Borron, Ambleside
Raymond E. Bowen, Dinas Powys
C. Stephen Briggs, Aberystwyth
June and Douglas Brooks, Ledbury
Eluned Brown, Cardiff
Revd Roger L. Brown, Welshpool
Delphine and Lindsay Bryant, Pencoed
M. Callaghan, Llanblethian
Muriel E. Chamberlain, Swansea
Jeff Childs, Dinas Powys
Dan Clayton-Jones, Mwyndy
Maureen Clifford, Cardiff
Mr and Mrs Austin O. Cole, London
D. J. Collier, Coychurch
Leonard Collings and Laurence Collings, Talygarn
B. M. Collins, Brynsadler
R. D. R. Collins, Llantrisant
Janice M. Connick, Crynant
Mrs Christopher Cory, Penllyn Castle
Robert E. Counsell, Pen-y-fai
F. G. Cowley, Swansea
Sylvia Crawshay, Newport
Jane Cresswell, St Athan
Brandon David Davies, Merthyr Tydfil
Brian W. Davies, Pontypridd
D. L. Davies, Cwmaman
Gareth Alban Davies, Llangwyryfon
Janet and John Davies, Cardiff
Margaret Rose Davies, Merthyr Tydfil
Michael G. Davies, Yelverton
Tom Davies, Blaendulais
Sir Christopher Davson, Rye
R. T. W. Denning, Cowbridge
Ian Dewar, Penarth
Captain Kenneth Dixon, Pontyclun
Lord Dynevor, Llandeilo

E. W. Edwards, Radyr
Keith H. Edwards, Aberthin
Martha Edwards, Pontyclun
N. M. and M. A. Elliott, Miskin
Peter Elmes, Dinas Powys
A. Weston Evans, Cardiff
D. Gareth Evans, Y Barri
G. E. Evans, Cardiff
Griffith J. Evans, Llantrisant
Hilda M. Evans, Trerhingyll
Jeff Evans, Yeovil
Lindsay Evans, Wrexham
Peter Graham Evans, Cheltenham, Victoria
Roger Everest, Talygarn
Michael Eyers, Bristol
Alan Fowler, Bridgend
Mr and Mrs C. Francis, Southerndown
David and Gloria Francis, Llanharry
Hywel Francis, Creunant
Madeleine Gray, Tongwynlais
The Griffiths family, Talygarn
Colin Griffiths, Llangors
Ralph A. Griffiths, Swansea
Rhidian Griffiths, Aberystwyth
George and Barbara Groves, Pentyrch
Malcolm J. Hackman, Talygarn
W. Hamlin, Cardiff
David Harbourne, Llandaf
Dr and Mrs David J. Harris, London, Ontario
R. C. Hastie, Bishopston
G. H. Haynes, Llanblethian
Dennis W. Heal, Penllyn
Mark Hebden, Talygarn
P. W. T. Henry, Porthcawl
T. F. Holley, Merthyr Tydfil
Andrew Hopper, Talygarn
E. H. Howell, Talygarn
John I. Howells, Cardiff
Kim Howells MP, Pontypridd
J. M. Hughes, Newport
John Vivian Hughes, Port Talbot

Vernon Hughes, Abergele
Laurence Ince, Solihull
Noel Israel, Talbot Green
Peter N. Jarvis, Bletchley
Peter Jarvis, Llandaff
Mr and Mrs R. P. Jenkins
Vic John, Llanharry
William H. John, Cardiff
Anthony L. Jones, Pencoed
Barrie Jones, Wormley, Hertfordshire
Beti Jones, Edinburgh
Bill Jones, Cardiff
D. Keith Jones, Cowbridge
David Lewis Jones, Dowlais
D. R. L. Jones, Maesteg
G. O. Jones, Port Talbot, and R. C. Clark, Pontrhydyfen
Gwenllian V. Jones, Newport
J. Gwynfor Jones, Cardiff
Melanie J. T. Jones, Cowbridge
Nev Jones, Pontyclun
Mr and Mrs Ossian Jones, Cowbridge
Stephen K. Jones, Wenvoe
Trevor H. Jones, Radyr
Michael John Keane, Merthyr Tydfil
J. and G. Keay, Llanblethian
Robert King, Resolven
Lesley G. Kingham, Hesket-Newmarket, Cumbria
Clive H. Knowles, Cardiff
Barbara Leech, Cardiff
The Lewis family, Talygarn
Sir David Mansel Lewis, Llanelli
Ceri W. Lewis, Treorci
Mr and Mrs Greg Lewis, Talygarn
J. M. Lewis, Llandaff
Richard Lewis, Milton Keynes
Mrs D. Llewellyn, Pentyrch
Nicholas Lloyd, Droitwich
Captain Norman Lloyd-Edwards, Llandaff
The Revd Chancellor B. M. Lodwick, Llandough
Chris Loyn, Penarth
Henry and Patricia Loyn, Penarth

Chris Lyddon, Pentyrch
John Lyons, Templeton, Pembrokeshire
M. A. McLaggan, Merthyr Mawr
Revd John D. Marshall, Cowbridge
Joanna Martin, Hitcham
Allan Mayne, Cwmbrân
A. G. Mein, Usk
R. G. T. Meyrick, Merthyr Tydfil
E. H. and A. Miles, Talygarn
J. L. S. Miles, Cowbridge
Julian Mitchell, Llansoy
Patricia Moore, Penarth
A. J. and E. Moreton, Merthyr Tydfil
David Morgan, Broad Haven, Pembrokeshire
Hugh Morgan, Clydach
Terry Morgan, Groesfaen
Anne L. Morris, Swansea
Bernard Morris, Swansea
Ichiro Nagai, Tokyo
John Newman, Sevenoaks
R. G. Norman, Pontyclun
Norma O'Leary, Llantrisant
Tyrone O'Sullivan, Hirwaun
J. E. Owen, Pontypool
John G. Owen, Caerphilly
Elizabeth Parkinson, Penarth
Derek Phillips, Dowlais
Teifion Phillips, Barry
Gwynedd O. Pierce, Creigiau
Violet Pole, Cefn Cribwr
Ray Price
Mrs John A. (Penny) Pugh, Glyntaff
Priscilla M. Quinn, Llanishen
Arthur Rees, Port Talbot
Gaynor Rees, Cowbridge
Iorwerth Rees, Cardiff
Kenneth Rees, Merthyr Tydfil
D. F. Renn, Great Bookham
Gwyn and Kathleen Rhys, Radyr
Joyce E. Richards, Ross-on-Wye
Peter Richards, Port Talbot

W. J. Cynfab Roberts, Aberystwyth
Paul Robeson, Junior
W. R. B. Robinson, Cheam
Sylvia B. Russell, Pontyclun
Susan Saunders, Pontyclun
Peggy Scott, Peterborough
Ron and Beryl Shepstone, Pontyclun
Leslie Shore, Ulverston
Eira M. Smith, Merthyr Tydfil
Jack Spurgeon, Aberystwyth
Agnes Stickings, Orpington
David Sturdy, Charlbury
Frederick C. Suppe, Muncie, Indiana
M. W. Tamplin, Brynsadler
Arnold Taylor, Chiddingfold, Surrey
The late Glyn J. Taylor, Llysworney
B. D. Thomas, Bridgend
Ceinwen H. Thomas, Caerdydd
D. Thomas, Newport
D. Brynmor Thomas, St Andrews
E. Hugh Thomas, London
H. G. Thomas, Neath Abbey
Hilary M. Thomas, Llandough
Chrystal Tilney, Llandaff
P. J. Ungoed, Maesteg
Hywel W. Vaughan, Raglan
Diane A. Walker, Cardiff
Graham and Betty Walker, Pontyclun
Huw Walters, Aberystwyth
T. M. Ll. Walters, Loughborough
Peter Watts, Sully
Peter V. Webster, Cardiff
Yvonne Weeding, Cowbridge
Chris Williams, Cardiff
Geoffrey J. Williams, Windsor
George Williams, Ludlow
Huw Williams, Dowlais
Jean M. Williams, Cardiff
L. H. W. Williams, Llancarfan
Maldwyn Williams, Talygarn
Matthew C. Williams, Cardiff

Alan and Coral Wilson, Pontypridd
Nigel Charles Wilson
C. W. Woodburn, Bosham, West Sussex
John Woods, Bridgend

Bridgend Library and Information Service
Cardiff County Library
Glamorgan Record Office
H. K. Lockyer (Booksellers), Abergavenny
Llantrisant History Society
Llyfrgell Genedlaethol Cymru/National Library of Wales, Aberystwyth
Merthyr Tydfil Historical Society
Museum of Welsh Life, St Fagans
National Art Library, Victoria and Albert Museum
The Library, National Museums & Galleries of Wales
Neath Port Talbot Library and Information Services
Pontyclun Institute Athletic Club
Pontyclun Primary School
Rhondda Cynon Taff Library Service, Treorchy Library
Salisbury Library, University of Wales Cardiff
The Library, Society of Antiquaries of London
South Wales Miners' Library, University of Wales Swansea
Torfaen Museum Trust Ltd.
University of Bristol Library
University of Wales Swansea Library
Vale of Glamorgan Libraries